Land Law

DIRECTIONS

6th Edition

SANDRA CLARKE

SARAH GREER

OXFORD

UNIVERSITY PRESS

OXFORD
UNIVERSITY PRESS

Great Clarendon Street, Oxford, OX2 6DP,
United Kingdom

Oxford University Press is a department of the University of Oxford.
It furthers the University's objective of excellence in research, scholarship,
and education by publishing worldwide. Oxford is a registered trade mark of
Oxford University Press in the UK and in certain other countries

Published in the United States of America by Oxford University Press
198 Madison Avenue, New York, NY 10016, United States of America

British Library Cataloguing in Publication Data
Data available

Library of Congress Control Number: 2018933979

ISBN 978-0-19-880955-5

Printed in Great Britain by
Bell & Bain Ltd., Glasgow

For our colleagues, past and present,
in the law schools at the University of
Greenwich and the University of Worcester

Guide to using the book

The sixth edition of *Land Law Directions* is enriched with a range of features designed to help support and reinforce your learning. This guided tour shows you how to fully utilize your textbook and get the most out of your study.

Learning objectives

These serve as a helpful signpost to what you can expect to learn by reading the chapter.

```
☐  LEARNING OBJECTIVES

By the end of this chapter, you will be able to:
● identify the legal freehold estate;
● distinguish the legal freehold from other estates and interests in land;
● understand how the legal freehold can be transferred;
● understand possible changes in the law.
```

Examples

We encounter real examples of land law every day, whether we recognize them or not. In each chapter you will find everyday scenarios illustrating how land law applies to real life situations.

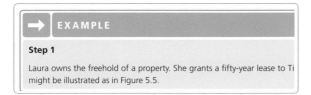

```
➡  EXAMPLE

Step 1
Laura owns the freehold of a property. She grants a fifty-year lease to Ti
might be illustrated as in Figure 5.5.
```

Diagrams and flowcharts

Numerous diagrams and flowcharts illustrate this book, providing a visual representation of concepts, processes, and cases. Use these in conjunction with the text to gain a clear understanding of even the most complex areas.

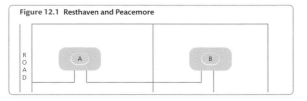

Figure 12.1 Resthaven and Peacemore

Photographs and sample documents

Photographs and sample legal documents demonstrate the role of land law in the real world, helping to clarify abstract ideas and develop skills to support your future career.

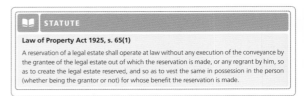

Form 15.1 Register of title for Anne's Cottage		
Edition Date: 1 December 2009		
Entry No.	**A. PROPERTY REGISTER**	
	containing the description of the registered land and the estate comprised in the title	
	Greenfordshire: Maryford	

Statute boxes

Land law is very much based on statute. Relevant provisions are set out and clearly explained in the text.

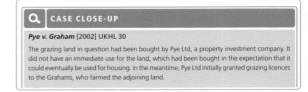

```
📖  STATUTE

Law of Property Act 1925, s. 65(1)
A reservation of a legal estate shall operate at law without any execution of the conveyance by
the grantee of the legal estate out of which the reservation is made, or any regrant by him, so
as to create the legal estate reserved, and so as to vest the same in possession in the person
(whether being the grantor or not) for whose benefit the reservation is made.
```

Case close-ups

Summaries of key cases are clearly highlighted for ease of reference and to develop your understanding.

```
🔍  CASE CLOSE-UP

Pye v. Graham [2002] UKHL 30
The grazing land in question had been bought by Pye Ltd, a property investment company. It
did not have an immediate use for the land, which had been bought in the expectation that it
could eventually be used for housing. In the meantime, Pye Ltd initially granted grazing licences
to the Grahams, who farmed the adjoining land.
```

Definition boxes

Key terms are highlighted and clearly explained when they first appear, helping you to quickly understand important terminology while reading. These terms are also collected in a glossary at the end of the book.

> ple—you will see numerous
> sewers might well be shared
> eeded; there may be a shared
> ts of light to windows in the
>
> **easement**
> a right enjoyed by the owner of land to a benefit from other land

Thinking points

Why was a particular decision reached in a certain case? Is the law on this point rational and coherent? Is land law fit for its purpose? Thinking points within chapters draw out these issues and help you to reflect.

> **THINKING POINT**
> What do you think showed the defendant's intention to possess? What had he done to the land to indicate his intention?
>
> As can be seen from the *Moran* case, the same acts that show physical possession often show in-

Cross references

Clearly marked cross references ensure the book is easy to navigate, pin-pointing particular sections where related themes or cases are covered.

> ▶ **CROSS REFERENCE**
> For easements, generally, and for the meaning of establishing an easement of light by prescription, in particular, see Chapter 12, 12.4.4.5.
>
> Bringing the register up to date involves a changed or because a right has been establi ment of light by prescription, that should be
>
> This provision also allows the register to be fraud is avoided. For example, in *Norwich* 116, the transfer was effected by the misus

Chapter summaries

The central points and concepts covered in each chapter are condensed into useful summaries. These provide a mechanism for you to reinforce your understanding and can be a helpful revision tool.

> **Summary**
> 1. The legal freehold is technically called the fee simple absolute in possession. An type of freehold estate cannot be legal, but takes effect as an equitable interest
> 2. As well as being a fee simple absolute in possession, the legal freehold must be ferred using the appropriate formalities, otherwise—at best—only an eq interest in land will be transferred.

End-of-chapter questions

Problem and essay questions at the end of each chapter help you to develop analysis, essay writing, and problem-solving skills, which are essential for successful study and in the workplace. You will find answers to these questions in the online resources at www.oup.com/uk/clarke_directions6e/.

> **?** **Questions**
> **Self-test questions**
> 1. Tajinder wants to buy a property. She looks on the land register and sees that th is registered to Paul. Tajinder goes to look at the property. She meets Suli, wh to be living there. She asks Suli whether she has any interest in the property. S not seem to want to answer Tajinder's questions. She just says that the house 'is

The bigger picture

Further advice, study suggestions, and additional cases are provided at the end of each chapter to help you build upon your knowledge of land law and prepare for assessments and examinations.

> ☐ **The bigger picture**
> • If you want to see how this area of land law fits into the rest of your studies, you at Chapter 15, especially 15.3. For some guidance on what sort of exam questio up in this area, see Chapter 16, 16.9.
> • One of the really interesting aspects of this area of law is the exploration of the r reform. Read the Law Commission reports, especially the later one:

Further reading

Selected further reading is included at the end of each chapter to provide a springboard for further study. These suggestions help you take your learning further and provide a guide to some of the key academic literature.

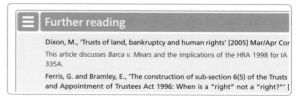

> ☰ **Further reading**
> Dixon, M., 'Trusts of land, bankruptcy and human rights' [2005] Mar/Apr Con
> This article discusses *Barca v. Mears* and the implications of the HRA 1998 for IA 335A.
> Ferris, G. and Bramley, E., 'The construction of sub-section 6(5) of the Trusts and Appointment of Trustees Act 1996: When is a "right" not a "right?"' [

Glossary

A useful one-stop reference point for clear definitions of all the keywords and terms used within the text.

> # Glossary
>
> **1925 property legislation** a series of Acts of Parliament that came into effect on 1 January 1926. These Acts consolidated earlier piecemeal changes in the law—particularly from 1922–24—and brought them all
>
> **bona fide** 'in good faith'
> **bona fide purchaser of the legal es without notice** broken down, thi someone who has bought the lega

Guide to the Online Resources

The online resources that accompany this book provides students with ready-to-use learning resources. The Resources are intended to be used alongside the book and are designed to maximize the learning experience.

 www.oup.com/uk/clarke_directions6e/.

Suggested approaches to end-of-chapter questions

Advice is given on answering the example problem and essay questions from the text to help you develop essential skills in analysing problems and constructing well-balanced arguments.

Self-test questions

Self-test questions for each chapter provide instant feedback to help you consolidate your knowledge of land law and prepare for assessments.

Web links

Don't spend time using search engines. The authors have selected links to useful websites so you can go directly to reliable sources of online information, allowing you to work efficiently and effectively.

Flashcard glossary

A series of interactive flashcards containing key terms and concepts allows you to test your understanding of land law terminology.

Regular updates

An indispensable resource that allows you to access recent changes and developments in the law that have occurred since publication of the book. These updates are accompanied by references to the textbook, so you can see how the new developments relate to the existing case law.

Advanced topics

Additional details on selected topics help to broaden and deepen your understanding of land law.

New to this edition

This edition includes a new chapter on proprietary estoppel, with detailed consideration of the case of *Davies v. Davies* [2016] EWCA Civ 463. This case neatly illustrates the two-stage process of establishing an equity and then identifying an appropriate remedy in cases of proprietary estoppel. It also reminds us—if we need reminding—that the court faces a difficult challenge in trying to reach an equitable outcome in cases involving family disputes spanning many years.

It also includes consideration of two new cases involving tenants or potential tenants. In the Supreme Court case of *McDonald v. McDonald* [2016] UKSC 28, their Lordships made the significant decision that it was not open to the court to consider proportionality when deciding whether or not to grant an order for possession brought by a private landlord against a residential tenant. Although Article 8 of the European Convention on Human Rights may well be engaged in such a case, the Court held that Parliament has already undertaken the requisite balancing exercise between the rights of the private landlord and the residential tenant in passing domestic legislation. The Convention rights were designed to protect individuals from infringement of their rights by the State, and not to be enforceable between private individuals. In *Watts v. Stewart* [2016] EWCA Civ 1247 a bold attempt to overturn the orthodoxy of *Street v. Mountford* [1985] AC 809 was rejected by the Court of Appeal. A legal right to exclusive possession was distinguished from a personal right of exclusive occupation, and the intention of the parties remains a determining factor in a dispute over whether the occupier has a lease or a licence of the property.

In the area of easements, *Regency Villas Title Ltd v. Diamond Resorts (Europe) Ltd* [2017] EWCA Civ 238, [2017] 2 P & CR DG8 (CA (Civ Div)) the Court of Appeal re-examined the leading case of *Re Ellenborough Park* [1955] 3 All ER 667 in respect of recreational rights over neighbouring land in modern times. Facilities used for pursuits such as tennis, croquet, and golf were accepted as capable of being easements. The case is, however, listed for appeal to the Supreme Court. There is also a new case on rights of way used to access land that was not originally part of the dominant tenement, *Gore v. Naheed & Ahmed* [2017] EWCA Civ 369, which distinguishes *Das v. Linden Mews* [2002] EWCA CIV 590.

In the law relating to freehold covenants, there is *Birdlip v. Hunter* [2016] EWCA Civ 603, [2017] 1 P & CR 1, in which the Court of Appeal set out the criteria to be applied in finding that there is a 'building scheme' imposing enforceable covenants on all the properties in a defined area of land.

The law of adverse possession continues to develop, despite the LRA 2002 appearing to strike it a near-mortal blow in 2003; the Privy Council case of *Smith v. Molyneaux* [2016] UKPC 35 followed the academically criticized decision in *BP Properties v. Buckler* [1987] 2 EGLR 168 on consent. The way the LRA 2002 works in adverse possession is one of the subjects in a much wider review of land registration in the Law Commission Updating the Land Registration Act 2002 consultation (Consultation Paper No. 227), so we can expect further changes to land registration in future.

Preface

We wrote the first edition of this book over a decade ago. The law in this area has continued to evolve and develop during this time, bringing us new directions and challenges. We have tried, as always, to make the often very complicated principles of land law as clear and accessible as we possibly can—although the courts do not always make that an easy task. We have dedicated this edition to our colleagues at our respective universities. We are grateful for their support, wisdom, and friendship over the years.

Thank you to Felicity Boughton, our Oxford University Press editor, for her help and good humour in the process of writing this edition. However, the biggest thank you, as always, must go to our families. Sarah would like to thank Steve and Hamish, as always. Sandra would like to thank her husband Pete and her Dad, Stan, for their unfailing support and love. Thanks also to Andrew and Stacey (formerly known as Lolly) and Dave and Becci for kindly buying houses this year—useful source material! The example in Chapter 6, 6.9.2.2 is, however, as with all of our examples, purely fictional, despite taking their names in vain.

Sandra Clarke and Sarah Greer

Publisher acknowledgements

Photo 1.5 is reproduced by kind permission of Scott Hortop

Figure 3.1 is reproduced by kind permission of Mr and Mrs S. C. Williams.

Form 3.1—Land Registry form TR1—is Crown copyright and is reproduced by kind permission of the Land Registry.

Form 5.1—Tenancy agreement—is reproduced for educational purposes only by kind permission of Oyez Professional Services Limited.

Contents

Table of cases

Bold page numbers indicate Case Close-ups. Other references may occur on the same page.

Table of legislation

Bold page numbers indicate where text is reproduced in full. Other references may occur on the same page.

UK Primary Legislation

UK Secondary Legislation

European Secondary Legislation

International Legislation

PART 1

INTRODUCTION

1 What is land?

> ### ☐ LEARNING OBJECTIVES
>
> **By the end of this chapter, you will be able to:**
>
> - recognize what is meant by 'land';
> - understand the extent of land—in particular, how it exists in three dimensions;
> - explain which objects form part of the land and which keep their separate character;
> - understand what is meant by 'intangible rights' in land;
> - discuss the ownership of objects found on, or within, the land, including the Crown's right to 'treasure'.

Introduction: how relevant is land law today?

Land law has always been important to people. From the beginning of civilization, people have needed to regulate land ownership and use. Although land law has ancient roots, it is of vital and growing importance in today's world. The rules relating to the ownership, occupation, and use of land affect everyone—we all need somewhere to live. Some people live in a freehold property; others live in a leasehold home. Although most people have heard the terms 'freehold' and 'leasehold', they are often unsure what they actually mean. Those about to buy a home need to understand the different rights and responsibilities accorded to freeholders and leaseholders. People renting from week to week, or month to month, also need to know what they can and cannot do in their homes. Even students living at home with parents, or people living in a property owned by a partner, need to know what rights, if any, they have in their homes. Land law is important—as important as the roof over your head.

Despite its very practical relevance, students sometimes say they find land law a difficult subject to study. Land law has a specialized vocabulary, with some words dating from medieval times, which can be off-putting at first. Words such as 'covenant' and 'ease-ment' have an old-fashioned sound, but they describe concepts that are as relevant today as they were when the words were first coined. Throughout this book, although we may use dusty old cases as authorities, we will also give modern examples and photographs of real pieces of land to illustrate and explain. Land law is a living, dynamic subject, and an increasingly relevant one in these days of housing shortages and increasing competition for land.

1.1 The definition of land

What exactly is land? Unfortunately, there is no simple answer: although there are many statutes that regulate land law, there is no single, authoritative, statutory definition of 'land'. Instead, there are a number of different definitions in various statutes which tend to repeat and expand upon one another in a less than helpful way.

A good starting point, however, is the partial definition of land in the Law of Property Act 1925 (LPA 1925), s. 205(1)(ix). The LPA 1925 is one among the body of statutes that makes up the 1925 prop-erty legislation: an impressive attempt to rationalize and codify the law relating to land.

 STATUTE

Law of Property Act 1925, s. 205(1)(ix)

'Land' includes land of any tenure, and mines and minerals, whether or not held apart from the surface, buildings or parts of buildings (whether the division is horizontal, vertical or made in any other way) and other corporeal hereditaments; also a manor, advowson, and a rent and other incorporeal hereditaments, and an easement, right, privilege, or benefit in, over, or de-rived from land; … and 'mines and minerals' include any strata or seam of minerals or sub-stances in or under any land, and powers of working and getting the same … ; and 'manor' includes a lordship, and reputed manor or lordship; and 'hereditament' means any real property which on an intestacy occurring before the commencement of this Act might have devolved upon an heir.

As a definition for a new student of land law, this leaves a lot to be desired. For a start, it is only a partial definition, because it begins '"Land" *includes*', which means that land may also include things that are *not* mentioned in this definition. It also uses some words and phrases that are not in common use today, so it can be difficult to grasp immediately what is meant.

Despite these shortcomings, however, it is worth persevering, because this definition can teach us quite a lot about the basics of land law. It also introduces some of the vocabulary needed for further study, which will make it much easier for you to understand later chapters.

1.1.1 **Land of any tenure**

▶ CROSS REFERENCE

For more on freehold land, see Chapter 3.

Firstly, the section states that land 'includes land of any tenure'. Broadly speaking, this means that both freehold and leasehold land count as land for land law purposes. The concepts of freehold and leasehold are dealt with in later chapters.

For now, it is sufficient to understand that freehold land is owned effectively 'forever', whereas leasehold land is owned by a tenant for a definite period, which may be short or long, but is not 'forever'. A leasehold is created out of a freehold.

CROSS REFERENCE

For more on leasehold land, see Chapter 5.

It might seem obvious to you that both are 'land', but, for historical reasons, this was not always the case. Originally, the distinction was not made between 'land' and other types of property, but between **real property (or realty)** and **personal property (or personalty)**. Personal property can also be described as chattels—a word that is thought to be derived from cattle, which were a common type of personal property in early farming societies.

> **real property, or realty** this term refers to freehold land
>
> **personal property, or personalty** all property that does not comprise freehold land
>
> **chattels** all property that is not real property, including leasehold land, and is also often used as the opposite to 'fixture'—see 1.1.3.1. Leasehold land came to have such importance, however, that it was called a 'chattel real', because it has many of the characteristics of real property.

Originally, all land was freehold, so real property meant freehold land. The word 'real' comes from the Latin *res*, which means 'the thing itself'. Real property could be protected in law by the real actions. This meant that a court action could be brought to restore the land itself to the true owner, rather than an award of money damages as compensation for its loss. It is still true today that courts will usually order specific performance of a contract to sell land—they will order the seller to transfer the land to the buyer rather than awarding damages.

By the time the idea of a lease developed, the definition of real property as freehold land was too fixed to be altered. Leasehold land was regarded as personal property, although it was clear that it was different from most types of personalty. The real actions were not available to leaseholders.

You will be relieved to hear that, because land now 'includes land of any tenure', leasehold land is now included squarely within the definition of land for all modern purposes.

CROSS REFERENCE

For more detail on 'tenure', see Chapter 2, 2.2.1.

1.1.2 **The extent of land**

Turning back to LPA 1925, s. 205(1)(ix), you can see that land includes mines and minerals, whether they are owned by the owner of the surface of the land or owned separately from it. This illustrates a very important fact about land, which is that land is three-dimensional. There is the surface of the land, the ground beneath the surface, and the airspace above. Different people can own different strata (or levels) of land.

 EXAMPLE

Anna owns a house that is built on land above a coalfield. She owns the surface of the land (and the house built on it), but the land beneath the surface—that with the coal in it—may be owned by the British Mining Company.

This same principle can be seen at work in the next part of the definition—that land includes 'buildings or parts of buildings (whether the division is horizontal, vertical or made in any other way)'. Not surprisingly, buildings form part of the land, but interestingly, different people can own different parts of buildings and the building can be divided in any way (see Figure 1.1).

Figure 1.1   Ways in which a building can be divided

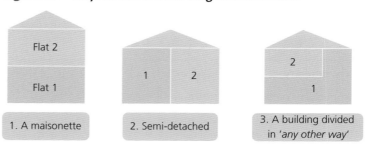

1. A maisonette

2. Semi-detached

3. A building divided in 'any other way'

> ### → EXAMPLE
>
> Maisonettes are buildings that are divided horizontally (1); semi-detached houses (2) are buildings that are divided vertically.
>
> There is, however, no reason why a building should not be divided unequally, so that one person owns all of the ground floor and part of the first floor, and the other person owns the rest of the first floor. This last example (3) is of a building divided in 'any other way'.

cuius est solum eius est usque ad coelum et ad inferos
'he who owns the land owns everything reaching up to the very heavens and down to the depths of the earth'

The extended definition of land is sometimes expressed in the maxim *cuius est solum eius est usque ad coelum et ad inferos*, or 'he who owns the land owns everything reaching up to the very heavens and down to the depths of the earth'. This maxim, approved in *Bocardo v. Star Energy* (see 1.1.2.1), is useful in reminding us that land includes not only the surface, but also the air above and the space beneath the ground. However, whilst it is true that land includes airspace and subterranean space (the space beneath the ground), it is not true that the owner's rights are unlimited, particularly with regard to airspace.

1.1.2.1 Subterranean space

The landowner owns the subterranean space below the surface of his land. He can dig down into it to form a cellar or underground room.

As s. 205(1)(ix) states, mines and minerals form part of the land—but certain minerals do not belong to the landowner and belong instead to the state. Gold and silver belong to the Crown as of right—*Case of Mines* (1568) 1 Plowd 310. The Crown is also entitled to oil, petroleum, coal, and natural gas (including shale gas obtained by fracturing the land or 'fracking') by statutory right—see the Coal Industry Act 1994 and the Petroleum Act 1998. In addition, the Crown has the right to treasure found in the land (see 1.2.3).

CASE CLOSE-UP

Bocardo v. Star Energy [2010] UKSC 35, [2011] 1 AC 380

This case contains an interesting point about ownership of the land 'down to the depths of the earth'. The claimants were the owners of an estate in Surrey. The defendants were holders of a licence under the Petroleum Act 1934 to search and drill for and pump out petroleum products from an oilfield that extended partly under the claimants' land. The defendants carried out their drilling operations from land next to the claimant's estate but, unknown to the claimants, their oil wells extended under the claimants' land.

The claimants eventually found out about the oil wells and claimed damages for trespass to their land. The defendants argued that the oil wells were so deep underground (a minimum depth of 800 ft) that they did not affect the claimants' use of the land in any way and therefore they did not trespass on the claimants' land.

The Supreme Court held that the oil wells were a trespass. Although they were deep below the surface, the subsoil belongs to the owner of the surface unless it has been granted to someone else. The petroleum products belonged to the state by statute (Petroleum Act 1934), but not the subsoil. It was not a trespass to remove the petroleum, but it was a trespass to drill wells under the claimants' land without permission. The defendants were therefore ordered to pay compensation to the claimants.

Recently, landowners have sought to use this decision to prevent fracking under their land. However, the Infrastructure Act 2015 provides that:

📖 **STATUTE**

Infrastructure Act 2015, s. 43 [Petroleum and geothermal energy: right to use deep-level land]

(1) A person has the right to use deep-level land in any way for the purposes of exploiting petroleum or deep geothermal energy.

…

(4) deep-level land is any land at a depth of at least 300 metres below surface level.

This right to use deep-level land expressly includes fracking under s. 44 of the Act. Provisions are made in later sections for notice and payments to landowners.

The land beneath the surface can be extended if land borders a roadway. There is a presumption that the landowner owns the subsoil of the roadway adjoining the land up to the middle of the roadway—**ad medium filum**, as the cases often say, meaning 'to the mid line'. Landowners can construct cellars that extend into this space below the ground.

> **ad medium filum**
> 'to the mid line'

Should you happen to be visiting a pub, take a closer look: often trap doors enabling delivery of barrels to the beer cellars are set in the pavement outside the pub (see Photo 1.1).

Photo 1.1 Pub trapdoor
© Sandra Clarke

1.1.2.2 **Airspace**

The owner of land also owns the airspace above that land—but he or she does not own 'up to the very heavens', as the case of *Bernstein v. Skyviews* [1978] QB 479 shows.

 CASE CLOSE-UP

Bernstein v. Skyviews [1978] QB 479

Lord Bernstein, the owner of a large country estate, brought an action in trespass against a company for flying over, and taking photographs of, his land. The case turned on whether the airspace formed part of the claimant's land.

Griffiths J held that the rights of the owner of land in the airspace above it extends 'to such height as is necessary for the ordinary use and enjoyment of his land and the structures upon it'. Above that height, the landowner has no more rights than the general public. Aircraft flying at a normal height do not trespass upon land, so Lord Bernstein lost the case.

It is clear, however, that lower regions of airspace do belong to the landowner. Cases have been brought in respect of overhanging signs, for example.

 CASE CLOSE-UP

Kelsen v. Imperial Tobacco Co [1957] 2 QB 334

The claimant leased a ground floor shop. The defendants had erected an advertising sign that projected into the airspace above his shop by about eight inches (30 cm). McNair J held that this was a trespass to the claimant's airspace, and granted him an injunction for the sign's removal.

Even if a neighbour has a real need to infringe on the landowner's airspace, this will not prevent an injunction being granted.

CASE CLOSE-UP

John Trenberth v. National Westminster Bank (1979) 39 P & CR 104

In this case, the defendant needed to repair his building, because it was unsafe. The claimant refused to allow scaffolding to be erected on his land, but the defendant proceeded anyway. The claimant was granted an injunction to prevent this. An earlier case, *Woolerton and Wilson Ltd v. Richard Costain Ltd* [1970] 1 WLR 411, in which an injunction had been delayed to allow time to complete the work, was not followed and the correctness of that decision was doubted.

It is also clear that the landowner does not have to prove that the trespassing object has affected his use of the land.

CASE CLOSE-UP

Laiquat v. Majid [2005] EWHC 1305 (QB)

In this case, there was an extractor fan at about 4.5 m above ground level, which protruded 750 mm into the claimant's garden.

Silber J, relying on *Kelsen v. Imperial Tobacco Co. Ltd* [1957] 2 QB 334, held that it was a trespass into the claimant's airspace. It was well within the height which the older authorities considered to be trespass, and it did not matter that the fan had not actually interfered with the claimant's normal use of his garden.

It is settled, then, that lower regions of airspace, to the height necessary for ordinary use of the land, form part of the land. Any objects intruding on that airspace from next door are a trespass and will entitle the landowner to either an injunction or damages, even if they do not, in fact, affect the ordinary use of the land.

It is interesting that the courts have held that there is a limit to the height above the land over which landowners have control, but apparently no limit to the depth over which they have control—see *Bocardo v. Star Energy* (see 1.1.2.1). In that case in the Court of Appeal Aikens LJ, at [2009] EWCA Civ 579 [61], said that it is not helpful to draw analogies between rights to airspace and rights to substrata, because there are many uses which can be made of airspace whilst the general public has no right to enter substrata, and because the use of airspace is regulated by statutes and regulations concerning aircraft. This view was endorsed by the Supreme Court, although as we have seen, Parliament has since intervened in respect of underground petroleum products and natural gas.

In the same way that cellars can extend under the surface, the owner of land next to a highway can build out over that highway above the height required for the passage of traffic.

Photos 1.2 and 1.3 show buildings that extend out over pavements and alleyways. Room is left for the passage of pedestrians underneath. It is quite possible for the part of the building over the alleyway in Photo 1.2 to be owned separately from other parts of the building. It may have no connection with the earth itself, but it is still 'land'. (Such pieces of land are sometimes called 'flying freeholds', although, for practical reasons that we shall see later on in the book, they are often leasehold rather than freehold.)

Photo 1.2　Building over alleyway

© Sandra Clarke

Photo 1.3　Balconies

© Terraxplorer

1.1.3 Corporeal hereditaments

It can be seen from the definition in LPA 1925, s. 205(1)(ix), that minerals and buildings are part of a wider category of **corporeal hereditaments**. This is a very old expression, but it is actually quite easy to understand. The word 'corporeal' means 'having a physical form', so it includes not only minerals and buildings, but also other physical things, such as plants, fences, etc.

> **corporeal hereditaments**
> any real property having a physical form

The word 'hereditaments', meanwhile, is defined in the last sentence of LPA 1925, s. 205(1)(ix), as *'any real property which on an intestacy occurring before the commencement of this Act might have devolved upon an heir'*. Again, this is a definition that is less than helpful for the new student: it is referring back to concepts that have little place in modern land law. It was meant at the time to indicate that the old cases on real property were to remain good law.

In the past, cases were brought to establish the extent of real property for inheritance purposes. This was because the heir was entitled to all real property, but not to chattels. It was therefore important to know which items formed part of the land (real property) and which remained separate from it (chattels). Despite their age, these cases are still authority in a more modern context for establishing the extent of land.

1.1.3.1 Fixtures

Many of the old cases that discussed real and personal property did so in the context of **fixtures**. The law on fixtures is important for reasons other than determining who should inherit property such as pictures fixed to the wall or statues standing in a garden.

> **fixture**
> an object that is attached to the land in such a way and for such a reason that it becomes part of the land

THINKING POINT

In today's world, when do you think it would be important to work out which objects form part of the land?

It is important when buying and selling land to know what is included within it, particularly when it is bought and sold at auction, as there is no further chance to bargain on what will be included in the sale. Also, if a mortgagee such as a bank or building society repossesses land where the borrower has defaulted on the loan, it needs to know what is included in its security, and what is not.

CROSS REFERENCE

For more on mortgages and repossession, see Chapter 14.

It can also be relevant for tax purposes to know whether an object forms part of the land.

Before land is sold, the freehold owner of the property may, of course, fix things to the property and remove them again at will (although different rules apply to tenants—see 'Tenant's fixtures'). It is only when land is to be sold, or when you need to know who owns an object for tax purposes, that the law on fixtures is relevant. When land is sold in the 'normal' way, by contract, the parties are free to come to an agreement about fixtures and fittings. They generally do this by filling in a list, supplied by their solicitors, in which they specify exactly what is included in the sale and what is excluded. It is only if this is not done that the general law on fixtures will be relevant.

EXAMPLE

Sandra bought a new house from Pete. Sandra and Pete specifically agreed that the carpets of the house were included in the sale, but that the curtains were excluded. It did not matter whether fitted carpets would form part of the land under the general law, because

Sandra and Pete had already reached an agreement about them. If, when he was moving out, Pete had changed his mind and taken the carpets, he would have been in breach of contract.

quicquid plantatur solo, solo cedit

'whatever is fixed to the land becomes part of it'

Yet again, there is an old Latin maxim that sums up the law on fixtures: **quicquid plantatur solo, solo cedit**, or 'whatever is fixed to the land becomes part of it'. However, you should approach the maxim with some caution: it is useful as a general guide, but it does not state the law with complete accuracy. You must look at the case law to understand which objects are likely to become part of the land and which will remain as chattels.

The best place to start is with the test in the leading case of *Holland v. Hodgson* (1872) LR 7 CP 328.

CASE CLOSE-UP

Holland v. Hodgson (1872) LR 7 CP 328

In this case, the question arose whether looms installed in a factory formed part of that factory—that is, were they part of the land?

Blackburn J said that whether an object is a fixture or a chattel depends on two tests:

1. the degree of annexation;
2. the purpose of the annexation.

In explaining the test, Blackburn J went on to say that articles that are attached to the land only by their weight are not usually considered to be part of the land, unless they were actually *intended* to form part of the land.

He gave the useful example of a dry-stone wall of the kind you often see when you are in the countryside. A pile of stones, randomly stacked in the middle of a field, would not be part of the land. However, stones that have been arranged, packed, and formed into a stone wall clearly are intended to be part of the land. It is for the person claiming that such an object is part of the land to prove it.

On the other hand, an object fixed to the land—however lightly—is initially considered to be part of the land, unless circumstances indicate that it was always intended to remain a chattel. In this case, it is for the person claiming that the object is a chattel to prove it.

This case tells us to look first at whether the object is attached in any way to the land. If it is, then it is to be classified as a fixture unless there is good reason to classify it as remaining a chattel. If it is not attached, the presumption is reversed: it is to be classified as a chattel unless there is good reason to classify it as a fixture. These rules have been considered in a large number of cases, of which only a selection can be considered here.

CASE CLOSE-UP

Berkley v. Poulett (1976) 120 Sol Jnl 836

The Court of Appeal considered whether pictures fitted into panelling on a wall, a heavy marble statue resting on a plinth in the garden, and a sundial formed part of land being sold by auction. The test in *Holland v. Hodgson* was applied.

The CA concluded that the pictures, although attached to the walls, were not fixtures: they were put on the walls to be enjoyed as pictures, rather than with the intention of making them part of the land. The statue, also, was not attached to the land, but was placed on a plinth that was attached to the land. The CA concluded that the plinth formed part of the land, but the statue did not, because there was no evidence that the statue was designed to go in just that spot in the garden as part of an 'architectural scheme'. The sundial was also held to be a chattel rather than a fixture, because it had been detached from its pedestal many years earlier.

Therefore, objects may remain chattels even though they are fixed to the building, if they were fixed only in order to be enjoyed as chattels. However, the reverse may be true—freestanding objects may be fixtures if the intention is for them to form a permanent part of the landscape:

 CASE CLOSE-UP

D'Eyncourt v. Gregory (1866) LR 3 Eq 382

The Court held that statues, figures, vases, and stone garden seats that were part of the architectural design of the grounds were fixtures, whether or not they were attached to the ground.

In 1997, the House of Lords considered the rules in *Holland v. Hodgson* and added a third category.

 CASE CLOSE-UP

Elitestone v. Morris [1997] 2 All ER 513

This case concerned a chalet or bungalow resting on concrete blocks on the ground, which had been brought onto the land many years before. It had been occupied by the defendants since 1971. The landowner and the occupiers assumed that the chalet belonged to the occupier, and rent was paid for the use of the land on which it stood.

A new landowner increased the rent steeply and notice was served on the occupiers to remove the chalet.

As part of their legal fight to stay on the land, the occupiers needed to argue that the chalet formed part of the land.

The Court of Appeal held that the chalet did not form part of the land, because it merely rested on—but was not attached to—the concrete blocks that formed its foundations.

This decision was reversed by the House of Lords. It found that the chalet was not designed to be removed from the land without being destroyed.

Lord Lloyd of Berwick said that he thought the terms 'fixture' and 'chattel' were confusing ones in the context of a house or building. He preferred a different approach, using a threefold classification:

An object which is brought onto land may be classified under one of three broad heads. It may be (a) a chattel; (b) a fixture; or (c) part and parcel of the land itself. Objects in categories (b) and (c) are treated as being part of the land.

> The chalet fell into category (c)—part and parcel of the land itself—as do most buildings. It appears that, if an object cannot be removed from the land except by destruction, it has become part and parcel of the land.

This case was applied in *Mew v. Tristmire* [2011] EWCA Civ 912.

 CASE CLOSE-UP

Mew v. Tristmire [2011] EWCA Civ 912

The claimants lived in old houseboats on wooden platforms around a harbour. Just like Mrs Morris, they wanted to claim that the houseboats formed part of the land so that they could remain there.

The Court of Appeal held that the houseboats were chattels. They had been brought to the harbour as moveable objects which could have been easily removed without being destroyed. They could not be considered as one object with the platforms onto which they had later been lifted. It did not matter that they were now very fragile and could not be moved without damage—it was the intention at the time they were brought to the land which was relevant.

The cases therefore point to the intention with which the object was brought on to the land as the dominant test. It is still relevant whether an object is fixed to the land or not, but intention may well alter that initial classification.

All these cases were considered in a modern context in a case concerning the sale of a valuable sculpture by a local council.

 CASE CLOSE-UP

London Borough of Tower Hamlets v. London Borough of Bromley [2015] EWHC 1954 (Ch)

'Draped Seated Woman', a sculpture created by the famous artist Henry Moore in 1957, was bought by the (since abolished) London County Council (LCC) and placed as a public work of art on Stifford Estate in Stepney, which is now owned by the claimant. The successor to the property of the LCC was the defendant.

The claimant wished to sell the statue, but the defendant disagreed. The issue was whether the statue formed part of the land when the LCC was dissolved and thus belonged to the claimant, or whether it remained a chattel and therefore belonged to the defendant.

The Court, using the authorities we have considered above, held that the sculpture remained a chattel. It had not been designed to go into that particular space, and might have been moved to another spot by the LCC. It was not part of an 'architectural design'. It was removable without damage, and had been moved successfully since that time. Therefore, the sculpture had not passed to the claimant with the land.

However, in a final twist to the story, the Court held that the defendant had not in fact brought the statue into its possession, and that the claimant had used it in a way inconsistent with the defendant's ownership, including loaning it to a sculpture park for several years. This meant that the defendant's claim to ownership was time-barred under the Limitation Act 1980, s. 2.

THINKING POINT

Look at Photo 1.4 of the Cutty Sark, a tea clipper built in 1869. She has been in dry dock in Greenwich since 1954 and has recently been restored and refixed into a glass exhibition centre.

Do you think that the Cutty Sark is a chattel, a fixture, or part and parcel of the land? Why?

Photo 1.4 The Cutty Sark

© Sandra Clarke

 THINKING POINT

What about the vessel pictured in Photo 1.5, the Gipsy Moth IV, in which Sir Francis Chichester sailed around the world. She was on display in Greenwich, close to the Cutty Sark.

Is she a fixture, a chattel, or part and parcel of the land? Why?

Does your answer differ from that which you gave for the Cutty Sark? Why?

Photo 1.5 How the Gipsy Moth IV was fixed to the ground
© Scott Hortop

  THINKING POINT

Finally, consider the boat pictured in Photo 1.6. It is a narrowboat moored on a canal and used as a houseboat.

Is she a chattel, a fixture, or part and parcel of the land? Why?

How does she differ from the Cutty Sark and Gipsy Moth IV?

It is submitted that the Cutty Sark forms part and parcel of the land, based on the fact that she was brought onto the land with the intention that she stay there permanently as a visitor attraction and has been in dry dock ever since. Gipsy Moth IV, on the other hand, is a chattel. Although she was attached to the land, it was simple to detach her from her fixings and take her elsewhere. In fact, she has been away from Greenwich for many years now and has since sailed around the world again! She was fixed to the land to display her as a chattel, not with the intention of making her part of the land.

Photo 1.6 A narrowboat moored on a canal

© Chris Crafter

Finally, the houseboat in Photo 1.6 is definitely a chattel, because she can be untied and moved at any time. Relevant cases are *Chelsea Yacht and Boat Club v. Pope* [2001] 2 All ER 409, in which it was held that a houseboat always remains a chattel, and of course, *Mew v. Tristmire*.

Everyday items

THINKING POINT

Have a look around at the room that you are in at the moment.

What do you think about the everyday items that you see?

What about carpets or curtains, or fitted kitchen units? Are they fixtures or chattels?

The best guidance on everyday items is the Court of Appeal decision in *Botham v. TSB plc* (1997) 73 P & CR D 1.

▶ CROSS REFERENCE

See Chapter 14 for more on mortgages.

> ### 🔍 CASE CLOSE-UP
>
> **Botham v. TSB plc (1997) 73 P & CR D 1**
>
> The appellant was behind with his mortgage payments, so the respondent bank was entitled to possession of his flat. The appellant claimed that he had transferred the contents of the property to his parents. The bank was entitled to anything that formed part of the land as a fixture, but not to chattels. The trial judge had divided the 109 items into nine categories and considered each of the categories. He found almost all of the items to be fixtures.
>
> The Court of Appeal differed, however, in its interpretation of the law. A summary of its decision can be seen in Table 1.1.
>
> It is important to note that all cases will depend upon their facts. If curtains or carpets were fixed in a different way, or were part of an 'architectural design', for example, the decision as to whether they are fixtures or chattels could vary. This case is, however, a very useful starting point in considering everyday items.

Table 1.1 Summary of the Court of Appeal's decision in *Botham v. TSB plc*

Item	Court of Appeal Decision
Fitted carpets	Held to be chattels, because they are easily removed
Lights fixed to walls or ceilings, some of which were in recesses in the ceilings and some of which were attached to the ceiling by tracks	Only those recessed into the ceiling were held to be fixtures; the others could be easily removed
Gas flame-effect fires	Held to be chattels, because they could be easily disconnected and removed
Curtains and blinds, including a shower curtain	Held to be chattels, because they are easily removed
Towel rails, soap dishes, and lavatory roll holders	Held to be fixtures, because they constituted a permanent improvement to the land
Fittings on baths and basins, such as taps, plugs, and shower heads	Held to be fixtures, because they constituted a permanent improvement to the land
Mirrors and marble panels on the walls in the fitted bathroom	Accepted by the defendants to be fixtures
Kitchen units and work surfaces, including a fitted sink	Held to be fixtures, because they constituted a permanent improvement to the kitchen
White goods in the kitchen, such as fridge-freezers, washing machines, and dishwashers	Held to be chattels, because they could be easily removed

Tenant's fixtures

The law on fixtures could act harshly in relation to tenants, because they occupy the land for a limited period only and have to return the land to their landlord at the end of the tenancy. If they have attached items to the land in such a way that the items have become fixtures, they become part of the land and belong to the landlord. In order to avoid such unfairness, a separate set of rules has been established concerning **tenant's fixtures**.

A tenant who attaches a tenant's fixture may remove it at any time during the tenancy or at the end of the lease, or even after the tenancy has ended, provided that he or she is still lawfully in possession. The tenant must make good any damage done in removing the fixture.

> **tenant's fixtures**
> fixtures attached to rented property by a tenant that the tenant is entitled to remove

 CASE CLOSE-UP

Mancetter Developments Ltd v. Garmanson Ltd [1986] QB 1212

The tenant had installed pipework and extractor fans in a factory. These were tenant's fixtures. When they were removed, large holes were left in the factory walls. The tenant was entitled to remove the fans and pipework, but was liable in damages for failing to make good the holes.

There are three categories of tenant's fixture: trade fixtures, ornamental fixtures, and agricultural fixtures.

- Trade fixtures
- These are objects used by the tenant in his or her trade. They have been held to include boilers, machinery, etc., and also the fittings of a public house. This is the category under discussion in *Mancetter Developments Ltd v. Garmanson Ltd*.

When looking at tenant's trade fixtures, it is important to consider the question in two steps:

1. Is it a fixture at all?

2. If it is a fixture, is it a trade fixture and therefore removable by the tenant? This may be decided by the wording of the lease: see *Peel Land and Property Ltd v. Sheerness Steel Ltd* [2014] EWCA Civ 100, in which the Court of Appeal held that the lease prevented the removal of any tenant's fixtures. The first instance decision, at [2013] EWHC 1658 (Ch) by Morgan J, contains a valuable discussion of fixtures and of tenant's fixtures in particular.

The reason for this two-step approach is that it is often necessary to decide whether an article is a fixture, even if it is a trade fixture that the tenant may ultimately have a right to remove. The ownership of the object may be important for tax or rent-review purposes during the tenancy. If it is a fixture, it belongs to the landlord until the tenant removes it under the tenant's fixture rules. If it is not a fixture, it is a chattel, which belongs to the tenant throughout.

- Ornamental fixtures
- Older cases—such as *Martin v. Roe* (1857) 7 E & B 237—recognized the tenant's right to remove articles attached to the land for ornamental purposes, which could be removed without damage to the land. It is arguable that, in the light of the 'purpose of annexation' test, these items would probably not be regarded as fixtures at all today and so would be removable by the tenant anyway.

- Agricultural fixtures
- Farm tenants are given statutory rights under Agricultural Tenancies Act 1995, s. 8, to remove any fixture they have affixed to the land. They must make good any damage caused by removal of their fixtures. Unlike trade fixtures, agricultural fixtures belong to the tenant at all times.

Finally, in an unusual case, *The Creative Foundation v. Dreamland Leisure Ltd* [2015] EWHC 2556 (Ch), [2016] Ch 253, it was held that a piece of rendering on a wall that had been covered with a graffito mural by the famous 'Banksy' could not be removed by the tenant and sold. The wall rendering was a landlord's fixture before its removal from the building, and became a landlord's chattel afterwards. Even if removed as 'repair' by the tenant, it belonged to the landlord.

1.1.3.2 **Water**

LPA 1925, s. 205(1)(ix), does not mention water at all, but the Land Registration Act 2002 does.

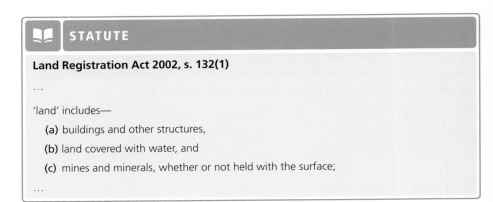

> ## 📖 STATUTE
>
> **Land Registration Act 2002, s. 132(1)**
>
> …
>
> 'land' includes—
>
> (a) buildings and other structures,
>
> (b) land covered with water, and
>
> (c) mines and minerals, whether or not held with the surface;
>
> …

Section 132(1) makes it clear that 'land covered with water' is still 'land' (and indeed, English law does not regard the water as being in separate ownership to the land it covers). Therefore, a lake or pond in the middle of your land is part of the land, and the bed of a river and the seabed also form part of the land.

So far, so good—but then it gets a little more complicated. Rights over the water itself depend on whether the water is still or flowing, and, if it is flowing, whether it is tidal or not. Still water, such as a pond or lake, is regarded as forming part of the land on which it rests and landowners can do as they like with it, subject to any statutory controls under the Water Resources Act 1991. Landowners have certain natural rights over rivers flowing through their land: they can fish in the river (unless that right has been granted to someone else) and they have the right to an undiminished flow of the water. They cannot, however, take water from the river to the detriment of landowners downstream and they are entitled to prevent owners upstream from abstracting (removing) water to a noticeable extent. In any case, abstraction is now regulated by statute.

In contrast, landowners have no natural right to water simply percolating through the land—that is, to water not in a defined stream, but just ground water. Subject to statutory restrictions, other landowners can pump out naturally percolating water, or even increase the amount of naturally percolating water reaching lower land, as long as they are acting reasonably—see the discussion of the law in *Palmer v. Bowman* [2000] 1 WLR 842.

If the boundary of land is a non-tidal river, the landowners on each side of the river own the bed of the river up to the centre line—*ad medium filum*. They can fish as far across the river as they can cast their lines.

Tidal water is treated somewhat differently. There is a starting presumption that the Crown owns the **foreshore**, although the Crown may have granted it to another body (for example, a local authority).

In addition, the public has rights of navigation and fishing over tidal waterways.

If the boundary of land is tidal water, the boundary may be fixed, or it may vary with the changing of the coastline over the years—see *Baxendale v. Instow Parish Council* [1982] Ch 14. In a more recent case the question of shifting sandbanks was discussed:

foreshore

the land between the high-water mark and low-water mark

CASE CLOSE-UP

Loose v. Lynn Shellfish Ltd [2016] UKSC 14

The extent of land over which a fishery (a right to harvest shellfish) could be exercised altered with the movement of the low-water mark (lowest astronomical tide) from time to time. However, the right did not extend to sandbanks which attached themselves to the foreshore at a specific time—this was not the gradual movement of the boundary, but a sudden one. The public still had the right to take shellfish from the sandbanks.

1.1.3.3 **Animals**

Wild animals and birds do not form part of the land while they are alive, and belong to landowners only when they are found dead on the land. Landowners, however, have the right to hunt them and thus bring them into possession by killing them.

1.1.3.4 **Plants**

Trees and other plants are attached to the land, and form part of it. It is possible to own the plants separately from the land—another example of land having different strata or levels.

 EXAMPLE

It is possible for Farmer Brown to own the land on which trees are planted, but for Forestry Ltd to own the trees.

1.1.4 **Incorporeal hereditaments**

Have another look at the definition in LPA 1925, s. 205(1)(ix).

 STATUTE

Law of Property Act 1925, s. 205(1)(ix)

'Land' includes land of any tenure, and mines and minerals, whether or not held apart from the surface, buildings or parts of buildings (whether the division is horizontal, vertical or made in any other way) and other corporeal hereditaments; also a manor, advowson, and a rent and other incorporeal hereditaments, and an easement, right, privilege, or benefit in, over, or derived from land; … and 'mines and minerals' include any strata or seam of minerals or substances in or under any land, and powers of working and getting the same … ; and 'manor' includes a lordship, and reputed manor or lordship; and 'hereditament' means any real property which on an intestacy occurring before the commencement of this Act might have devolved upon an heir.

You will have noticed that it also includes reference to **incorporeal hereditaments**.

'Incorporeal' means things without a physical form (intangible property), such as rights to receive rent from the land, rights of way, rights of light, and the two ancient rights mentioned in the definition in LPA 1925, s. 205(1)(ix)—an 'advowson' and a 'manor'. You need not worry about an advowson (the right to present a priest to a parish), because it is largely obsolete. Manorial rights, meanwhile, are mainly ceremonial nowadays—but there have been two modern cases showing that manorial rights are not quite dead and buried:

> **incorporeal hereditaments**
> intangible rights in land

CROSS REFERENCE

If you want to know more about this case, see Chapter 12, 12.4.4.1.

 CASE CLOSE-UP

Bakewell Management Ltd v. Roland Brandwood and Ors [2004] UKHL 14

A businessman who bought the lordship of a manor tried to charge large sums of money for granting rights of way over the common land of the manor to the residents who owned houses around the common. They had been driving over the common to reach their houses for years, but he claimed that they had no right to do so. He was eventually unsuccessful, but the residents had to appeal all the way to the House of Lords to stop him.

 CASE CLOSE-UP

Crown Estate Commissioners v. Roberts [2008] EWHC 1302 (Ch)

The defendant bought up a number of titles to ancient manors and tried initially to claim ownership of large areas of the foreshore of the Pembrokeshire coastline. This claim failed because of a decision in an earlier case (*Roberts v. Swangrove Estates* [2008] EWCA Civ 98), so Mr Roberts instead claimed a number of manorial rights, including wreck de mer, a several fishery, treasure trove, sporting rights, and estrays (these ancient terms are explained in a glossary in an appendix to the judgment). However, all he was able to prove title to was 'a moiety' (half) of a right to wreck.

Although both these cases led to very little in the final analysis, there was a good deal of expensive litigation and anxiety before the matters were settled. It might be better if such ancient rights were either abolished or their extent set out clearly by statute.

Incorporeal hereditaments form part of the land just as much as corporeal hereditaments. If you reflect for a moment, you will see why this is.

 EXAMPLE

Ali lives in a first-floor flat. The stairs and hallways belong to his landlord, Ben. If Ali is to use his flat, he must have a right of way over the stairs and hallways. This right of way needs to form part of land and needs to be transferred with the physical land each time it is transferred to a new owner, or the flat will be valueless.

It is therefore necessary, when looking at the extent of a piece of land, to consider the incorporeal hereditaments that may form part of it. These rights form an important part of the land.

The other side of the coin is that other people may have rights over your land. These may be incorporeal hereditaments, such as rights of way—Ben, in the example just given, has a right of way over his land that will bind any future owner of it. Such rights are described as **proprietary rights**. They are not personal to the original parties, as are ordinary contractual rights, but are binding on future owners, who were not parties to the original contract.

proprietary rights
rights that are not personal to the original parties, but which are binding on future owners

Many of these proprietary rights will be studied in later chapters, but it is worth noting now that the courts have always sought to limit the number of proprietary rights, precisely because they have such far-reaching effects. In the leading House of Lords decision, *National Provincial Bank Ltd v. Ainsworth* [1965] AC 1175, Lord Wilberforce made the following statement:

 CASE CLOSE-UP

National Provincial Bank Ltd v. Ainsworth [1965] AC 1175

Per Lord Wilberforce at 1247:

> Before a right or an interest can be admitted into the category of property, or of a right affecting property, it must be definable, identifiable by third parties, capable in its nature of assumption by third parties, and have some degree of permanence or stability.

This definition means that a proprietary right needs to have three qualities:

1. It must be definable—that is, it must be possible to say what the right is and what it is not.
2. It must be able to be transferred to a new owner—that is, it must not be personal to the person now claiming that right.
3. It must last a reasonable amount of time—that is, it must not be a very fleeting right, or one that changes frequently.

This is somewhat circular, in that the *consequence* of a right being proprietary is that it can be transferred to a new owner and the *definition* is that it is a right that can be transferred to a new owner. Also, the degree of stability of the right will depend in some measure on whether it is held to be proprietary. This definition however, does set out the most important features of proprietary rights and, in practice, the law is slow to add new rights to the category of proprietary rights, although this can still happen.

1.2 Objects lost and found in and on the land

Sometimes questions arise as to the rights of landowners to objects found lost or hidden on, or buried within, the land. The rules that apply differ depending on whether the object is found in (or attached to) the land or on the surface of the land. In both cases, however, these rules apply only if the true owner of the object (the person who lost or hid it) cannot be found.

1.2.1 **In the land**

Objects found in, or attached to, the land belong to the occupier of the land.

 CASE CLOSE-UP

AG of the Duchy of Lancaster v. Overton (Farms) Ltd [1981] Ch 333

In this case, the Court had to decide whether coins were treasure trove (see 1.2.3) or not. It was accepted that if they were not they would belong to the owner of the soil in which they were found.

1.2.2 **On the land**

Objects found on the surface of the land may belong either to the finder or to the occupier of the land. The lost object can be claimed by the occupier only if a manifest intention to control the land can be shown.

 CASE CLOSE-UP

Parker v. British Airways Board [1982] 1 All ER 834

A passenger found a gold bracelet on the floor of the executive lounge. He handed it to an employee of British Airways, with a request that it be returned to him if the true owner was not found. British Airways could not find the owner, so they sold the bracelet and kept the proceeds. The claimant sued for damages, on the basis that he had a better right to the bracelet than British Airways. The Court of Appeal held that the claimant did, indeed, have a better right to the bracelet.

The bracelet was not attached to the ground, so the occupier did not have automatic priority over the finder. The claimant was lawfully in the lounge and not a trespasser, and he did not have dishonest intentions. The test, therefore, was whether the defendants had shown 'a manifest intention to exercise control over the lounge and all things which might be in it'. They had not done so, because there was no evidence that they searched regularly, or at all, for lost articles.

It was accepted by the court in *Parker v. British Airways* that, in some circumstances, there was a clear 'manifest intention to exercise control' by the very nature of the premises. Donaldson LJ agreed that a bank vault would fall into such a category. At the other end of the spectrum, a public park clearly gives rise to no such implications. Most premises fall somewhere in between these two extremes.

 CASE CLOSE-UP

Waverley Borough Council v. Fletcher [1995] 4 All ER 756

In this case, the defendant, who was using a metal detector in a park owned by the claimant council, found a brooch some 9 inches (23 cm) below the surface of the land. He dug it up and reported his find to the Coroner, who determined that it was not treasure trove (see 1.2.3). The question arose as to who had the better right to the brooch: the finder or the landowners.

The Court of Appeal held that the claimant council had the better right to the brooch. It had been found within, or attached to, the land, rather than on the surface, so that it belonged to the owner of the soil in which it had been found. The defendant's claim that he was enjoying lawful recreation in the park was rejected, because metal detecting and digging for finds were not recreations of the sort permitted in local parks.

Both of these cases show the importance of the lawfulness of the finder's presence on the land. A trespassing finder will have no right to the found object. This may occur because the finder was not invited onto the land at all, or because the limits of the permission (known in land law as a licence) that was granted by the landowner have been exceeded. For example, in *Waverley Borough Council v. Fletcher* the defendant had a licence to be in the park for recreation, but not to use a metal detector, nor to dig up the park.

1.2.3 **Treasure**

At common law, items of gold or silver found hidden in land belonged to the Crown.

In *AG of the Duchy of Lancaster v. Overton (Farms) Ltd*, it was held that coins had to contain a substantial quantity of gold or silver to be **treasure trove**. Finders of treasure trove were paid compensation.

The common law was defective however, in not protecting archaeological finds unless they were of gold or silver and so the Treasure Act 1996 was enacted with effect from 24 September 1997. This Act abolished treasure trove and made fresh provision in relation to treasure. It removed the requirement that the objects had to have been hidden in the land to be treasure, it defined the amount of precious metal that had to be present for a find to count as treasure, and it made provision for other items of archaeological importance found with treasure to be included within the definition.

> **treasure trove**
> under common law before 1997, items of gold and silver found in a concealed place, having apparently been hidden by their owner and not reclaimed, to which the Crown had the right of possession, now replaced by the Treasure Act 1996

 STATUTE

Treasure Act 1996, s. 1 [Meaning of 'treasure']

Treasure is—

any object at least 300 years old when found which—

   (i) is not a coin but has metallic content of which at least 10 per cent by weight is precious metal;

  (ii) when found, is one of at least two coins in the same find which are at least 300 years old at that time and have that percentage of precious metal; or

 (iii) when found, is one of at least ten coins in the same find which are at least 300 years old at that time;

any object at least 200 years old when found which belongs to a class designated under section 2(1);

any object which would have been treasure trove if found before the commencement of section 4;

any object which, when found, is part of the same find as—

   1. an object within paragraph (a), (b) or (c) found at the same time or earlier; or

   2. an object found earlier which would be within paragraph (a) or (b) if it had been found at the same time.

Treasure does not include objects which are—

unworked natural objects, or

minerals as extracted from a natural deposit,

or which belong to a class designated under section 2(2).

Under s. 2(1) of the Act, the Secretary of State was given power to designate further objects as treasure and, under the Treasure Designation Order 2002, SI 2002/2666, the following items were added to the definition of treasure.

📖 **STATUTE**

Treasure Designation Order 2002, art. 3 [Designation of classes of objects of outstanding historical, archaeological or cultural importance]

3.   The following classes of objects are designated pursuant to section 2(1) of the Act.

   (a) any object (other than a coin), any part of which is base metal, which, when found, is one of at least two base metal objects in the same find which are of prehistoric date;

   (b) any object, other than a coin, which is of prehistoric date, and any part of which is gold or silver.

The Act and the Order apply to objects within these definitions that are found anywhere within England, Wales, and Northern Ireland, whether attached to or within land, or on the surface. In practice, most treasure is discovered during archaeological digs or by people using metal detectors. Very little treasure is likely to be found on the surface of land.

Finds of items that might be treasure have to be reported to the Coroner within fourteen days and an inquest held to determine whether the find is treasure or not. It is a criminal offence not to report a find. A Code of Practice for offering finds to museums, and for rewarding finders and landowners has been drawn up—see the Treasure Act 1996 Code of Practice (second revision). This Code sets out the division of the reward between the finder and the landowner. It starts with the presumption that the reward is to be split 50/50, but an agreement between the finder and landowner as to the split may be observed. If the finder is a trespasser or has committed an offence related to finding, or dealing with, the treasure (such as not declaring it in a timely way to the Coroner), his or her reward may be reduced or refused altogether.

1.2.4 **Summary**

The law on objects lost and found in and on the land is summarized in Figure 1.2.

Figure 1.2 A summary of the law on objects lost and found in and on the land

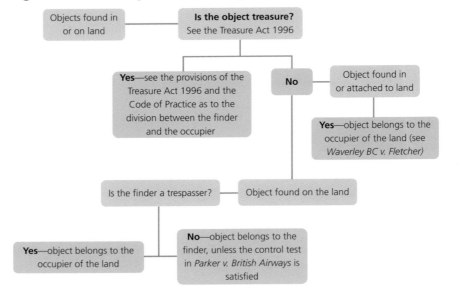

Summary

1. Land extends both below and above the ground.

2. Both corporeal and incorporeal hereditaments form part of the land.

3. The law distinguishes between fixtures and chattels, and the test used by the courts to identify them relates to the degree and (more importantly) purpose of annexation.

4. Items lost or hidden on land belong to their true owner if they can be found, or, if they cannot, to the occupier of the land within which the items are buried or to which they are attached.

5. If the item is merely on the surface of the land, however, the finder may well have better rights than the landowner, depending on the 'manifest intention to control' test. An exception to these rules is found within the law of treasure.

The bigger picture

- If you want to see how this area of land law fits into the rest of your studies, you can look at Chapter 15, especially 15.2.1 and 15.2.2. Before you can answer any question on land law, you need to be able to identify the land!

- For some guidance on what sort of exam questions come up in this area, see Chapter 16.3.

- If you need to find extra cases for research on coursework in this area, the following may be helpful.

Extent of land

Anchor Brewhouse Developments Ltd v. Berkley House (Docklands Developments) Ltd [1987] 2 EGLR 173
London & Manchester Assurance Co Ltd v. O & H Construction Ltd [1989] 2 EGLR 185
Mitchell v. Mosley [1914] 1 Ch 438 (this case was approved by the Supreme Court in *Bocardo v. Star Energy*)

Fixtures

Caddick v. Whitsand Bay Holiday Park Ltd [2015] UKUT 0063 (LC)
Hamp v. Bygrave [1983] 1 EGLR 174
Melluish v. BMI (No. 3) Ltd [1996] AC 454
Smith v. City Petroleum Co Ltd [1940] 1 All ER 260
Stokes v. Costain Property Investments Ltd [1984] 1 WLR 763
Young v. Dalgety plc [1987] 1 EGLR 116
Webb v. Frank Bevis Ltd [1940] 1 All ER 247

Objects found on or in land

Armory v. Delamirie (1722) 1 Stra 505, 93 ER 664
Bridges v. Hawksworth (1851) 15 Jur 1079
Elwes v. Brigg Gas Co (1886) 33 Ch D 562
Hannah v. Peel [1945] KB 509

? Questions

Self-test questions

1. Daisy's neighbour has started to build an extension to his house. The extension adjoins Daisy's back garden. The foundations for the extension and the new drainage pipes run under Daisy's garden. Has Daisy any grounds for complaint?

2. Mai Ling's neighbour has just installed a new boiler. The flue extends some 10 cm into Mai Ling's garden, at a height of about 4 m. Has Mai Ling any grounds for complaint?

3. Olu has just bought a house. When he saw the house before buying it, the garden contained a large shed and a number of beautiful plants. The shed and some of the plants were removed before he moved in. Does Olu have any grounds for complaint?

4. Haminder is walking across Farmer Jones's field when he sees a golden bracelet half-buried in the soil. He loosens it with his fingers and takes it home to clean it up. Haminder hands the bracelet to the police, but they have handed it back, saying that they cannot trace the owner. Can Haminder keep the bracelet?

Exam questions

1. Abdul owns a metal detector, which he enjoys using to find objects buried below the surface of land. Early in 2003, he went out with his metal detector onto Bill's farm. Bill was a tenant farmer, leasing his farm from Cuthbert.

   Abdul had seen Bill a few days earlier and asked if he could look for 'buried treasure' in Bill's fields. Bill had laughed and said: 'Okay, but I doubt you'll find anything there—I plough it up pretty regularly.'

   In fact, Abdul found a cache of metal objects, which turned out to be silver goblets and arm-rings, dating from Saxon times. They have been valued at £250,000. He also found a Rolex watch lying on the surface of the field. No one knows who lost or buried any of the items.

   Advise Abdul whether he can lawfully keep these items and, if not, to whom they belong.

2. 'As a matter of legal definition, "land" is both the physical asset and the rights which the owner or others may enjoy in or over it.' (M. Dixon, *Principles of Land Law*, 8th edn)

   Discuss.

 You will find answers to these questions online at www.oup.com/uk/clarke_directions6e/.

☰ Further reading

Caldwell, D. , 'Don't get in a fix over fixtures' (2014) 164(7616) NLJ 15

This article examines the case of *Peel Land and Property Limited v. TS Sheerness Limited* [2014] EWCA Civ 100.

Conway, H. , 'Case comment on *Elitestone v. Morris*' [1998] Conv 418

This case comment examines the leading case of *Elitestone v. Morris*.

Iljadica, M. 'Is a sculpture land?' (2016) 3 Conv 242–50

This article considers *London Borough of Tower Hamlets v. London Borough of Bromley* [2015] EWHC 1954 (Ch).

Thompson, M. P. , 'Must a house be land?' [2001] Conv 417

This article looks at the case of *Chelsea Yacht and Boat Club v. Pope*, and considers the nature of land and of dwelling houses.

 Online Resources

For more advice relating to this chapter, including self-test questions and an interactive glossary, visit www.oup.com/uk/clarke_directions6e/.

2 The structure of land law

LEARNING OBJECTIVES

By the end of this chapter, you will be able to:

- understand the origins of the structure of modern land law;
- explain the doctrines of tenure and estates;
- identify the different roles of common law and equity in land law;
- understand the doctrine of notice and why it was replaced by registration;
- identify the significance of the 1925 property legislation;
- understand registration of land charges and be aware of registration of title.

Introduction

Arguably, the single most important provision in land law is in the Law of Property Act 1925, s. 1.

STATUTE

Law of Property Act 1925, s. 1

(1) The only estates in land which are capable of subsisting or of being conveyed or created at law are—

   (a) An estate in fee simple absolute in possession;

   (b) A term of years absolute.

(2) The only interests or charges in or over land which are capable of subsisting or of being conveyed or created at law are—

   (a) An easement, right, or privilege in or over land for an interest equivalent to an estate in fee simple absolute in possession or a term of years absolute;

   (b) A rentcharge in possession issuing out of or charged on land being either perpetual or for a term of years absolute;

(c) A charge by way of legal mortgage;

(d) … and any other similar charge on land which is not created by an instrument;

(e) Rights of entry exercisable over or in respect of a legal term of years absolute, or annexed, for any purpose, to a legal rentcharge.

(3) All other estates, interests, and charges in or over land take effect as equitable interests.

…

This section lies at the heart of modern land law, because it sets out the estates and interests in land that can exist at law and then says that all other interests in land are equitable.

The section raises a huge number of questions for someone with no knowledge of land law:

- What is an estate?

- What does it mean to be 'conveyed at law'?

- What is the difference between an estate 'at law' and an 'equitable interest'?

- Why does it all matter?

The aim of this chapter is to explain what land lawyers mean by legal estates and equitable interests, and why it matters which you own.

2.1 The historical context

At first sight, the history of land law may seem completely irrelevant—after all, why does it matter what the law used to be? Surely what is important is the modern law, not what used to happen in the past?

Our experience, however, suggests that some explanation of the history of land law is vital to understanding the modern law. Many of the concepts and words that confuse students starting out in land law have ancient origins. Explaining these means that the structure of land law becomes clearer, so it is easier to understand how land law works today.

Table 2.1 sets out the main periods in the development of land law. This chapter does not cover any of these in depth, but uses them to explain the main concepts.

Table 2.1 A historical outline of land law

Period	Development
1066 (the Norman Conquest)–c. 1300	**Tenures and estates** Land law in England and Wales dates from 1066. During this early period, the doctrines of tenure and estates were established, as the common law courts worked out the fundamental principles of land law. At the end of this period, in 1290, the statute Quia Emptores was passed, which began to end the feudal system.

(continued)

Table 2.1 (Continued)

Period	Development
1300–1535	**Common law and equity**
	The body of law known as equity grew and became established. Equitable estates and interests came to exist alongside common law estates and interests. One of the most important developments of equity was the 'use', which later developed into the trust.
1535–c. 1650	In 1535, the Statute of Uses was passed. This was intended to abolish 'uses'—the forerunners to trusts. In fact, lawyers found ways round the statute and a great deal of new law was created as a result.
c. 1650–c. 1800	In 1660, the Tenures Abolition Act was passed, which further reduced the effect of the feudal system of tenure. Trusts were developed further, the strict settlement was invented, and the modern form of mortgage was developed.
1800–1925	During this period, there was a series of statutory reforms of land law. These culminated in the 1925 property legislation—a series of Acts of Parliament that consolidated earlier changes in the law.
1926–	Since the 1925 property legislation, there have been further developments in equity, such as 'new model' constructive trusts and proprietary estoppel. In addition, there have been further statutory reforms, the most important of which have been the Trusts of Land and Appointment of Trustees Act 1996, and the Land Registration Act 2002.

CROSS REFERENCE

For more on modern trusts, see Chapters 8, 9, and 11.

For more on mortgages, see Chapter 14.

CROSS REFERENCE

For more on proprietary estoppel, see Chapter 10.

For more on the Trusts of Land and Appointment of Trustees Act 1996, see Chapter 11, 11.1 and 11.2.

CROSS REFERENCE

For more on the Land Registration Act 2002, see Chapter 4.

2.2 The earliest developments: tenures and estates

The structure of land law traditionally dates from 1066: the date of the Norman Conquest. William, Duke of Normandy, invaded England and fought the Saxon King, Harold, at the Battle of Hastings. King Harold was killed and the victorious Duke became King William I, the first Norman King of England.

The significance of this event for English land law was that the Normans brought with them their own system of landholding, known as the **feudal system**. Under that system, only the King was able to own land outright. All others were granted land by the King, to hold from him for a certain period of time. This holding of land is known as **tenure** and the period of time for which it is held is known as an **estate**.

> **feudal system** a political, economic, and social system under which only the monarch was able to own land outright
>
> **tenure**
> 1. *freehold tenure*—in the feudal system, the grant of an estate in land by a lord to a tenant. The tenant 'holds the land of the lord' for the period defined by the estate.
> 2. *leasehold tenure*—the relationship between a landlord and a tenant in leasehold land

> **estate** the length of time for which land has been granted to a tenant under the system of tenure. It means the duration of the grant. Note that this is a use of the word 'estate' that differs from the general use of the word; estate is used in this technical sense in land law.

2.2.1 Tenures

In this chapter, we will be looking at the first meaning of tenure—that is, freehold tenure.

When William I became King of England, he became the 'paramount lord' of all the land in England, which gave him the power to make grants of that land to anyone he wished. In practice, he no doubt left many of the Saxon noblemen in residence on their land and either granted estates in that land to them, or granted an estate in it to a Norman lord, who would, in turn, grant an estate in it to the Saxon already in residence. In return for the grant of the estate, the new tenant would be obliged to perform services for his new lord.

▶ CROSS REFERENCE
For more on leasehold tenure, see Chapter 5.

 EXAMPLE

The King might grant the Duke of Borsetshire an estate in the whole of Borsetshire, in return for the provision of 100 fully equipped soldiers for 100 days each year. The Duke might provide these soldiers by making grants of parcels of his land to ten lesser noblemen, in return for ten soldiers each for 100 days a year. He might also make grants to farmers in return for quantities of food, etc.

Each of the tenants might, in their turn, make grants of part of their land in return for services.

Tenure also carried with it certain 'incidents', which meant payments to the lord or rights that the lord could exercise. For example, when an estate in land passed on the death of a tenant to his heir, a sum of money was usually payable to the lord. If a tenant died without leaving an heir, the estate would revert back or **escheat** to the lord.

> **escheat** the right of the lord to the tenant's land if he were to die without leaving an heir. This survives into modern times as the right of the Crown to land left without an owner (bona vacantia), although it is now regulated by the Administration of Estates Act 1925. Common law escheat survives, under which land is disclaimed by a debtor on insolvency (bankruptcy).

The granting of estates in land in return for services and incidents led to the development of the feudal pyramid.

Figure 2.1 The feudal pyramid under William I

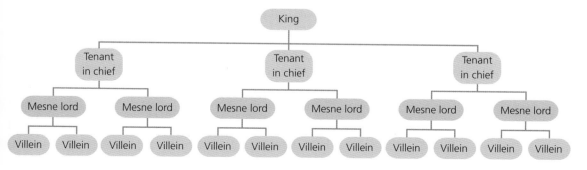

As you can see, the King is at the top of the pyramid as the owner, or more correctly, as 'paramount lord' of all land in the kingdom. The 'tenants in chief' held estates directly from him; the 'mesne' lords held from the tenants in chief, etc. At the very bottom are the 'villeins' or peasants, who held on the 'unfree tenures'. They would be granted strips of land in their lord's fields, to grow their own food, in return for working on the lord's land for part of the time. It is important to note that there could be many more levels in the feudal pyramid than are shown in Figure 2.1. New grants could be made at any time and the process of making such grants of land was called **subinfeudation**.

subinfeudation

the process of making new grants of land under the feudal system

The feudal system's use of the land as a means to obtain services did not last very long. Over time, many services were replaced by a payment of money instead. With inflation, those sums of money became less valuable.

In 1290, the statute Quia Emptores (which is still in force) began the dismantling of the feudal system, because it prohibited subinfeudation. From the passing of that statute to present times, estates in land can be transferred only by **substitution**—that is, one owner taking the place of another. No further levels could be added to the feudal pyramid and, over the course of time, the pyramid began to flatten.

substitution

the process of transferring estates in land under which one owner takes the place of another

This flattening process was accelerated by the Tenures Abolition Act 1660 and completed by the Law of Property Act 1925 (LPA 1925). Today, there is only one form of tenure left and only one lord. Everyone holds their land directly from the Crown on 'freehold tenure in socage', a tenure that has no services and only one relevant incident—escheat. So, the feudal pyramid has flattened completely, as shown in Figure 2.2.

Figure 2.2 The feudal pyramid today

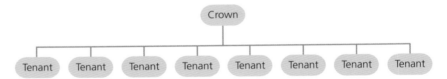

It is fair to say that the doctrine of tenure itself now has limited importance in everyday land law in England and Wales. But it 'is a doctrine which could not be overturned without fracturing the skeleton which gives our land law its shape and consistency', according to Brennan J of the High Court of Australia in the case of *Mabo v. Queensland (No. 2)* (1992) 175 CLR 1 FC 92/014.

See the online resources for an excerpt from this case, with some questions.

 **CASE CLOSE-UP**

Mabo v. Queensland (No. 2) **(1992) 175 CLR 1 FC 92/014**

The doctrine of tenure was minutely examined to establish whether, when the Crown acquired sovereignty over Australia, this destroyed all prior interests held by Aboriginal Australians. It was held that the Crown's 'radical title' as paramount lord did not destroy native title rights that had existed since before the Crown acquired sovereignty; it was only if the Crown had granted the land to settlers or used the land itself that native title had been destroyed.

The case contains a fascinating discussion of the details of the doctrine of tenure.

2.2.2 Estates

The doctrine of estates follows on directly from the doctrine of tenure and is a consequence of it. If land is to be 'held of' a lord, then the parties must specify the length of time for which it is to be held. This length of time is the estate in land. In the very ancient *Walsingham's Case* (1573) 2 Plowd 547, it was said that: 'An estate in the land is a time in the land, or land for a time.'

Before 1925, there were three common freehold estates, as shown in Table 2.2.

Table 2.2 Types of common freehold estate pre-1925

Estate	Duration
Fee simple	For as long as there were heirs to inherit. The estate would not end unless all possible heirs (blood relations of the grantee or any of his heirs, etc.) were dead. The estate could therefore potentially last forever. It would come to an end only if the present tenant were to die without leaving an heir.
Fee tail	For as long as the grantee's lineal descendants (children, grandchildren, etc.) lasted. A variant of the fee tail was the fee tail male, under which only male lineal descendants could inherit. (Note that these estates could, in later times, be 'barred' to create a fee simple.)
Life estate	For as long as the life of the grantee or the life of a named person. Note that this is not a fee, because it is not inheritable.

The common feature of all the freehold estates is that they are of uncertain duration: no one can say with certainty when a person will die, or when all of his or her heirs will die. This is the hallmark of the freehold estates and distinguishes freehold from leasehold.

One question that might occur to you is how to know what sort of estate is under **conveyance** (being transferred): did the **conveyancer** intend to transfer the fee simple, the fee tail, or merely a life estate?

Historically, conveyancers have used 'words of limitation'—a particular phrase that is known to have the correct legal effect—to mark out the limits of the estate they intended to transfer. In modern times, however, this is simplified by statute under LPA 1925, s. 60.

 STATUTE

Law of Property Act 1925, s. 60(1)

A conveyance of freehold land to any person without words of limitation, or any equivalent expression, shall pass to the grantee the fee simple or other the whole interest which the grantor had power to convey in such land, unless a contrary intention appears in the conveyance.

Therefore, the grantor is assumed to have transferred the largest estate he or she held in the land, unless it is made clear in the transfer that a lesser interest was intended.

2.2.3 Crown land

Unlike everyone else, the Crown can own land outright (**allodial land**) and not as an estate held of a lord. This includes **desmesne land**.

conveyance
the transfer of a legal estate in land from one person to another

conveyancer
a person who specializes in the transfer of estates in land—usually a solicitor or licensed conveyancer

allodial land
land that is owned outright, rather than as an estate held of a lord

demesne land
'land belonging to [the monarch] in right of the Crown'

STATUTE

Land Registration Act 2002, s. 132

…

'demesne land' means land belonging to Her Majesty in right of the Crown which is not held for an estate in fee simple absolute in possession;

…

> **CROSS REFERENCE**
>
> For clarification of the meaning of 'foreshore', see the definition at Chapter 1, 1.1.3.2.

Examples of demesne land include the foreshore and land that has escheated to the Crown, as well as land that has belonged to the Crown since ancient times and in which an estate was never granted.

2.3 Common law and equity

> **common law**
>
> the law developed by the Royal Courts—that is, the law applicable to the whole country, not purely local law

Tenures and estates are creations of the **common law** and their development dominates most of the early history of English land law. At that time, however, the common law itself was developing, as law moved out of local courts and into the Royal Courts (the King's Bench, the Common Pleas, and the Exchequer). Actions in these courts were by 'writs', which were very prescriptive. Like many modern-day government forms, these writs were appropriate only for certain cases. Other cases simply could not be 'fitted into' any writ, so it was difficult to bring the case at all—particularly after the Statute of Westminster II 1285, which severely restricted the invention of new writs. This led to obvious injustice in a number of cases.

The remedy for such injustice was for the injured party to appeal directly to the King as the 'fountain of all justice'. The King's Council, including the King's most important minister, the Chancellor, heard these petitions and, gradually, the Chancellor rather than the King's Council came to be responsible for hearing such claims. In this way, the Court of Chancery developed.

From the end of the seventeenth century until the Constitutional Reform Act 2005, only lawyers were appointed to the post of Lord Chancellor and each sat as a judge in the Court of Chancery. The system of justice called **equity** developed, from one-off decisions in the early stages, to become a body of law that was as settled as the common law. The principles of equity, however, were based on conscience, in contrast to the common law's emphasis on technicality.

> **equity**
>
> the law developed by the Lord Chancellor and the Court of Chancery to remedy defects in the common law

Because equity developed from the position of the King as fountain of all justice, in cases of conflict between the two systems, equity prevailed over the common law. This means that, if there are two possible answers to a legal problem—one given by the common law and one given by equity—the equitable answer takes priority.

> **CROSS REFERENCE**
>
> For an example of this rule in action, see *Walsh v. Lonsdale* in Chapter 5, 5.4.2.

Eventually, by the Judicature Acts 1873 and 1875, the two systems of law came to be administered by all courts, so that there were no longer courts of common law and courts of equity. The two systems of law still operate side by side, and, even today, it is possible to distinguish equitable rights and remedies from legal ones.

2.3.1 **The effect of equity on land law**

The easiest way to describe the effect of equity on land law is by giving examples of the types of interest rejected by the common law, but recognized by equity. One important example is the **trust**.

CROSS REFERENCE

For the use of trusts in modern land law, see Chapter 11.

> **trust** an arrangement by which someone (called a 'settlor') transfers property to others (called 'trustees') on terms that the trustees will hold that property for the benefit of certain persons (called the 'beneficiaries')

To understand how the trust developed, think about the following example.

EXAMPLE

Sir Robin of Locksley was about to go off to war abroad. He wanted to ensure that his family was provided for while he was away. He therefore transferred his estate in Locksley Hall to his good friend, Sir Guy of Gisborne, trusting him to use the property for the benefit of Sir Robin's wife, Lady Marian, and children.

In this example, Sir Robin was the settlor, Sir Guy was the trustee, and Lady Marian and the children were the beneficiaries.

The common law courts, after a little hesitation, refused to recognize the rights of beneficiaries under trusts. The common law recognized only the trustee as having legal rights in the land, because he was the person with legal title to the land: it had been transferred to him. The courts of equity, meanwhile, recognized the rights of the beneficiaries.

EXAMPLE

Suppose that after three years, Sir Guy of Gisborne received news that Sir Robin was dead. He decided to keep Locksley Hall for himself and therefore threw Lady Marian and the children out into the streets.

If Lady Marian had brought an action in the common law courts for the return of the land, she would have been unsuccessful. The common law courts recognized only the legal title of the trustee.

If Lady Marian had gone to the Court of Chancery, however, she might have obtained a remedy. The Court recognized the equitable rights of the beneficiaries as the true or 'beneficial' owners of the estate. The Court would have issued an order to the trustee (Sir Guy) to carry out the terms of the trust, and Lady Marian and the children could have moved back in.

> *in rem*
> a right enforceable against everyone—that is, a right in the property itself

The order for the trustee to carry out the terms of the trust is an example of equity acting *in personam*—that is, 'on the person'. Because equity acts on the conscience of the individual, equitable rights are enforceable only against those 'whose conscience is affected by them'. This can be contrasted with the common law, under which legal rights can be enforced against anyone, no matter what the state of their conscience. Legal rights are said to be *in rem*—that is, in the property itself, rather than against a particular person.

> *in personam*
> a right enforceable against certain persons or classes of persons

The history of the development of the trust is a fascinating one, but its details are outside the scope of this book. It started as the 'use', developed in the fifteenth century. The use proved so effective as a means of avoidance of feudal dues (taxes) that it was prohibited by Parliament in the Statute of Uses 1535. Lawyers found ways around the statute, however, and the use returned as the trust. Trusts are still used for tax avoidance today, as well as for many other purposes in land law and other areas of law.

Another example of the effect of equity on land law is the development of the **mortgage**.

❯ CROSS REFERENCE

For more on mortgages, see Chapter 14.

mortgage
a way of using land as security for a loan

equity of redemption
the rights of a mortgagor over the mortgaged property—particularly, the right to redeem the property

charge
a legal or equitable interest in land, securing the payment of money

The earliest type of modern mortgage dates from the seventeenth century. The borrower would convey (transfer) his estate in the land to the lender, in return for the loan. The lender would promise to reconvey (return) the land to the borrower on a date that was fixed for the repayment of the loan. The common law was inflexible about this date for repayment, even if the failure to pay was as the result of an accident or mistake. Equity began to intervene in these cases to extend the date for repayment; at first, where there were special circumstances, but eventually in all cases. Over time, the equitable right of the borrower (mortgagor) to redeem the land long after the agreed date had passed became a recognized right in the land called the **equity of redemption**. Although modern mortgages do not work by conveyance and reconveyance, but by way of a **charge**, the equity of redemption is still a valuable right.

Because the courts of equity regularly upheld both the interests of the beneficiaries under trusts and the equity of redemption held by the mortgagor, these rights came to be equitable estates and interests in land. Therefore, a beneficiary under a trust (such as Lady Marian in our examples) had an equitable estate in the land, whereas her trustee (Sir Guy) had a **legal estate** in the land. This is still true today, although the interests of beneficiaries are nowadays referred to as **equitable interests** rather than as estates, in line with the wording used in LPA 1925, s. 1(3).

legal estate
an estate in land that is recognized by the common law

equitable interest
an interest in land that is recognized by equity

2.4 Legal and equitable estates and interests

From 2.3, you should have understood that two kinds of estates and interests developed in land law: those recognized by the common law (legal rights) and those recognized by equity (equitable rights).

If you take a minute to look back at the introduction to this chapter, you will see that this distinction is a fundamental one in the modern law and that LPA 1925, s. 1, lists those estates and interests in land that can be legal, and then says that all other rights in land can only be equitable. We have established so far what we mean by estates in land, and what we mean by legal and equitable rights—but why does it matter whether you hold a legal estate or an equitable interest?

The main difference stems from the way in which common law and equity enforce rights. As we saw earlier, common law acts *in rem*, whereas equity acts *in personam*. You can understand the difference that this makes in practice by thinking about the following situation.

> **THINKING POINT**
>
> Consider again the trust in the examples above. Sir Guy of Gisborne is the legal owner of Locksley Hall, but Lady Marian and the children are the equitable owners of Locksley Hall. As we established earlier, the Court of Chancery would oblige Sir Guy to carry out the terms of the trust, as he had originally agreed to do.
>
> Suppose that Sir Guy were to sell Locksley Hall to the Sheriff of Nottingham and keep the money for himself. The Sheriff would become the legal owner of Locksley Hall, because he has bought Sir Guy's legal estate in the land. The vital question, however, is whether he would have to hold it on trust for Lady Marian and the family—after all, he did not agree to be a trustee.
>
> If Lady Marian's rights in Locksley Hall had been legal rights, they would have been enforceable against anyone, because they would be rights *in rem*. As equitable rights, however, they would be enforceable only *in personam*—against certain persons. Would the Sheriff of Nottingham be such a person?

The answer to this question can be found in the origins of equity as a doctrine of conscience. Equity would enforce the trust against anyone whose 'conscience was affected' by it. This would come down, ultimately, to whether that person had notice of (knew about) the equitable interest. Therefore, the answer to the question whether the Sheriff of Nottingham would be affected by Lady Marian's equitable interest under the trust would depend upon whether the Sheriff knew about it.

If the Sheriff bought the land knowing of Lady Marian's equitable interest, he would be ordered by the Court of Chancery to carry out the trust. If he knew nothing about the trust, the Court of Chancery would not require him to carry it out, so Lady Marian would have no remedy against him. Instead, she would have to bring an action against Sir Guy of Gisborne, against whom equity could act *in personam*. The problem with that solution, however, would be that Sir Guy no longer owned the land. Therefore, he could only be ordered to pay damages. If he had run away with the money and could not be found, Lady Marian would be left with no remedy at all.

This demonstrates a major disadvantage of equitable estates and interests over legal ones.

2.4.1 **The doctrine of notice**

Gradually, the rule developed that equitable interests could be enforced against anyone *except* those who bought a legal estate in the land and who had no notice of the equitable interest in it. There is a classic statement of this rule in the old case of *Pilcher v. Rawlins* (1872) LR 7 Ch App 259, which sets out the importance of someone now referred to as the **bona fide purchaser of the legal estate for value without notice**.

> **bona fide purchaser of the legal estate for value without notice** broken down, this phrase refers to someone who has bought the legal estate in the land—the 'purchaser of the legal estate'—who has acted honestly in the purchase—that is, in good faith or 'bona fide'—and has bought the land without knowing about the equitable interest in the land—that is, 'without notice'

Such a person was held to have an 'absolute, unqualified, unanswerable defence' to any claim in equity. He could not be deprived of the full value of his legal estate by equity, but had to be allowed to 'depart in possession' of it.

The differences between legal and equitable interests might therefore be expressed as in Table 2.3.

Table 2.3 The differences between legal and equitable interests

Legal estates and interests	Enforceable against everyone—that is, 'good against the whole world'
	Common law acts *in rem*
Equitable estates and interests	Enforceable against everyone *except* the 'bona fide purchaser of the legal estate for value without notice'
	Equity acts *in personam*

We next need to consider what exactly is meant by the 'bona fide purchaser of the legal estate without notice', who is sometimes quaintly referred to as 'equity's darling'.

2.4.1.1 'Bona fide'—in good faith

bona fide

'in good faith'

It is clear from James LJ's statement of the law in *Pilcher v. Rawlins* that **bona fides** (good faith) is a separate requirement from that of notice and one that may be tested by the courts. In *Midland Bank v. Green* [1981] AC 513, Lord Wilberforce defined it as 'genuine and honest'. In practice, it is closely related to the lack of notice and particularly to the doctrine of constructive notice, which is considered at 2.4.1.4.

2.4.1.2 'Purchaser of the legal estate'

> CROSS REFERENCE

For more on the fee simple absolute in possession, see Chapter 3, 3.1.

For more on the term of years absolute, see the definition at Chapter 5, 5.1.

This means that the person must buy a legal estate in the land. In the past, this could have meant any freehold estate, or a legal lease. Since 1925, it means a fee simple absolute in possession, or a term of years absolute, which are the two remaining legal estates under LPA 1925, s. 1(1).

A purchaser is someone who gives value for the land—so someone who receives it as a gift, or as an inheritance, for example, would not qualify. The meaning of purchaser is extended to those who take 'a charge by way of legal mortgage' under LPA 1925, s. 87(1): that is, a person who lends money on the security of a mortgage over the estate.

Note that the definition is limited to those who purchase a legal estate in the land; it does not apply to someone who buys only an equitable interest. If an equitable interest is purchased, then the rule 'if equities are equal, the first in time prevails' applies, meaning that an earlier equitable interest will usually be enforceable against the purchaser of a later equitable interest.

2.4.1.3 'For value'

'Value' means consideration in money or money's worth. Historically, it also included marriage, which was viewed as consideration for a transfer of property. It does not mean that full value must have been paid for the land. For example, in *Midland Bank v. Green* [1981] AC 513, a payment of £500 for land worth £40,000 was held to be within the definition of 'a purchaser for money or money's worth'.

2.4.1.4 'Without notice'

The doctrine of notice lies at the heart of the definition of the person against whom equity would enforce interests. A bona fide purchaser for value of the legal estate who had no notice of the equitable interest would not be bound by it—but notice was not confined to matters of which the purchaser actually knew. It was extended to situations in which the purchaser should have known of the equitable interest.

There are three types of notice: actual notice, constructive notice, and imputed notice.

Actual notice

A purchaser had actual notice of any interests about which he actually knew, by whatever means. He need not, however, attend to vague rumours—*Barnhart v. Greenshields* (1853) 9 Moo PCC 18.

Constructive notice

A purchaser had constructive notice of any interests about which he was deemed to know:

 CASE CLOSE-UP

Jones v. Smith (1841) 66 ER 943

In this case, Lord Wigram identified two categories of constructive notice:

1. cases in which the purchaser has knowledge of some defect or incumbrance in relation to the property, enquiry into which would reveal others, so is deemed to have notice of what those enquiries would have revealed;
2. cases in which the purchaser has deliberately abstained from enquiries to avoid having notice.

The first type of constructive notice means that, if a purchaser discovers a problem with, or equitable interest in, the estate being purchased, further enquiries must be made. The purchaser will be deemed to have notice of any interest that would have been discovered by further enquiries, whether or not they were actually made.

The second type of constructive notice means that a purchaser cannot decide to make no enquiries at all, in the hope that this will avoid being fixed with notice of any equitable interests. In this case, the purchaser will be treated as if he knew anything that proper enquiries would have revealed.

A third category of constructive notice is that the purchaser is also deemed to have notice of all those matters that a reasonable or prudent purchaser, acting with skilled legal advice, would have investigated—*West v. Reid* (1843) 2 Hare 249.

These rules are now summarized by statute, under LPA 1925, s. 199.

 STATUTE

Law of Property Act 1925, s. 199

1. A purchaser shall not be prejudicially affected by notice of—

   ...

   (ii) any other instrument or matter or any fact or thing unless—

      (a) it is within his own knowledge, or would have come to his knowledge if such inquiries and inspections had been made as ought reasonably to have been made by him;

      ...

The purchaser therefore needs to investigate the title to the estate to the same standard as a skilled lawyer. There is also a requirement to inspect the land and to make enquiries of the occupiers as to their rights. A purchaser who fails to do these things might be fixed with notice of matters which should have been discovered.

Imputed notice

This is notice imputed to the purchaser by virtue of actual or constructive knowledge possessed by the purchaser's agent.

 STATUTE

Law of Property Act 1925, s. 199(1)(ii)(b)

(b) in the same transaction with respect to which a question of notice to the purchaser arises, it has come to the knowledge of his counsel, as such, or of his solicitor or other agent, as such, or would have come to the knowledge of his solicitor or other agent, as such, if such inquiries and inspections had been made as ought reasonably to have been made by the solicitor or other agent.

A purchaser is deemed to know what his or her solicitor (or other agent) knew and even what that solicitor would have known if the job had been done properly.

 THINKING POINT

Do the doctrines of constructive notice and imputed notice make it easier or harder for someone to be a bona fide purchaser of the legal estate for value without notice?

These doctrines make it harder, because they expand the meaning of 'notice'. It includes not only what the purchaser actually knew, but also what they, or their solicitor, ought to have known if they had made proper enquiries. Therefore, equitable interests affect more purchasers than they otherwise would have done.

2.4.2 Summary

The situation before 1925, therefore, was that legal estates 'bound the whole world'—that is, that any person coming to own a legal estate in land would be bound to give effect to any existing legal interest in it.

 EXAMPLE

Sir Guy of Gisborne granted a legal lease (tenancy) of one wing of Locksley Hall to John Little. When Sir Guy sold Locksley Hall to the Sheriff of Nottingham, there is no doubt that John Little's lease would have been binding on the Sheriff; the Sheriff could not have thrown John Little off the land, but would have had to permit him to remain there for the term of his lease.

A person coming to own a legal estate in land would be bound by existing equitable interests in it only if he was *not* a bona fide purchaser of the legal estate without notice.

EXAMPLE

Consider again the position of Lady Marian after Locksley Hall had been sold to the Sheriff. She did not have a legal estate or interest in the land; she had only an equitable interest in it. Therefore, the Sheriff would have had to give effect to her interests only if he was not a bona fide purchaser of the legal estate for value without notice. This would have depended upon whether the Sheriff knew, or ought to have known, about the trust. If Lady Marian and the children were actually living in Locksley Hall, it is very likely that at the very least, the Sheriff would have had constructive notice of their interests and would thus have been bound by them. This would have meant that Lady Marian and the children could continue living in the hall.

2.5 The 1925 property legislation

The **1925 property legislation** marks a watershed in the history of land law. Although based on older concepts and previous reforms, the effect of this body of legislation cannot be overstated. In many ways, modern land law can be dated from this legislation.

By the nineteenth century, land law in England and Wales had become hopelessly complex. Attempts at reform were made throughout the nineteenth century, but most of them were concerned with the process of conveyancing (transferring land), rather than with the substantive law. It was not until after World War I that professional legal opinion finally accepted the need for real reform of land law. It was this acceptance that led to the 1925 property legislation.

1925 property legislation a series of Acts of Parliament that came into effect on 1 January 1926. These Acts consolidated earlier piecemeal changes in the law—particularly from 1922–24—and brought them all together as a body of law, which made substantial changes to the common law of property.

The Acts that are bundled together under this heading are (in alphabetical order):

- Administration of Estates Act 1925;
- Land Charges Act 1925;
- Land Registration Act 1925;
- Law of Property Act 1925;
- Settled Land Act 1925;
- Trustee Act 1925.

As you might expect after more than ninety years, all of these Acts have been amended, and some of them have been repealed and replaced by later legislation. Nonetheless, the 1925 property legislation remains a fundamental landmark in the development of modern land law and the basic scheme that it introduced continues.

It is, of course, very difficult to sum up the policy of so many Acts of Parliament in a few words, but some underlying themes can be seen running through them.

Put simply, the legislation tried to achieve two main objectives:

1. Land must be freely alienable—that is, it must be possible to transfer it (and interests in it) to others.

2. Land must be capable of fragmentation of ownership, for both family reasons and commercial reasons—that is, it must be possible to create numerous different interests in land in favour of others.

These two objectives are in tension with each other: if land is to be easy to transfer, the fewer interests that exist in it, the better. A purchaser is less likely to buy land if he or she cannot buy the estate free of **prior adverse interests**.

> **prior adverse interests**
>
> interests that come before an estate in time and that are not for the present landowner's benefit

 EXAMPLE

It is 1800. Locksley Hall, and its surrounding outbuildings and land, are now owned by the Earl of Huntingdon. He, however, has only a life estate in the Hall, after which it is to go to his eldest son, Lord Locksley for life, then to his eldest son in fee tail. The Earl of Huntingdon's mother, Lady Huntingdon, has a life interest in one of the houses in the grounds, as well as an annuity (annual payment of income) secured on the estate. Under the terms of the settlement (trust) that governs the Hall, various other beneficiaries—such as the Earl's sisters—have rights in parts of the property. There are several mortgages on the Hall—some legal and some equitable—and some of the land has been leased to the Huntingdon Mining Corporation.

It is clear that this kind of complexity will make it very difficult to sell Locksley Hall. No one has the right to sell an unencumbered freehold in the Hall: the Earl has only a life estate and so does his eldest son. The land is encumbered (burdened) with many different interests, some of which are legal and some equitable. A purchaser would have to work very hard to pay all of these off and to be sure that every interest had been discovered.

This example shows that land is capable of fragmentation of benefit—many different people have rights in it, and the land is being used to support a whole family and some commercial purposes. But it lacks alienability—it is much harder to transfer.

If land is to be more freely alienable, then the number of interests allowed to exist in it must be limited in some way and/or those interests must not be binding on a purchaser. This, however, would decrease the availability of fragmentation of benefit, which could be a disadvantage in utilizing the land fully. In other words, it would make it easier to sell the land, but it would make it harder for different people to own a share in it.

Although landowners before 1926 could easily share the land (fragment the benefit), the differences between legal and equitable rights could leave some beneficiaries vulnerable. Those with equitable interests had a share in the land, but they might lose it to a purchaser.

 EXAMPLE

Under the settlement, Jane Goodwill, the Earl's cousin, has been granted a right to live in one of the cottages on the estate. While she is away on holiday, the Earl grants a legal lease of the cottage for ten years to Peter Farmer.

Because Peter Farmer has purchased a legal estate in the land (a lease) and Jane's rights are equitable, Jane will be unable to enforce her rights against Peter unless he has had notice of them. If he is held to have had neither actual nor constructive notice, she may lose her home for the next ten years.

On the other hand, if Peter Farmer had no actual notice of Jane's rights when he took the lease, but is deemed to have had constructive notice, then he will be bound to give effect to her interests. This could be very unfair to Peter, who planned to live in the cottage.

In both cases, there would be a remedy against the Earl, but that would lie in damages only and would depend on him having enough money to pay damages. It would also not result in the injured party keeping the land—a remedy that he or she would probably prefer.

So, if we consider the position before 1925, some problems become clear. A purchaser of a legal estate in land might have had to deal with a number of interests already existing in the land: some of them legal and some of them equitable.

As we have seen, a purchaser who had no notice of an adverse right in land would be bound by that right if it was legal, but not if it was equitable—and this had two consequences:

1. The more legal rights there were in land, the more difficult it was for a purchaser to know whether he or she was buying an estate free of adverse rights.

2. Because of the doctrine of notice, the more equitable rights there were, the more difficult it was to be certain of property rights. On the one hand, equitable rights could be lost if the legal estate in the land was bought by a bona fide purchaser for value without notice; on the other hand, a purchaser might be deemed to have constructive notice of equitable rights even though he or she did not, in fact, know of them. Neither situation was entirely fair or satisfactory.

The solution of the 1925 property legislation was to alter radically the system of legal and equitable interests in land. Some of the main outcomes of this are that:

- the range of legal rights that can exist in land was reduced to two estates and a limited number of interests under LPA 1925, s. 1, as we saw at the start of this chapter;

- provision was made for registration of interests in land, so that the effect of the doctrine of notice was reduced;

- a way was devised for some equitable interests to be 'lifted off' the land and transferred into the purchase price paid for the legal estate. This is known as 'overreaching' (see 2.5.3).

2.5.1 The two legal estates

The two legal estates are a fundamental provision of LPA 1925, s. 1, which we introduced at the beginning of the chapter. Having looked at the history of the law, and established what an estate is, what legal and equitable rights are, and why it mattered whether an interest in land was legal or equitable, we can look at the section in more depth.

 STATUTE

Law of Property Act 1925, s. 1(1)

The only estates in land which are capable of subsisting or of being conveyed or created at law are—

(a) An estate in fee simple absolute in possession;
(b) A term of years absolute.

▶ CROSS REFERENCE

For more on the fee simple absolute in possession, see Chapter 3, 3.1.

For more on the term of years absolute, see the definition at Chapter 5, 5.1.

The very first section of the LPA 1925 reduces the number of legal estates that can exist in land to only two. This is the meaning of the words 'capable of subsisting or of being conveyed or created at law'. The first legal estate is the **fee simple absolute in possession**, or freehold estate. The second is the **term of years absolute**, or leasehold estate.

> **fee simple absolute in possession** this refers to the legal freehold estate
>
> **term of years absolute** this refers to the leasehold estate

▶ CROSS REFERENCE

For more on these trusts, see Chapter 11.

Before 1926, there could also be equitable freehold estates in land, but this is no longer possible: former equitable estates are now equitable interests and can exist only as beneficial interests under a trust. Therefore fees tail, life interests, etc. are now equitable interests, rather than estates in land as they were formerly. The fee simple absolute in possession (the legal freehold) is held on trust to give effect to these lesser interests in equity.

2.5.1.1 Legal interests in land

Having reduced the number of legal estates to two, LPA 1925, s. 1, goes on to limit the number of **legal interests** that can exist in land.

> **legal interests**
>
> interests in land that can exist at common law, rather than in equity

STATUTE

Law of Property Act 1925, s. 1(2)

The only interests or charges in or over land which are capable of subsisting or of being conveyed or created at law are—

   (a) An easement, right, or privilege in or over land for an interest equivalent to an estate in fee simple absolute in possession or a term of years absolute;

   (b) A rentcharge in possession issuing out of or charged on land being either perpetual or for a term of years absolute;

   (c) A charge by way of legal mortgage;

   (d) … and any other similar charge on land which is not created by an instrument;

   (e) Rights of entry exercisable over or in respect of a legal term of years absolute, or annexed, for any purpose, to a legal rentcharge.

This subsection contains a list of interests in land that can exist at common law, rather than in equity. Some of these will be considered in later chapters of this book. For present purposes, it is important to note that this is only a short list of interests. Other interests in land were not abolished, but LPA 1925, s. 1(3), provides that, unless an interest in land falls within the list in LPA 1925 s. 1(2), it will be equitable rather than legal.

STATUTE

Law of Property Act 1925, s. 1(3)

All other estates, interests, and charges in or over land take effect as equitable interests.

2.5.1.2 **Summary**

The combined effect of these provisions is to limit the number of legal estates and interests in land, and thus to limit the number and types of rights that will bind a purchaser without notice. This therefore carries out the first of the objectives of the 1925 property legislation.

Next, we will consider the second part of the reforms: the introduction of a system of registration.

2.5.2 **Registration**

The idea of **land registration** was not new in 1925. There had been a number of previous attempts to bring in systems of registering interests in land, particularly in densely populated areas, such as London, but the 1925 legislation was the first time that a compulsory, nationwide system of registration was introduced.

It is important to grasp at the outset that the 1925 legislation introduced not one, but two systems of registration: one of these, registration of title, is intended to be permanent; the other, registration of land charges, is intended to be temporary, although it will continue to exist for some time to come. The differences between the two are summarized in Table 2.4.

> **land registration**
> the system of registering certain legal estates and interests in land

Table 2.4 The two systems of land registration

Registration of title	The nationwide, compulsory system started in 1925 by the Land Registration Act 1925. The idea behind the system is that title to the land should be registered, and that the register should reflect all of the estates and interests affecting the land.	Land already included in this scheme is known as *registered land*
Registration of land charges	This is intended to be a temporary solution to the unfairness of the doctrine of notice until title to all land is registered. It enables certain categories of equitable interest in land to be entered on a register. Purchasers must inspect the register to see what equitable interests exist. Constructive and imputed notice does not apply to such interests. Owners of registered equitable interests can be sure that a transfer of the legal estate will not destroy their interests.	This type of registration applies only to land that is not yet registered land, known as *unregistered land*

 THINKING POINT

Why do you think a temporary system of registration was necessary, as well as a permanent one?

The answer to this question is a practical one. It takes time to create a register of all of the titles to land in England and Wales. The authors of the legislation were aware of this and therefore decided that a partial reform applying to unregistered land was necessary as well. By April 2015, 84 per cent of the land area of England and Wales was registered, although well over 90 per cent of titles (over 24 million) are registered, because it is mainly owners of larger areas of land who have not yet registered their titles.

There is, therefore, a large area of unregistered land to which the temporary system of registration of land charges still applies, although the government have recently announced a key commitment to comprehensive registration of title by 2030.

In this chapter, we will look at the details of the temporary system only; detailed consideration of the system of registration of title requires a chapter of its own, and you will find this in Chapter 4.

2.5.2.1 Unregistered land—registration of land charges

> **unregistered land**
>
> land to which the title has not yet been registered at the Land Registry. Title to such land has to be proven by documentary evidence, known as 'title deeds'.

The system of registration that was introduced for **unregistered land** was a partial reform only of the doctrine of notice: it applies only to certain equitable interests granted in unregistered land. The legislation is now contained in the Land Charges Act 1972. Not all equitable interests can be registered and those that cannot still rely on the old doctrine of notice.

Registrable interests

The categories of registrable interests are contained in Land Charges Act 1972, s. 2. A summary of these can be seen in Table 2.5.

Table 2.5 The categories of registrable interests

Category	Definition	Summary
Class A	'rent or other annuity or principal money … which is a charge on land … created pursuant to the application of some person under … an Act of Parliament'	These are charges on land in respect of certain statutory payments made—for example, by landlords to tenants in relation to improvements
Class B	'a charge on land (not being a local land charge) … created otherwise than pursuant to the application of any person'	These are charges created automatically by statute to ensure the repayment of costs or expenses—for example, the costs of legal aid should land be recovered or preserved by the case
Class C	'(i) puisne mortgage, (ii) limited owner's charge, (iii) a general equitable charge, (iv) an estate contract'	This is an important category of charges. A puisne (pronounced 'puny') mortgage is one that is not protected by deposit of title deeds. The usual way for a first legal mortgage of unregistered land to be protected is for the mortgagee (lender) to take physical possession of the documents proving title to the land. This will prevent the land being sold without the mortgagee's consent. A second or subsequent mortgagee (legal or equitable) cannot have the title deeds, however, because the first mortgagee already has them. Therefore, he or she can enter a charge on the land charges register to protect their interest in the land. A limited owner's charge is a charge to protect the repayment of money spent on the land by someone who has only a limited interest in it—for example, money spent by someone who has only a life interest under a settlement

> **CROSS REFERENCE**
>
> For more on mortgages, see Chapter 14.

> **CROSS REFERENCE**
>
> For more on settlements, see Chapter 11, 11.6.1.

Table 2.5 Continued

Category	Definition	Summary	
		The general equitable charge is a sort of 'sweeping up' category, defined by reference to all of the things it is not—see Land Charges Act 1972, s. 2(4)(iii). It includes, for example, a charge on land that a vendor (seller) of the land has in respect of unpaid purchase money.	
		An estate contract is defined as '*a contract by an estate owner … to convey or create a legal estate, including a contract conferring … a valid option to purchase, a right of pre-emption or any other like rights*' under Land Charges Act 1972, s. 2(4)(iv). An option to purchase is a right that is granted to another person to buy the estate in land within a certain period of time. If the right is exercised, the estate owner is obliged to sell. A right of pre-emption is a right of 'first refusal': if the estate owner decides to sell, he or she must offer the land to the holder of the right of pre-emption first.	
Class D	'(i) an Inland Revenue charge, (ii) a restrictive covenant, (iii) an equitable easement'	An Inland Revenue charge is a charge on land registered by the Inland Revenue in relation to unpaid Inheritance Tax	⟩ CROSS REFERENCE For more on restrictive covenants, see Chapter 13, 13.5.
		A restrictive covenant is an agreement contained in a deed that a landowner will refrain from doing something on his or her land (see Chapter 12). Such covenants may be enforceable between subsequent landowners, as well as between the persons who actually entered into the agreement—hence they are registrable as land charges.	
		An easement is a right for the benefit of one piece of land over another piece of land—for example, a right of way (see Chapter 11). If such a right is equitable (rather than legal), it must be registered as a land charge.	⟩ CROSS REFERENCE For more on easements, see Chapter 12.
Class E	An annuity created before 1 January 1926 and not registered in the register of annuities	These are old annuities and increasingly unlikely to be encountered	
Class F	A charge affecting land by virtue of the Family Law Act 1996, Pt IV	This is a charge in respect of a spouse's (or civil partner's) statutory right to occupy a matrimonial (or partnership) home of which he or she is not the owner	

This is a very long list of interests and you do not need, at this stage, to understand what they all mean. The important thing to note is that most of these interests are the kind that are likely to have been granted in return for money or money's worth—they are commercial interests rather than 'family' interests.

So, for example, Class C land charges include estate contracts, which would include a contract to buy the land, either immediately or in the future (an option contract). Class D land charges include equitable easements, which would include rights of way and other rights over neighbouring land. The reason why these sorts of interest can be considered commercial is that they would usually be granted for money, or would increase the price that someone would pay for their land. It is therefore important that they are not destroyed when the land is sold.

'Family interests', on the other hand, are those types of interest that one would not expect to continue in relation to the land once it has been sold to someone else. For example, the family home may be subject to equitable interests in favour of family members who have paid for its purchase. These interests can be satisfied by a share of the purchase money once the house is sold; they do not need to continue to bind the land in the hands of a purchaser and therefore are not registrable under the Land Charges Act 1972.

Effect of registration

If the interest is one that can be registered under the Land Charges Act 1972, registration is both necessary and sufficient. The owner of the equitable interest must register it and, if that is done, the interest will be protected because registration is deemed to constitute actual notice to the purchaser of the legal estate under LPA 1925, s. 198(1).

 STATUTE

Law of Property Act 1925, s. 198(1)

The registration of any instrument or matter in any register kept under the Land Charges Act 1972 or any local land charges register shall be deemed to constitute actual notice of such instrument or matter, and of the fact of such registration, to all persons and for all purposes connected with the land affected, as from the date of registration or other prescribed date and for so long as the registration continues in force.

Because the effect of registration is to constitute actual notice, once an equitable interest is registered under the Land Charges Act 1972, it will be binding upon any subsequent owner of the land.

Consequences of failure to register

We have already stated that registration is both necessary and sufficient: if you *can* register the interest, then you *must* do so. The inevitable consequence of this is that, if you do not register it, your interest may well be lost if the land is sold to a new owner. Under Land Charges Act 1972, s. 4, if a registrable interest is not registered (see Table 2.6), it will be void (which means it will have no effect) as against:

Table 2.6 Those unaffected by an unregistered land charge

'a purchaser of the land charged with it, or of any interest in such land'	classes A, B, C(i) (ii) (iii), and F.
'a purchaser for money or money's worth of the legal estate in the land charged'	classes C(iv) and D

Note that both of these apply to a purchaser. Someone who receives land as a gift or inheritance, for example, will be bound by all prior equitable interests, registered or not.

The legislation is clear in rejecting any 'conscience' element in registration, for fear of bringing back constructive notice by the back door. Even actual notice on the part of the purchaser is not sufficient to protect an unregistered interest.

Q CASE CLOSE-UP

Midland Bank v. Green [1981] AC 513

A family farm was originally owned by Walter Green. He granted an option to purchase the farm, which was unregistered land, to his son, Geoffrey.

This option was an estate contract and therefore should have been registered as a Class C(iv) land charge—but Geoffrey failed to register it.

Walter fell out with Geoffrey and, intending to defeat the option, sold the land to his wife (Geoffrey's mother, Evelyn) for £500. The farm was worth £40,000 at that time.

The question arose whether this sale was valid to defeat the unregistered option. There was no doubt that the sale was a breach of contract by Walter. Equally, there was no doubt that Evelyn knew of the option. Under what is now the Land Charges Act 1972, s. 4(6), however, an unregistered estate contract is void against 'a purchaser for money or money's worth of the legal estate in the land charged'.

Two main arguments were put forward for Geoffrey:

1. that the word 'purchaser' should be interpreted as meaning purchaser 'in good faith';
2. that 'money or money's worth' should be interpreted to exclude nominal or inadequate consideration.

Lord Wilberforce (who gave the only substantive judgment) rejected both of these arguments, saying:

> The case is plain: the Act is clear and definite. Intended as it was to provide a simple and understandable system for the protection of title to land, it should not be read down or glossed: to do so would destroy the usefulness of the Act. Any temptation to remould the Act to meet the facts of the present case, on the supposition that it is a hard one and that justice requires it, is, for me at least, removed by the consideration that the Act itself provides a simple and effective protection for persons in Geoffrey's position—viz.—by registration.

It can be seen from this case that the House of Lords applied the Land Charges Act 1972 strictly, refusing to alter its plain meaning so as to bring it more into line with the equitable doctrine of notice. It is worth noting that Geoffrey was not left without remedy: he was awarded damages against his solicitors for negligence and against his father for breach of contract. Neither of these remedies, however, entitled him to enforce the option against his mother.

Problems with registration of land charges

Registrable equitable interests in unregistered land must be 'registered against the name of the estate owner whose estate is intended to be affected' under the Land Charges Act 1972, s. 3(1). Because the land itself is not registered, the only possible way for equitable interests to be registered is against the name of the estate owner. This means that a purchaser has to search the register for entries made against that name.

This has led to two problems, as follows:

1. The owner of the equitable interest may not know the full name of the estate owner, or may be mistaken about it. He or she may therefore register against the wrong name.

2. The purchaser of unregistered land may not know all of the possible names against which to search, because documents of title dating from as early as 1925 may have been lost in the meantime. Therefore the purchaser may not search against a relevant name.

An example of the first problem—the incorrect name—is shown in the case of *Oak Co-operative Building Society v. Blackburn*.

 CASE CLOSE-UP

***Oak Co-operative Building Society v. Blackburn* [1968] Ch 730**

The estate owner in this case was Francis David Blackburn. He agreed to sell the house to a Mrs Caines, who moved in. The house was not legally transferred to her and so the agreement to buy the house was an estate contract, which was required to be registered as a Class C(iv) land charge. This was eventually done, against the name of *Frank* David Blackburn, a name by which Mr Blackburn was known in the neighbourhood.

Subsequently, Mr Blackburn mortgaged the property to the claimant building society. They made a search of the land charges register against the name Francis *Davis* Blackburn and did not find the registration of the estate contract. The question to be decided by the Court of Appeal was whether the building society was bound by the estate contract.

It was held that it was. The Court held that registration against a version of the estate owner's true name was effective against a purchaser who did not search at all, or who searched (as here) against an incorrect name. It would not, however, be effective against a purchaser who searched against the full, correct name (see *Diligent Finance Co. Ltd v. Alleyne* (1972) 23 P & CR 346).

⊃ CROSS REFERENCE

For more on transfers of unregistered land, see Chapter 3, 3.3.

---

title deeds

the documentary evidence that shows how land came to its present owner

---

In this case, the Court seems to have taken a practical view and to have tried to get the legislation to work as well as possible. Any system based on names, however, is going to give rise to these sorts of difficulty.

The second problem is one that is caused by the age of the system of registration of land charges. It has now been in place for over ninety years, during which time land may have changed hands many times. The main proof of title for unregistered land is the collection of **title deeds**—conveyances and other documents showing how land came into the possession of the present owner.

These documents must go back at least fifteen years. Often, there will be documents going back further than this—but not always. There may be names against which land charges have been validly registered in the past, but against which the purchaser does not know to search.

 EXAMPLE

Bleak House, which is unregistered land, was conveyed to Anna in 1925. Since then, the transfers have been as follows.

1932 Anna transferred it to Ben.

1946 Ben transferred it to Chris, who granted an equitable right of way (easement) over Bleak House in favour of the house next door, Windy Corner. This equitable easement has been correctly registered against Chris's full name.

1958 Chris transferred Bleak House to Edie.

1965 Edie transferred Bleak House to Fatima.

1973 Fatima transferred the house to Gopal.

1989 Hari inherited the property from Gopal.

In 2017, Hari contracted to sell Bleak House to Ines. The land is still unregistered. To prove good title, Hari must produce a conveyance (transfer) going back at least fifteen years. This means that he must show how he inherited the property, and the conveyance to Gopal in 1973. These will give Ines the names of Fatima, Gopal, and Hari, and she can search against these names in the land charges register. But there is no guarantee that the conveyances from 1946 or 1958 will have been kept, so Ines may not be able to search against Chris's name. Therefore she will not discover the right of way, but will still be treated as if she had actual knowledge of it under LPA 1925, s. 198(1).

This problem has been addressed by statute, in the Law of Property Act 1969, which introduced a scheme of compensation to deal with undiscoverable land charges that are not within the actual knowledge of the purchaser.

 STATUTE

Law of Property Act 1969, s. 25 [Compensation in certain cases for loss due to undisclosed land charges]

(1) Where a purchaser of any estate or interest in land under a disposition to which this section applies has suffered loss by reason that the estate or interest is affected by a registered land charge, then if—

(a) the date of completion was after the commencement of this Act; and

(b) on that date the purchaser had no actual knowledge of the charge; and

(c) the charge was registered against the name of an owner of an estate in the land who was not as owner of any such estate a party to any transaction, or concerned in any event, comprised in the relevant title;

(d) the purchaser shall be entitled to compensation for the loss.

The purchaser remains bound, therefore, by the equitable interests that were correctly registered, but which they could not discover, but unless the purchaser actually knew about those interests at the time of purchase, compensation will be paid. It is a partial solution, although not as good a solution as ensuring that all registered interests can be discovered.

Both of these problems are examples of the intended temporary nature of registration of land charges when compared to the permanent system of registration of title.

2.5.2.2 Registered land

The nationwide, compulsory system of land registration was started in 1925 by the Land Registration Act 1925, although there had been previous systems in place, particularly in London. The idea be-

registered land

land to which the title is registered with the Land Registry. Title to such land is guaranteed by the Land Registry and proven by a search of the register.

hind the system is that title to all land should be registered, and that the register should reflect all of the estates and interests affecting the **registered land**.

Under the Land Registration Act 2002, which replaced the LRA 1925, the Land Registry keeps a register of all land in England and Wales. Each title is identified by number, and is related to a map reference and plan that is based on the Ordnance Survey Map, not to the name of the estate owner. This means that there is no need to keep title deeds for registered land—they are replaced by the register, which is now kept electronically. There is also no need to register land charges against the name of the estate owner; instead similar rights can be registered on the register of title.

Once title to land is registered, all dealings with it are subject to the registration system. We will deal with the details of this in Chapter 4.

2.5.3 Lifting equitable interests off the land: overreaching

The last of the three main principles of the 1925 property legislation was to establish a method of selling land free from the 'non-commercial' or 'family' equitable interests that existed within it. The method devised for doing this is called **overreaching** and is dealt with in LPA 1925, s. 2.

overreaching

the process by which interests in land are converted into corresponding interests in money arising from the sale of the land

Overreaching does not apply to 'commercial' interests, such as those registrable under the Land Charges Act 1972—see LPA 1925, s. 2(3)–(5).

Overreaching allows trustees of land, for example, to sell that land free from the interests of the beneficiaries. It is important that any provisions are complied with—particularly the provision of LPA 1925, s. 27, that any capital money is paid to two trustees.

▶ CROSS REFERENCE

To find out what occurs if money is not paid to two trustees, see from Chapter 7, 7.2.3.

The effect of overreaching is that the equitable interests no longer exist in the land itself, but in the purchase money that has been paid for it. In other words, the equitable interests are lifted off the land and transferred into the money. Instead of owning an interest in land, the beneficiary owns an interest in money. This makes it much easier to sell the land, because the purchaser has a simple way of ensuring that it can be bought free from 'family'-type interests.

▶ CROSS REFERENCE

Overreaching is considered in more detail in Chapter 7, 7.3.1.

2.6 Conclusion

Since 1925, land can be divided into land to which title is registered (registered land) and land to which title is not yet registered (unregistered land).

Within unregistered land, legal rights bind 'the whole world', without need for registration (except for puisne mortgages—see Table 2.5). Equitable interests are divided into three groups:

- overreachable rights, which are not registered and which will not bind a purchaser as long as he or she complies with the overreaching provisions;
- registrable rights, which must be registered under the Land Charges Act 1972 against the name of the estate owner whose estate is intended to be affected;
- equitable interests, which do not fit into either category and which depend upon the doctrine of notice for their enforceability against a purchaser.

Within registered land, legal rights do need to be registered, including the title to the estate and legal interests in land such as mortgages and rights of way.

Some equitable rights must be noted on the register if they are to be binding on future purchasers, and these are broadly the same equitable rights as were registrable under the LCA 1972 in unregistered land.

Most 'family' rights are not registrable, and will not bind a purchaser as long as he or she complies with the overreaching provisions. However, if those provisions are not complied with, the rights may be binding on purchasers in certain circumstances (see Chapter 7, 7.3.3 onwards for more details).

The scheme for registration of title is far more comprehensive and therefore more complex than that for unregistered land—but the rules will become clearer in the subsequent chapters, in which they will be explained in context.

> CROSS REFERENCE

For more details on registered land, see Chapter 4.

 ## Summary

1. Land law has ancient origins and some of those ancient concepts—such as estates—survive into the modern day.

2. Land law has been influenced by both common law and equity, with the development of the trust and the mortgage being particularly important features introduced by equity.

3. Legal and equitable estates and interests differed in their effects on purchasers of the land, because common law acts *in rem* and equity *in personam*. This gave rise to the doctrine of notice.

4. Problems with the increasing numbers of estates in land and with the doctrine of notice eventually led to the 1925 property legislation, a series of Acts of Parliament that reformed the way in which land law worked.

5. There are now two legal estates in land under LPA 1925, s. 1(1): the fee simple absolute in possession (freehold) and the term of years absolute (leasehold).

6. There are a limited number of legal interests in land under LPA 1925, s. 1(2), which include easements, profits à prendre, and mortgages.

7. All other interests in land exist in equity only—LPA 1925, s. 1(3).

8. The LPA 1925 introduced compulsory registration of title and there are now two systems: registered land and unregistered land.

9. Unregistered land is governed by the Land Charges Act 1972 and is a system of partial registration of certain equitable interests against the name of the estate owner.

10. Registered land is a comprehensive system of registration of titles to land. It is based on maps and title numbers. It is hoped that, eventually, all titles to land will be registered.

 ## The bigger picture

- This chapter covers the theoretical structure of land law. You can find out more about how land law fits together under the system of registration of title by looking at Chapter 15, and in particular 15.6. See also Chapter 16, 16.4 for ideas on how to answer questions on the areas covered by this chapter.

- If you are really interested in the history of land law, a good starting point is A. W. B. Simpson (1961) *An Introduction to the History of Land Law*, Oxford: Oxford University Press. For later history, see J. Stuart Anderson (1992) *Lawyers and the Making of English Land Law 1832–1940*, Oxford: Oxford University Press.

- There are other suggestions in the 'Further reading' section, and more on the *Mabo v. Queensland* case on the online resources.

? Questions

Self-test questions

1. From what historical event did the doctrines of tenure and estate originate? How important are they in the modern law?

2. What were the main differences between legal and equitable interests in land before 1925?

3. Which estates in land can now exist 'at law'? What has happened to the other former estates?

4. What is the difference between 'registered' and 'unregistered' land?

5. How are equitable interests protected in unregistered land?

Exam question

1. What were the main objectives of the 1925 property legislation?

 You will find answers to these questions online at www.oup.com/uk/clarke_directions6e/.

≡ Further reading

Bright, S. and Dewar, J. (eds) (1998) *Land Law Themes and Perspectives*, Oxford: Oxford University Press, chs 1, 4, and 11

Chapter 1 discusses the idea of property in land and explains the abstract nature of English property law concepts. You might find it useful if you want to understand different theoretical models of property ownership.

Chapter 4 deals with the thinking behind the 1925 property legislation.

Chapter 11 deals with Australian indigenous land rights.

Butt, P., 'Native land rights in Australia: the Mabo case' [1995] Conv 33

This article deals with the *Mabo* case and Australian indigenous land rights.

Gardner, S. and MacKenzie, E. (2015) *An Introduction to Land Law* (4th edn), Oxford: Hart, chs 1–3

These chapters give a brief, but illuminating, theoretical explanation of rights *in rem*, ownership, and registration, as well as looking at the human rights aspect of land law.

Law Commission/HM Land Registry (1998) Land Registration for the Twenty-First Century: A Consultative Document, Law Com No. 254, available online at http://www.lawcom.gov.uk/project/land-registration-for-the-21st-century/#land-registration-for-the-21st-century-consultation.

This report sets out the reasons behind the reform of the law in the LRA 2002.

McFarlane, B. (2008) *The Structure of Property Law*, Oxford: Hart, Part 1

This book explains the tensions behind land law and how the law is structured to deal with those tensions.

Registering land or property with Land Registry. https://www.gov.uk/registering-land-or-property-with-land-registry.

This is a simple guide to the basics of registration of title.

Online Resources

For more advice relating to this chapter, including self-test questions and an interactive glossary, visit www.oup.com/uk/clarke_directions6e/.

PART 2

LEGAL ESTATES

3 The freehold estate

LEARNING OBJECTIVES

By the end of this chapter, you will be able to:

- identify the legal freehold estate;
- distinguish the legal freehold from other estates and interests in land;
- understand how the legal freehold can be transferred;
- understand possible changes in the law.

Introduction

In the last chapter, we saw that the 1925 property legislation made important changes to land law. One of the most fundamental was the reduction of the number of legal estates in land to just two:

- the fee simple absolute in possession (freehold estate);
- the term of years absolute (leasehold estate).

In layman's terms, the freehold estate is the closest English law gets to 'ownership' of the land forever, whereas a leasehold estate is for a defined period of time, which can be very short (six months is a typical term) or very long (even thousands of years) but which always has an end point, and during which the leaseholder or tenant is always in a contractual relationship with the lessee or landlord.

In this chapter, we will be looking at the characteristics of the fee simple absolute in possession, which is the technical name for the freehold estate.

3.1 The fee simple absolute in possession

In order to understand more fully the nature of the legal freehold, we have to consider each of the terms that make up its legal definition: the 'fee simple absolute in possession'. This is a very technical phrase, but unless an estate satisfies each part of it, the estate cannot be a legal freehold, but must instead be an equitable interest in land.

3.1.1 Fee simple

> **fee**
> the estate is inheritable, meaning that it can be left in a will after someone dies

A **fee** is an inheritable estate which can pass from one generation to another, unlike a life interest, which ends on the death of the owner. This is what gives the freehold estate the potential to last forever, because it lasts until the owner for the time being dies without leaving an **heir**.

In modern times, **fee simple** means that the estate continues for as long as there is anyone to inherit it, whether by will, or upon an intestacy (when someone dies without leaving a will) under the Administration of Estates Act 1925. If there is no will and no one to inherit under that Act, the estate will go back to the Crown.

> **heir**
> originally, the person entitled to inherit freehold land (usually the eldest son); now someone who inherits property under a will

Other fees do exist—in particular, the **fee tail**. They cannot nowadays be legal estates in land, but can exist as equitable interests only.

> **fee tail** an estate that is inheritable for as long as there are lineal descendants of the owner

> **fee simple**
> an estate that is inheritable for as long as there are general heirs of the owner

3.1.2 Absolute

The word **absolute** means that the fee simple must belong to the owner outright, without the possibility of being brought to an end (other than on the failure of heirs). In other words, the estate must not be limited in any way. There are two types of fee simple that are not absolute: determinable fees and conditional fees.

> **absolute**
> complete; unconditional; not qualified

3.1.2.1 Determinable

 CROSS REFERENCE

See Chapter 2, especially Table 2.2.

The **determinable fee simple** is an estate that might last forever, but which may be cut short by a specified but unpredictable event.

> **determinable fee simple**
> an estate that may last forever, but which may be cut short by a specified but unpredictable event

 EXAMPLE

Abishek may transfer his house to Biljana on the following terms: '… in fee simple until she passes her land law exam'.

💬 **THINKING POINT**

If the grant had been made to Biljana 'until she dies', would that also be a determinable fee?

The determining event must be unpredictable: that is, it must not be certain to happen. Although we hope Biljana will pass her land law exam, it is not certain. Unfortunately, death is a certain event for all of us, including Biljana, at some point. This grant would have created a life interest, which is something very different.

3.1.2.2 **Conditional**

A **conditional fee simple** is an estate that might last forever, but which may be brought to an end on the satisfaction of a **condition subsequent**—a conditional event that may occur after the estate has been created.

> **conditional fee simple**
>
> an estate that might last forever, but which may be brought to an end on the satisfaction of a condition subsequent

---

 EXAMPLE

Abishek may transfer his house to Biljana on the following terms: ' … in fee simple on condition that she does not pass an exam in land law'.

Again, the occurrence of the conditional event must be unpredictable.

> **condition subsequent**
>
> a condition that may be fulfilled after the estate has been created

3.1.2.3 **Differences between determinable and conditional fees**

As you will note from the two examples, a similar result can be achieved by a determinable fee and a conditional fee, which raises the question of why we should bother distinguishing between them. The answer is that the two estates actually have different legal effects. The law regards the coming to an end of the two estates differently: while a determinable fee comes naturally to an end as soon as the determining event happens, a conditional fee potentially lasts forever and is cut short only if the condition is satisfied—that is, if the conditional event occurs. In practice, this is shown by the difference in wording—examples of which are shown in Table 3.1.

Table 3.1 **Differences in wording between determinable and conditional fees**

Words that indicate a determinable fee	Words that indicate a conditional fee
while	provided that
during	on condition that
as long as	but if
until	if it happen that

The first legal difference is that a determinable fee comes to an end immediately and automatically when the determining event occurs.

 EXAMPLE

Abishek transferred his house to Biljana 'in fee simple until she passes her land law exam'. As soon as Biljana passes her land law exam, her estate in the house will come to an end. Abishek need not take any action to end it.

Conditional fees, on the other hand, give the grantor (the person who transferred the estate to the owner of the conditional fee) the right to enter and bring the estate to an end when the event occurs.

EXAMPLE

Abishek transferred his house to Biljana 'in fee simple on condition that she does not pass an exam in land law'. When Biljana passes her land law exam, Abishek (the grantor of the estate) has a right to put an end to Biljana's estate in the land. If he does not do so, however, the estate will continue.

forfeiture

the bringing to an end of an estate as the consequence of an offence or a breach of an undertaking

Because a conditional fee contains this right to **forfeiture** (bringing the estate to an end), the courts have construed such conditions strictly. It must be possible to say with certainty when such a condition has been breached, so vague conditions will be struck out. In addition, the courts have struck down certain conditions if they make it impossible for land to be transferred, or if they are against public policy. In general, conditions that wholly prohibit marriage, or which encourage illegal or immoral behaviour, have been struck out. Conditions forbidding marriage to certain classes of persons, however, or forbidding a person from following certain religions, have been upheld.

 CASE CLOSE-UP

Blathwayt v. Lord Cawley [1975] 3 All ER 625

A condition in a settlement stated:

> if any person who under the trusts hereof shall become entitled … to the possession of [the settled property] shall … be or become a Roman Catholic … the estate hereby limited to him shall cease and determine and be utterly void.

This condition was held not to be void as against public policy. Lord Wilberforce agreed that public policy must move with the times, but said:

> Discrimination is not the same thing as choice: it operates over a larger and less personal area, and neither by express provision nor by implication has private selection yet become a matter of public policy.

It is possible that the provisions seen in _Blathwayt v. Lord Cawley_ would now be incompatible with the beneficiary's human rights—in this case, the 'right to freedom of thought, conscience and religion' under the European Convention on Human Rights (ECHR), Art. 9. Lord Wilberforce was referred to the ECHR in the _Blathwayt_ case, but declined to apply its standards to a will taking effect in 1936 (which was before the ECHR was drafted). Since the enactment of the Human Rights Act 1998, which incorporates the ECHR into domestic law, the courts might be inclined to take a different view.

A second legal difference between determinable fees and conditional fees is that conditional fees are capable of being legal estates, whereas determinable fees are always equitable interests only. The reason for this distinction is the Law of Property Act 1925 (LPA 1925), s. 7, which was amended for historical reasons that are not relevant today.

 STATUTE

Law of Property Act 1925, s. 7 [Saving of certain legal estates and statutory powers]

A fee simple which, by virtue of the Lands Clauses Acts, … or any similar statute, is liable to be divested, is for the purposes of this Act a fee simple absolute, and remains liable to be divested as if this Act had not been passed, [and a fee simple subject to a legal or equitable right of entry or re-entry is for the purposes of this Act a fee simple absolute].

As a consequence of the amendment in the square brackets in this section, most conditional fees—as long as they contain a legal or equitable **right of re-entry**, which almost all do—are treated as fees simple absolute and are therefore capable of being legal estates, rather than as equitable interests.

right of re-entry

a legal or equitable right to resume possession of land, here as the result of forfeiture

The situation is consequently as follows:

- the fee simple absolute can be a legal estate;
- the determinable fee simple can only ever be an equitable interest;
- the conditional fee simple can be a legal estate under LPA 1925, s. 7(1), if it is subject to a right of re-entry. Otherwise, it will be an equitable interest.

3.1.3 **In possession**

The final requirement for a legal freehold is that the fee simple absolute must be **in possession**. This means that the estate must confer upon its owner the immediate right to enjoy the land, or the rents and profits of the land, from the date on which the estate is granted—LPA 1925, s. 205(1)(xix).

in possession

the estate must confer upon its owner the immediate right to enjoy the land, or the rents and profits of the land, from the date of the grant

The owner may be in possession either by occupying the property or by receiving the rents and profits from it.

 EXAMPLE

Peter owns a fee simple absolute in Mulberry House. He works abroad and therefore does not live in his house, which is leased to Jane.

Peter is in receipt of the rent from Mulberry House paid by Jane. This means that his fee simple absolute is 'in possession' and is a legal freehold estate. Jane has a leasehold estate in Mulberry House.

There are two types of estate that are not in possession: estates in remainder and estates in reversion.

3.1.3.1 **In remainder**

An **estate in remainder** is an interest that gives its owner the present right to future enjoyment of that estate. This is best explained by looking at an example.

estate in remainder

an interest that gives its owner the present right to future enjoyment

 EXAMPLE

Peter grants Mulberry House 'to Abigail for life, remainder to Belinda in fee simple absolute'.

Abigail has a life interest in the house, which is in possession—she can enjoy the land now. Even if Mulberry House is still leased to Jane, as in the earlier example, Abigail is entitled to the rents and profits, so her life estate is in possession.

Belinda has a fee simple absolute, but it is not in possession. It will fall into possession when Abigail dies. She has a fee simple absolute in remainder.

Notice that neither Abigail nor Belinda has a legal estate—a fee simple absolute in possession—in Mulberry House. Abigail does not have a fee at all, because she has only a life interest, which can only be equitable. Belinda has a fee simple absolute, but not in possession: it is in remainder and is therefore an equitable interest.

> In this situation, a trust of land will have been created. The legal freehold (fee simple absolute in possession) will be held by trustees to give effect to Peter's dispositions.

vested remainder

the present right to a future interest

In the example, Belinda's fee simple in remainder is said to be a **vested remainder**. This means that Belinda is certain to get Mulberry House at some point in the future, because Abigail is certain to die. Even if Abigail were to live longer than Belinda, she would still die at some time, and then Belinda's successors—the persons to whom she has left her equitable fee simple in Mulberry House after her death—will be entitled in possession.

contingent remainder

a future interest that can only come into being on meeting a condition precedent

The opposite of a vested remainder is a **contingent remainder**. This is a future interest which may or may not come into being, depending upon the fulfilment of a **condition precedent**—the occurrence of some specified event before the estate comes into being, as in the following example.

condition precedent

a condition that must be met before the estate comes into being

→ **EXAMPLE**

Peter grants Mulberry House 'to Abigail for life, remainder to Belinda in fee simple provided that she survives Abigail'.

Abigail has a life interest in possession in Mulberry House. Belinda has a fee simple absolute in remainder, but only if she lives longer than Abigail. The phrase *'provided that she survives Abigail'* is a condition precedent. If Belinda dies first, she (or her successors) will not be entitled to Mulberry House. Instead, unless there are other remainders, Mulberry House will revert to Peter (see 3.1.3.2). If Abigail dies first, Belinda becomes entitled to the fee simple absolute, which will then become a legal estate vested in possession.

Both vested and contingent remainders are equitable interests under the 1925 property legislation. There are rules against contingent remainders vesting after too long a lapse of time and thus tying up the land too far into the future: rules against remoteness of vesting and the rule against perpetuities. The details of these rules are, however, outside the scope of this book.

3.1.3.2 **In reversion**

estate in reversion

an interest that is retained by the grantor, because the fee simple estate in the land has not been transferred to anyone

An **estate in reversion** is an interest that is retained by its owner (the grantor), because the fee simple estate has not been transferred to anyone else. There was an example of an estate in reversion in the example in 3.1.3.1, in which Mulberry House reverted to Peter. Another example of an estate in reversion is as follows:

→ **EXAMPLE**

Peter grants Mulberry House 'to Abigail for life'.

Abigail has a life interest in possession in the house, but there is no further grant of the house to take effect when she dies. This means that Peter has not disposed of the fee simple in the house: he has a fee simple absolute in reversion in Mulberry House, which is an equitable interest. When Abigail dies, Peter's fee simple absolute will fall into possession.

An estate in reversion arises by operation of law. It is not the same as the 'possibility of reverter' that occurs when there is a determinable fee simple, or the right of re-entry that accompanies a conditional fee simple. An estate in reversion is always a vested interest, because it is any part of the full legal fee simple absolute that the grantor has not transferred and which therefore remains with them. Estates in reversion are always equitable interests.

3.1.4 **Summary**

In order, therefore, to have a legal freehold, it must be shown that the estate meets all the parts of the description 'fee simple absolute in possession'. It might be useful to think of each of the terms as a hurdle that must be cleared before the estate owner can reach the goal of a legal freehold. If any of the hurdles is 'knocked down'—for example, if it is a life estate only and therefore not a 'fee', or if it is in remainder and therefore not 'in possession'—then the estate can exist in equity only.

It is also important to remember that a legal freehold must exist in each piece of land, unless it is held outright by the Crown. If no individual appears to hold the fee simple absolute in possession, then, since 1925, either a settlement or a trust must have arisen.

Since 1997, the fee simple absolute in possession that is not vested in a single person will, in the vast majority of cases, be held by trustees as a trust of land.

Even if the estate owner does have a fee simple absolute in possession, he or she still may not hold a legal estate if the correct formalities for creation or transfer of the estate have not been observed.

CROSS REFERENCE

For more on subinfeudation and Quia Emptores, see Chapter 2, 2.2.1

CROSS REFERENCE

For more on settlements and trusts, see Chapter 11.

CROSS REFERENCE

For more on joint owners and trusts of land, see chapter 8.

3.2 The creation of a legal freehold

The creation of a legal freehold is not possible except by the Crown. This is because other freehold owners are no longer able to create new freeholds out of their own freeholds by subinfeudation, which was outlawed by Quia Emptores in 1290.

The Crown can grant freeholds to others out of Crown land and these will then constitute new fees simple absolute in possession, which will have to be registered at the Land Registry as a new estate in land (first registration of title).

Since the Land Registration Act 2002 (LRA 2002) came into force, the Crown can also grant itself freeholds—something that was impossible at common law. This means that the Crown can register those freeholds at the Land Registry.

CROSS REFERENCE

For more on subinfeudation and Quia Emptores, see Chapter 2, 2.2.1.

CROSS REFERENCE

For more on first registration, see Chapter 4, 4.5.

3.3 Transfer of the legal freehold

Although freehold owners cannot create new freeholds, they are generally free to transfer all, or part, of the freehold that they own to someone else. If that freehold is in unregistered land, the owner has wide powers under which to deal with it at common law, as preserved by LPA 1925, s. 1(4). If the freehold is in registered land, the registered proprietor has wide powers of disposal under LRA 2002, s. 23.

STATUTE

Land Registration Act 2002, s. 23 [Owner's powers]

(1) Owner's powers in relation to a registered estate consist of—

    (a) power to make a disposition of any kind permitted by the general law in relation to an interest of that description, other than a mortgage by demise or sub-demise, and

    (b) power to charge the estate at law with the payment of money.

. . . .

Subsection (1)(a) means that the owner can make any kind of disposal of the land—for example, selling it, leasing it, etc.—other than creating a mortgage of it by the old-fashioned method known as 'demise', or 'sub-demise'. Subsection (1)(b) allows a mortgage to be granted by way of a charge over the land. This has, for years, been the way in which land is mortgaged, so the LRA 2002 was simply tidying up the law to reflect modern practice.

In some cases these wide powers may be limited in some way—for example, if the owner is a trustee. If the land is unregistered, the limitation may be apparent from the terms of the conveyance, or may be registrable as a land charge, or may depend on the doctrine of notice. In the case of registered land, the notice is given by placing a restriction in the proprietorship register. Some restrictions must be placed there by the Chief Land Registrar; others are voluntary and the registered proprietor must apply for them to be entered—LRA 2002, s. 42.

Although the owner of the freehold is generally free to transfer his or her land, English law has always required a certain element of formality in transfers of land. Reasons for this include deterring fraudulent transactions and helping to ensure certainty of ownership. Nowadays, that formality is satisfied in the requirements for formal documentation and in the requirements for registration.

In explaining the formalities needed to transfer estates in land, it is helpful to set out the four main steps in the process of buying and selling land, or **conveyancing**, as it is generally called:

1. negotiation and agreement;

2. formation of the contract and exchange of contracts;

3. transfer or conveyance of the legal estate;

4. registration.

3.3.1 Negotiation and agreement

At this first stage, the purchaser (buyer) will look at the property and decide, in principle, to buy it. This results in an agreement to buy the land 'subject to contract'. This is not a legally binding agreement: either party is free to withdraw. During this stage, the purchaser will usually arrange a loan with which to pay for the property, unless he or she is lucky enough to be wealthy enough not to need one. The loan will usually be secured by the grant of a **mortgage** by the purchaser over the land. This is often called 'arranging a mortgage', but you should note that the mortgage, or charge, is properly the name of the security for the loan. It is not the bank or other lender who grants the mortgage, but rather the purchaser, in return for the loan. Of course, the purchaser does not own the land at the time of the arrangement to borrow the money, but agrees to grant a mortgage as soon as he or she becomes the owner. The paperwork for the mortgage and the purchase will later be sent to the Land Registry together.

> **CROSS REFERENCE**

For more on mortgages, see Chapter 14.

> **CROSS REFERENCE**

For more on first registration, see Chapter 4, 4.6.

> **CROSS REFERENCE**

For more on sole owners and trusts of land, see Chapter 7, 7.2.2 onwards.

For more on the rights of the sole owner of land, see 7.1.

conveyancing

the process of transferring a legal estate in land from one person to another

> **mortgage**
> properly, the name for the charge over land that is the security for the loan granted by a bank to the purchaser of the land, rather than the name for the loan itself

The purchaser will usually have one of three types of survey, or report, completed in order to establish the condition of the property:

▶ **CROSS REFERENCE**
For more on mortgages, see Chapter 14.

- A full structural survey

  This is the most expensive of the surveys, because it is most detailed. It is most appropriate for older properties, or if the buyer has concerns about the house.

- A home condition report

  This is not as detailed as a full structural survey, but should discover any major defects in the property and many minor ones as well.

- A valuation report

  This type of report is not very detailed, because the surveyor is concerned only with establishing that the house is worth the amount of money for which the vendor (seller of the property) is asking.

If a mortgage is to be granted in return for a loan, a valuation survey will be a requirement of the lender. Following completion of the survey, there may be further negotiations on price, either as a result of defects found in the survey, or because the value of land is rising or falling at the time of the negotiations.

Sometimes, at this stage, a vendor will threaten to pull out of an agreement because he has received a higher offer—referred to as **gazumping**, or sometimes the purchaser may refuse to proceed unless the vendor accepts a lower price—sometimes called **gazundering**, or the vendor may pull out of selling altogether because of uncertainty and a lack of available properties to buy—referred to as **gazanging**. This stage of the house-buying process is often very stressful, because the purchaser will be incurring costs in arranging loans and having surveys carried out, as well as paying a solicitor or licensed conveyancer for the early stages of conveyancing (such as proof of title and local authority searches). If the transaction does not eventually go ahead, those costs will be wasted.

> **gazumping** the process of a third party offering, or the vendor accepting, a higher offer on a property on which a sale price has already been agreed, but for which agreement no binding contract is yet in place
>
> **gazundering** the process of the purchaser demanding a lower price on a property after a sale price has already been agreed, but for which agreement no binding contract is yet in place
>
> **gazanging** the vendor pulling out of the sale altogether at the last moment

It is often the case that the vendor is a purchaser as well, because many house-buying transactions take place in chains—that is, there are a number of transactions that are dependent on each other.

 EXAMPLE

Ben and Belinda live in a small house. They want to move into a larger house. They look at Callum's house and offer to buy it.

Ben and Belinda however, cannot, afford to own both their present house and Callum's house at the same time. They must find someone to buy their house before they can formally agree to buy Callum's house.

Ali is looking for a small house to buy as his first home. He looks at Ben and Belinda's house, and agrees to buy it.

Ali, Ben and Belinda, and Callum are all part of a 'chain' of transactions:

A ———————B and B ——————— C

If any of the parties change their minds, or if something goes wrong, all of the purchases and sales come to a stop, and may 'fall through'.

Clearly, this chain could be even longer. Callum may be moving to a new house as well—say, Diljot's house—in which case, his purchase is also part of the chain, as might be Diljot's purchase:

A ———————B and B ——————C —————D —————?

All chains are only as strong as their weakest link, so the longer the chain, the greater the chance of a breakdown.

In 2007 it was estimated that 28 per cent of property transactions failed after terms have been agreed and that over £350m each year was wasted in costs of purchases and sales that did not go ahead. The then government tried to address the issue of wasted costs by introducing Home Information Packs (HIPs) which contained important information about the property for sale and which could be relied upon by any purchaser without the costs of searches, etc. being repeatedly incurred. However, HIPs did not lead to a dramatic reduction in wasted costs, and were unpopular with those selling homes as they cost up to several hundred pounds. They were suspended from 21 May 2010 and abolished in 2012. All that is now required is an Energy Performance Certificate.

3.3.2 Formation of the contract and exchange of contracts

Once the parties have agreed terms, they can enter into a formal contract for the sale and purchase of the land. The agreement is not legally binding until both parties have entered into a formal contract. Contracts for the sale of land are required to be made in writing incorporating all of the terms of the agreement, under Law of Property (Miscellaneous Provisions) Act 1989 (LP(MP)A 1989), s. 2.

 STATUTE

Law of Property (Miscellaneous Provisions) Act 1989, s. 2 [Contracts for sale etc. of land to be made by signed writing]

(1) A contract for the sale or other disposition of an interest in land can only be made in writing and only by incorporating all the terms which the parties have expressly agreed in one document or, where contracts are exchanged, in each.

(2) The terms may be incorporated in a document either by being set out in it or by reference to some other document.

(3) The document incorporating the terms or, where contracts are exchanged, one of the documents incorporating them (but not necessarily the same one) must be signed by or on behalf of each party to the contract.

...

(5) This section does not apply in relation to—

(a) a contract to grant such a lease as is mentioned in section 54(2) of the Law of Property Act 1925 (short leases);

(b) a contract made in the course of a public auction; or

[(c) a contract regulated under the Financial Services and Markets Act 2000, other than a regulated mortgage contract [, a regulated home reversion plan, a regulated home purchase plan, or a regulated sale and rent back agreement];]

and nothing in this section affects the creation or operation of resulting, implied, or constructive trusts.

...

Before this section came into force, contracts for the sale of land were governed by LPA 1925, s. 40. This required the contract to be *'evidenced in writing'*, which meant that an oral contract could be given validity by a later written memorandum. This is no longer possible. It also provided an exception for transactions of which there had been *'part performance'*—most typically, situations in which the purchaser was allowed to move into the premises before the conveyance. However, any act of part performance could make the contract enforceable, provided the act was *directly referable* to the contract. LPA 1925, s. 40, no longer applies, but it is useful to be aware of it when reading older cases.

► CROSS REFERENCE

For more on implied, resulting, and constructive trusts, see Chapter 11.

It is still possible for an informal agreement to take effect if it can be shown that it has given rise to a resulting, implied, or constructive trust, because LP(MP)A 1989, s. 2(5), specifically provides that the section is not to affect the creation or operation of such trusts. It is this exception which has led to most case law. In particular, there has been debate about whether proprietary estoppel can be used to save an informal transaction that does not comply with this section, although it is not specifically mentioned in s. 2(5). *Yaxley v. Gotts* [2000] Ch 162 seemed to indicate that this was possible, by finding that the proprietary estoppel gave rise to a constructive trust. However, a claimant who fails to enter into a formal agreement, particularly in a commercial situation, will not always succeed.

🔍 CASE CLOSE-UP

Cobbe v. Yeoman's Row Management Ltd [2008] UKHL 55

The claimant was a property developer who spent large sums of money in obtaining planning permission for the development of property belonging to the defendant. He was relying on an 'in principle' oral agreement that he could buy the property from the defendant, develop it, and then they would both get further sums from the sale of the units developed. However, once planning permission had been granted, the defendant went back on his agreement and refused to sell the property to the claimant after all. Since there was no written contract complying with LP(MP)A 1989, s. 2(1), no claim could be brought to enforce the contract. Therefore, the claimant brought an action claiming that there was a proprietary estoppel in his favour, or that alternatively there was a constructive trust, both of which would have given him a proprietary interest in the property. He also made claims based on restitution and unjust enrichment, as well as a claim to a *quantum meruit*.

The House of Lords, reversing the Court of Appeal ([2006] EWCA Civ 1139), held that there were no grounds for holding that there was either a proprietary estoppel or a constructive trust. There was no proprietary estoppel because there was no certain interest in land that it was expected would be transferred; there were to be further negotiations on the exact terms of the agreement. The claimant, an experienced property developer, knew that the agreement was binding 'in honour' only. There was no constructive trust because the defendant withdrawing unconscionably from the agreement was not enough to found such a trust. The property had been owned by the defendant long before the agreement was reached.

The claimant was entitled to damages based on unjust enrichment and *quantum meruit* for the sums he had spent, but not to an interest in the property.

CROSS REFERENCE

For more on proprietary estoppel, see Chapter 10.

See the 'Advanced topics' in the online resources for more detail on the interpretation of LP(MP)A 1989, s. 2.

> **specific performance**
> a remedy for breach of contract that demands the fulfilment of obligations under the contract

Whittaker v. Kinnear [2011] EWHC 1479 (QB) has also held that proprietary estoppel in cases relating to land has not been abolished by the LP(MP)A 1989.

In practice, the Law Society's Standard Conditions of Sale are normally used as the terms of the contract. It is common practice for each party to sign a separate copy of the contract, each of which is then 'exchanged'—often by agreement over the telephone, rather than physically—when both parties are ready to proceed. Once contracts have been exchanged, the parties are bound to carry out the transaction. If one party backs out, he or she will be in breach of contract. The most usual remedy for breach of a contract to sell land is **specific performance**—that is, the court will order the transfer of the land from the vendor to the purchaser.

The availability of specific performance as a remedy leads to an important consequence for the vendor and purchaser: after contracts are exchanged, the property belongs to the purchaser in equity. In other words, after exchange, a trust is imposed upon the vendor to hold the property in trust for the purchaser. One important consequence of this is that the purchaser must insure the property from the moment of exchange.

3.3.3 **Transfer or conveyance of the legal estate**

3.3.3.1 **Proof of title**

After contracts have been exchanged, the purchaser's solicitor will conduct searches to establish that the vendor has title to the land and to establish what encumbrances—third-party rights, such as rights of way, restrictive covenants, etc.—exist on the land.

The requirement to prove title will be met in different ways depending upon whether the land is registered or unregistered.

Registered land

If the land is registered, the proof of title lies in the Land Registry entry for that land. The registered proprietor has the power to transfer the land, unless there are restrictions entered on the proprietorship register. Entry as the registered proprietor is conclusive proof of ownership of the legal estate in the land.

CROSS REFERENCE

For more on registered land, see Chapter 4.

The purchaser should also inspect the land itself, however, not least to see if there are any potential overriding interests, which are binding on purchasers without being registered.

CROSS REFERENCE

For more on legal and equitable interests, see Chapter 2.

Unregistered land

If land is unregistered, there is, of course, no Land Registry entry to consult. Instead, the vendor must provide a documentary root of title going back at least fifteen years—Law of Property Act 1969, s. 23. This root of title is likely to be a conveyance to the present owner of the property. Older conveyances may be handwritten.

CROSS REFERENCE

Figure 3.1 is the original conveyance of the piece of land considered in Chapter 4, Form 4.1.

An example of the beginning of an old conveyance is shown in Figure 3.1. (The original is five pages long.)

The purchaser will also have to search the land charges register for registered land charges, and be aware that other legal and equitable interests in the land may exist. These can most easily be discovered by inspecting the land itself.

> **deed**
> a formal document that makes it clear, on its face, that it is intended to be a deed and which is executed as a deed

3.3.3.2 **The requirement for a deed**

The main requirement for formality in transferring land in modern times is that a legal estate in land must be transferred by **deed**.

Figure 3.1 An old-fashioned conveyance

STATUTE

Law of Property Act 1925, s. 52 [Conveyances to be by deed]

(1) All conveyances of land or of any interest therein are void for the purpose of conveying or creating a legal estate unless made by deed.

…

STATUTE

Law of Property (Miscellaneous Provisions) Act 1989 [as amended by the Regulatory Reform (Execution of Deeds and Documents) Order 2005], s. 1 [Deeds and their execution]

…

(2) An instrument shall not be a deed unless—

(a) it makes it clear on its face that it is intended to be a deed by the person making it or, as the case may be, by the parties to it (whether by describing itself as a deed or expressing itself to be executed or signed as a deed or otherwise); and

(b) it is validly executed as a deed—

(i) by that person or a person authorised to execute it in the name or on behalf of that person, or

(ii) by one or more of those parties or a person authorised to execute it in the name or on behalf of one or more of those parties.

(2A) For the purposes of subsection (2)(a) above, an instrument shall not be taken to make it clear on its face that it is intended to be a deed merely because it is executed under seal.

> **(3)** An instrument is validly executed as a deed by an individual if, and only if—
>
>   **(a)** it is signed—
>
>   **(i)** by him in the presence of a witness who attests the signature; or
>
>   **(ii)** at his direction and in his presence and the presence of two witnesses who each attest the signature; and
>
>   **(b)** it is delivered as a deed …
>
> …

These requirements are set out in LP(MP)A 1989, s. 1, which replaced the old common law requirement from 1 January 1990. Before that time, a deed had to be 'signed, sealed and delivered'.

As you can see from LP(MP)A 1989, s. 1(2A), the execution of a document under seal is no longer enough to show that it is a deed. It must comply with the new provisions. The requirement for a seal had become largely obsolete since sealing wax and seal rings fell out of use, and it was replaced by the requirement for attestation (witnessing) by the required number of witnesses.

The modern requirements for a deed can thus be summarized as in Table 3.2.

Table 3.2 The requirements for a valid deed

Requirement	Details
Declares on its face that it is a deed	Either by: (i) 'describing itself as a deed'—usually by the document beginning 'this deed'; (ii) expressing itself to be 'signed or executed as a deed'—usually by words such as 'executed as a deed' at the end of the document; or (iii) otherwise—that is, anything else that makes it clear it is a deed—see *HSBC Trust v. Quinn* [2007] EWHC 1543 (Ch).
Signed	Either: (i) by the party making the deed; or (ii) at his or her direction and in his or her presence—that is, by someone other than the vendor, if he or she is too ill to sign the deed, or cannot write.
Attested (witnessed)	If signed by the maker of the deed, by one witness who must be present when the deed is signed. If signed at his or her direction, by two witnesses, who must be present when the deed is signed.
Delivered	This used to mean physical delivery to the other party to the transaction, but nowadays means that the deed is irreversible. The fact that the deed is to be delivered is usually stated at the end of the document, just above the signature.

The requirement to use a deed is set out in LPA 1925, s. 52.

Under LPA 1925, s. 205(1)(ii), 'conveyance' includes a mortgage, a charge, and a lease, as well as a straightforward transfer of the land.

There are a number of exceptions to this requirement in s. 52(2), some of which will be encountered later in this book. Since this chapter deals with express transfers of the legal freehold, s. 52(1) applies and a deed must be used.

Nowadays, the document used to transfer the land is invariably the Land Registry form, TR1 (see Form 3.1). This is used for both registered and unregistered land, because it contains the right information to enable the estate to be correctly registered after transfer. All transfers of the legal freehold must be registered (see 3.3.4).

Form 3.1 Land Registry transfer form TR1

© Crown copy right

Land Registry
Transfer of whole of registered title(s)

TR1

If you need more room than is provided for in a panel, and your software allows, you can expand any panel in the form. Alternatively use continuation sheet CS and attach it to this form.

Leave blank if not yet registered.	**1** Title number(s) of the property: UG23456
Insert address including postcode (if any) or other description of the property, for example 'land adjoining 2 Acacia Avenue'.	**2** Property: 36 Hillendale Road, Ruxhurst, London, RU1 3BW
	3 Date: 05/08/2009
Give full name(s).	**4** Transferor: Stanley Clifford Wentworth and Patricia Anne Wentwoth both of 36 Hillendale Road Ruxhurst, London RU1 3BW
Complete as appropriate where the transferor is a company.	<u>For UK incorporated companies/LLPs</u> Registered number of company or limited liability partnership including any prefix: <u>For overseas companies</u> (a) Territory of incorporation: (b) Registered number in England and Wales including any prefix:
Give full name(s).	**5** Transferee for entry in the register: Sandra Clarke and Sarah Greer both of 12 Brixton Road Greenwich London SE9 1 LS
Complete as appropriate where the transferee is a company. Also, for an overseas company, unless an arrangement with Land Registry exists, lodge either a certificate in Form 7 in Schedule 3 to the Land Registration Rules 2003 or a certifed copy of the constitution in English or Welsh, or other evidence permitted by rule 183 of the Land Registration Rules 2003.	<u>For UK incorporated companies/LLPs</u> Registered number of company or limited liability partnership including any prefix: <u>For overseas companies</u> (a) Territory of incorporation: (b) Registered number in England and Wales including any prefix:
Each transferee may give up to three addresses for service, one of which must be a postal address whether or not in the UK (including the postcode, if any). The others can be any combination of a postal address, a UK DX box number or an electronic address.	**6** Transferee's intended address(es) for service for entry in the register: 36 Hillendale Road, Ruxhurst, London RU1 3BW
	7 The transferor transfers the property to the transferee

Form 3.1 Continued

Place 'X' in the appropriate box. State the currency unit if other than sterling. If none of the boxes apply, insert an appropriate memorandum in panel 11.	**8 Consideration** ☐ The transferor has received from the transferee for the property the following sum (in words and figures): ☐ The transfer is not for money or anything that has a monetary value ☐ Insert other receipt as appropriate:
Place 'X' in any box that applies. Add any modifications.	**9 The transferor transfers with** ☐ full title guarantee ☐ limited title guarantee
Where the transferee is more than one person, place 'X' in the appropriate box. Complete as necessary.	**10 Declaration of trust. the transferee is more than one person and** ☐ they are to hold the property on trust for themselves as joint tenants ☐ they are to hold the property on trust for themselves as tenants in common in equal shares ☐ they are to hold the property on trust:
Insert here any required or permitted statement, certificate or application and any agreed covenants, declarations and so on.	**11 Additional provisions**
The transferor must execute this transfer as a deed using the space opposite. If there is more than one transferor, all must execute. Forms of execution are given in Schedule 9 to the Land Registration Rules 2003. If the transfer contains transferee's covenants or declarations or contains an application by the transferee (such as for a restriction), it must also be executed by the transferee.	**12 Execution**

WARNING

If you dishonestly enter information or make a statement that you know is, or might be, untrue or misleading, and intend by doing so to make a gain for yourself or another person, or to cause loss or the risk of loss to another person, you may commit the offence of fraud under section 1 of the Fraud Act 2006, the maximum penalty for which is 10 years' imprisonment or an unlimited fine, or both.

Failure to complete this form with proper care may result in a loss of protection under the Land Registration Act 2002 if, as a result, a mistake is made in the register.

Under section 66 of the Land Registration Act 2002 most documents (including this form) kept by the registrar relating to an application to the registrar or referred to in the register are open to public inspection and copying. if you believe a document contains prejudicial information, you may apply for that part of the document to be made exempt using Form EX1, under rule 136 of the Land Registration Rules 2003.

The information required for the transfer can be seen in the form.

Box 1 deals with the title number of the property. If the property were unregistered land, this box would be left blank and a title number would be assigned by the Land Registry when the land is registered.

Box 2 describes the property. Because it is already registered and will be identifiable on a plan filed at the Registry, only the address need be given. If it were unregistered land, it would have to be described in such a way as to be identifiable. This would usually be by reference to the description in one of the documents relied upon as a good root of title.

> **EXAMPLE**
>
> When 36 Hillendale Road was transferred to Stanley and Patricia Wentworth, the description given was: '… the land comprised in a Conveyance dated the 31st day of July 1928 made between J. W. Ellingham Limited of the one part and Albert Edward Gales of the other part'.
>
> The conveyance referred to is that in Figure 3.1.

Box 4 gives the name of the transferor. In this case, there are two transferors: Stanley and Patricia Wentworth. They are the vendors in this case.

In Box 5, Sandra Clarke and Sarah Greer are named as the transferees (the purchasers in this case).

Box 6 requires an address for service. It is important to make sure that the Land Registry has at least one up-to-date address for the service of any notices or other communications to do with the land. Here, the transferees have given the address of the property itself, so they probably intend to live there. If they had bought the property to let out to tenants, for example, they would have given an alternative address. It is also possible to add an email address.

Box 7 contains the words that actually carry out the transfer of the land: 'The transferor transfers the Property to the Transferee.'

Box 8 deals with the consideration paid for the transfer. Note that there need not be any consideration: the deed itself 'imparts consideration' and can be sued upon even if no consideration is paid—but it is usual for some consideration to be paid.

Box 9 deals with the title guarantee. This is a conveyancing matter that is beyond the scope of this book.

Box 10 contains a declaration of trust, to set out whether the transferees are to hold the property as joint tenants or as tenants in common in equal shares.

Box 11 can be used to write in any special agreements the parties have made.

> **CROSS REFERENCE**
>
> For more on joint tenants and tenants in common, see Chapter 8.

> **EXAMPLE**
>
> If Mr and Mrs Wentworth want Sandra and Sarah to promise not to build any further buildings on the land, this agreement or 'covenant' could be recorded in Box 11 on the transfer form. The Land Registry would then be able to enter the covenant in the charges register of the title.

In the last box on the form, there is space to execute the form as a deed. The formalities referred to earlier must be observed. Thus, in this case, the transferors must sign the document in the presence of a witness, who must attest the signature. If Sandra and Sarah have made any promises—for example, the covenant mentioned in the example—they must execute the deed as well.

Form TR1 will be sent to the Land Registry along with any other relevant documents—such as the old conveyance if the land is to be registered for the first time—and any documents relating to a mortgage being granted by Sandra and Sarah over the land.

3.3.4 **Registration**

After the transfer of the freehold estate has taken place, it must be completed by registration at the Land Registry. For details of first registration of title, and registrable dispositions of registered land, please see Chapter 4, 4.5 and 4.6.

 Summary

1. The legal freehold is technically called the fee simple absolute in possession. Any other type of freehold estate cannot be legal, but takes effect as an equitable interest in land.

2. As well as being a fee simple absolute in possession, the legal freehold must be transferred using the appropriate formalities, otherwise—at best—only an equitable interest in land will be transferred.

3. A contract for the sale or other disposition of a legal freehold must be made in writing and must incorporate all the terms of the contract—LP(MP)A 1989, s. 2.

4. A conveyance of a legal freehold must be made by deed—LPA 1925, s. 52.

5. The conveyance of a legal freehold must be completed by registration, whether or not the land was registered before the transfer—LRA 2002, ss. 4 and 27(2).

The bigger picture

- If you want to know more about registers of title, look at Chapter 15, especially 15.1. For possible exam questions on this area, see Chapter 16, 16.5. If you need more detailed information on the formation of a contract for the sale of land under LP(MP)A 1989, s. 2, please see the 'Advanced topics', Chapter 3 in the online resources.

- More information on registration can be found in Chapter 4.

- If you need more information for coursework, see the cases listed below.

Absolute, determinable, and conditional fees

Blanchfield v. AG of Trinidad and Tobago [2002] UKPC 1
Fraser v. Canterbury Diocesan Board of Finance (No. 2) [2005] UKHL 65
Re Da Costa [1912] 1 Ch 337
Re Leach [1912] 2 Ch 422
Re Moore (1888) 39 Ch D 116
Re Tepper's Will Trust [1987] Ch 358
Walsingham's Case (1573) 2 Plowd 547

Contracts for the disposition of land—LP(MP)A 1989 s. 2

Firstpost Homes v. Johnson [1997] 1 WLR 38

Helden v. Strathmore Ltd [2011] EWCA Civ 542

Herbert v. Doyle [2010] EWCA Civ 1095

Joyce v. Rigolli [2004] EWCA Civ 79

Matchmove Ltd v. Dowding [2016] EWCA Civ 1233

McLaughlin v. Duffill [2008] EWCA Civ 1627, [2010] Ch 1

Record v. Bell [1991] 1 WLR 853

Rollerteam Ltd v. Riley [2016] EWCA Civ 1291

Spiro v. Glencrown Properties Ltd [1991] Ch 537.

Target Holdings Ltd v. Priestley (1999) 79 P & CR 305

? Questions

Self-test questions

1. Anna is the registered proprietor of Green Cottage. She grants Barry a life interest in Green Cottage. Will this estate be legal or equitable?

2. Anna grants Barry a life interest in Green Cottage, with remainder in fee simple to Cassie. Will Cassie have a legal estate in Green Cottage:

   (a) before Barry's death?

   (b) after Barry's death?

3. Donald transfers his house to Edwin 'until he qualifies as a barrister'. What kind of estate will this be? Is it legal or equitable?

4. Look back at Question 1: when Barry dies, who will be the owner of Green Cottage?

5. Gary wants to buy Frank's house. They have entered into an agreement 'subject to contract'. What rights does this give Gary over Frank's house?

6. Frank has entered into a written contract to sell his house to Gary. What interest, if any, does Gary have in Frank's house?

Exam question

1. Frank executes a deed transferring his house, which is unregistered land, to Gary. What interest does Gary have in the house? What difference would it make to your answer if the house had been registered land at the time of the transfer?

 You will find answers to these questions online at www.oup.com/uk/clarke_directions6e/.

Further reading

On Crown Land

Law Commission/HM Land Registry (2001) *Land Registration for the Twenty-First Century: A Conveyancing Revolution*, Law Com No. 271, available online at http://www.lawcom.gov.uk/project/land-registration-for-the-21st-century/, paras 2.7, 11.5–11.19

This Law Commission/HM Land Registry report introduced the LRA 2002. You can see here details of provisions about Crown land.

On LP(MP)A 1989, s. 2

Chambers, K., 'Property supplement: Yeoman's scope' (2008) 158 NLJ 1629

Pawlowski, M., 'Oral Agreements: estoppel, constructive trusts and restitution' (2008) 12 L and T Rev 163

These two articles discuss the effect of *Cobbe v. Yeoman's Row Management Ltd* [2008] UKHL 55.

On Electronic Conveyancing

Hatfield, E., The e-conveyancing re-revolution [2015] 2 Conv 148–51

This article discusses renewed initiatives to introduce e-conveyancing and compares progress here with that in other common law jurisdictions.

https://www.gov.uk/government/organisations/land-registry

This is the website of the Land Registry. It features publications explaining land registration and you can look at the forms required to register land.

 Online Resources

For more advice relating to this chapter, including self-test questions and an interactive glossary, visit www.oup.com/uk/clarke_directions6e/.

4 Registration of title

LEARNING OBJECTIVES

After reading this chapter, you will be able to:

- appreciate the main features of the system of registration of title to land;
- be able to read a register of title
- distinguish between first registration of title and registrable dispositions;
- understand substantive registration, interests protected by notice, and over-riding interests;
- understand what is meant by alteration and rectification of the register;
- know when an indemnity will be payable as the result of a mistake in the register.

Introduction

From reading Chapter 2 of this book, you should have understood that one of the main reforms introduced by the 1925 property legislation was the introduction of compulsory, nationwide registration of title to land.

> **1925 property legislation** A series of Acts of Parliament that came into effect on 1 January 1926. These Acts consolidated earlier piecemeal changes in the law—particularly from 1922–24—and brought them all together as a body of law, which made substantial changes to the common law of property

CROSS REFERENCE

For more on the 1925 property legislation and registration of title, see Chapter 2, 2.5, particularly 2.5.2.2.

In this chapter we will look at that permanent system of registration, which now underpins all dealings with land, and is thus of fundamental importance in land law. The disadvantage to explaining land registration in detail so early in the book is that, as yet, you have not had a chance really to understand the interests in land that need to be registered. This inevitably makes it more difficult to explain clearly what is being registered and why. What we suggest is that, after reading through this chapter, you dip into it again later in your land law course and use it to fill in any gaps in your understanding.

4.1 The principles of registration

There are three main principles of registration of title, first set out by Theodore Ruoff, a former Chief Land Registrar, as follows:

1. **The mirror principle**

   The register should be a mirror of the estates and interests affecting the land.

2. **The curtain principle**

   The details of any trusts affecting the land should be kept off the title.

3. **The indemnity principle**

   An indemnity (compensation) is payable by the state if loss is caused by errors in the register.

As we go through the chapter, we will consider whether and to what extent these principles are applied in the current legislation.

---

mirror principle the principle in registration of title that the register should be a mirror of the estates and interests affecting the land

curtain principle the principle in registration of title that the details of any trusts affecting the land should be kept off the title

indemnity principle
an indemnity (compensation) is payable by the state if loss is caused by errors in the register

---

4.2 The legislative framework

The current system of registration of title was introduced by the Land Registration Act 1925 (LRA 1925), which was in force for 77 years. However, in 1998, the Law Commission and the Land Registry published a joint consultative document recommending changes to the system of registration. In 2001, a second Law Commission report was published, to which was attached a draft Bill, which eventually became the Land Registration Act 2002 (LRA 2002).

The LRA 2002 did not simply tidy up the legislation relating to land registration; it also changed some aspects of the law. Its stated objectives included the introduction of electronic conveyancing and making fundamental changes to the law of registration of title, with the aim of enabling a purchaser to make fewer enquiries about, and inspections of, the land than was formerly the case with unregistered title.

The LRA 2002 is now itself the subject of a consultation exercise by the Law Commission (Updating the Land Registration Act 2002 A Consultation Paper, Consultation Paper No. 227) which is looking in particular the interests that can be registered; how interests are protected on the register; the effect of registration; the extent of the guarantee of title that registration provides; and the development of electronic conveyancing. It is due to report in spring 2018.

4.3 The register of title

The main, practical effect of registration of title is that the old system of 'title deeds' described in Chapter 3, 3.3.1 and illustrated in Figure 3.1 is replaced by one much simpler document kept electronically at the Land Registry. Each title is identified by number, and is related to a map reference and plan that is based on the Ordnance Survey Map, not to the name of the estate owner.

There are three parts to the register of each title:

1. **The property register**

    This contains a description of the land, including incorporeal hereditaments, such as easements over other land, restrictive covenants, etc., for the benefit of the land.

2. **The proprietorship register**

    This gives the names of the estate owner(s), the type of title, and any restrictions to which they are subject when dealing with their title.

3. **The charges register**

    This contains those things that are a charge or encumbrance on the land—that is, those things that do not benefit the land, but rather are a burden on it. Examples include mortgages and rights of way over the land (as opposed to those over other land for the benefit of this land).

> **CROSS REFERENCE**
> For more on incorporeal hereditaments, see Chapter 1, 1.1.4.

> **property register** first part of the register of title, containing a description of the land by address and postcode, and including incorporeal hereditaments, such as easements over other land and restrictive covenants benefiting the land
>
> **proprietorship register** second part of the register of title giving the names of the registered proprietor, the type of title, and any restrictions to which the registered proprietor is subject when dealing with their title
>
> **charges register** third part of the register of title, containing charges or encumbrances over land such as mortgages, easements, and restrictive covenants burdening the land

Form 4.1 shows an example of a register of title. At the top, you can see the title number, which is the Land Registry's unique reference number for that estate in land. The register is then divided into the three parts listed earlier.

The first part, the property register, gives the address of the land (36 Hillendale Road, Ruxhurst) and refers to a plan filed at the Registry. It also states that the land is freehold land. The property register then lists an easement existing for the benefit of this land—rights of drainage over neighbouring properties. The easement, being an incorporeal hereditament, forms part of the definition of the land in this title.

The second part, the proprietorship register, gives the names of the proprietors (owners) of the estate in land—Stanley and Patricia Wentworth. There are no restrictions entered on the proprietorship register limiting their power to deal with the title.

The third part, the charges register, contains any encumbrances on the land:

1. The first entry in this section concerns an easement—rights of drainage. Read in combination with the similar entry in the property register, it looks as though the drains for this property and neighbouring ones run under a number of properties. Each of the properties carries with it a right to use all of the drains, not only the bit that runs under its own land.

> **CROSS REFERENCE**
> For more on easements, see Chapter 12.
> For more on restrictive covenants, see Chapter 13, 13.5.
> For more on mortgages, see Chapter 14.

2. The second entry refers to restrictive covenants into which a previous owner of the land entered. These covenants are listed in a schedule at the end of the register, and include restrictions on the type and number of houses that may be built on the land. Such restrictive covenants may still be enforceable against the present proprietors.

3. The third entry is a charge, or mortgage over the land, and the proprietor of the charge (the lender)—in this case, the Barnebridge Building Society—is shown below it.

The legal authority behind the register of title is found in LRA 2002, s. 1, which provides that 'there is to continue to be a register of title kept by the registrar', and goes on to provide for the making of rules about the keeping of the register. These rules take form in the Land Registration Rules 2003, SI 2003/1417 (LRR 2003), which have subsequently been amended, most recently in 2011.

Form 4.1 Example of a register

```
---------------------------------------------------------------------------
--------
TITLE NUMBER : UG234567
A PROPERTY REGISTER
This register describes the land and estate comprised in the title.
---------------------------------------------------------------------------

GREATER LONDON      LONDON BOROUGH    Ruxley

1. (23 November 1967) The Freehold land shown edged with red on the
plan of the above Title filed at the Registry and being 36 Hillendale
Road, Ruxhurst.

2. (23 November 1967) This property enjoys rights of drainage over
neighbouring properties.

END OF A REGISTER
---------------------------------------------------------------------------

TITLE NUMBER : UG234567
B PROPRIETORSHIP REGISTER
This register specifies the class of title and identifies the owner.
It contains any entries that affect the right of disposal.
TITLE ABSOLUTE
---------------------------------------------------------------------------

1. (25 March 1988) Proprietor: STANLEY CLIFFORD WENTWORTH and
PATRICIA ANNE WENTWORTH both of 36 Hillendale Road, Ruxhurst, London.

END OF B REGISTER
---------------------------------------------------------------------------

TITLE NUMBER : UG234567
C CHARGES REGISTER
This register contains any charges and other matters that affect the
land.
---------------------------------------------------------------------------

1. (23 November 1967) The land is subject to rights of drainage.

2. (23 November 1967) A Conveyance of the land in this title dated 21
July 1928 made between (1) J.W. Ellingham Limited (Vendor) and (2)
Albert Edward Gales (Purchaser) contains covenants details of which
are set out in the schedule of restrictive covenants hereto.

3. (25 March 1988) REGISTERED CHARGE dated 1 June 1988 to secure the
monies including the further advances therein mentioned.

PROPRIETOR OF Charge dated 1 June 1999 Barnebridge Building Society
of Barnebridge House, Crown Street, Barnebridge BR2 9QT.
```

Form 4.1 Example of a register (continued)

```
------------------------------------------------------------------

TITLE NUMBER : UG234567
SCHEDULE OF RESTRICTIVE COVENANTS
------------------------------------------------------------------

The following are details of the covenants contained in the
Conveyance dated 31 July 1928 referred to in the Charges Register:-

1. No house or other building shall be erected on the land except in
accordance with these stipulations;

2. One house only of the cost of at least Five hundred pounds and in
all respects according to front elevations to be approved of by the
Vendor or the surveyor of the Vendor shall be erected on the land and
for the purposes of this stipulation the cost of every house shall be
taken to be the net first cost thereof in labour and materials alone
(exclusive of ornamental fittings) to be estimated by the surveyor
for the time being of the Vendor at the lowest current prices.

3. No hoarding shall be erected or placed on the land for
advertisements and no hut shed caravan house on wheels or other like
erection movable or otherwise intended or adapted or capable of
adaption for use as a dwelling or sleeping apartment shall be erected
or placed or be allowed to be or remain on the land.

4. No road or way shall be made or permitted across the land hereby
conveyed for access to or regress from any adjoining lands and
premises.

END OF REGISTER
NOTE: The date at the beginning of an entry is the date on which the
entry was made in the Register.
```

The Chief Land Registrar, who is also the chief executive of the Land Registry, officially keeps the register. Registration is carried out by staff appointed by the registrar.

The registrar may refer any disputes about land registration to the Land Registration division of the Property Chamber First-tier tribunal, which may avoid the need for the parties to go to court.

LRA 2002, s. 2, sets out the scope of title registration.

 STATUTE

Land Registration Act 2002, s. 2 [Scope of title registration]

This Act makes provision about the registration of title to—

  (a) unregistered legal estates which are interests of any of the following kinds—

   (i) an estate in land,

   (ii) a rentcharge,

   (iii) a franchise,

   (iv) a profit à prendre in gross, and

   (v) any other interest or charge which subsists for the benefit of, or is a charge on, an interest the title to which is registered; and

  (b) interests capable of subsisting at law which are created by a disposition of an interest the title to which is registered.

THINKING POINT

Look carefully at LRA 2002, s. 2, above. What is the difference between subsections (a)(i)–(iv) and subsections (a)(v) and (b)?

Subsections (a)(i)–(iv) deal with estates or interests in land that have not yet been registered (unregistered land). Subsections (a)(v) and (b) deal with interests in and dispositions of registered land.

Interests in land that can be registered with their own title are listed as follows.

1. Estates in land

   You will remember from LPA 1925, s. 1(1), that there are only two legal estates in land: the freehold and the leasehold.

CROSS REFERENCE

For the meaning of a bare trust, see Chapter 7, 7.2.2.

   The owner of a freehold estate in land may apply to be registered as owner of that estate. A person who is entitled to have a freehold estate vested in him or her by reason of a bare trust may also apply to be registered as owner of that estate.

   Not all leasehold estates may be registered with their own title. This is because short leases, such as typical residential shorthold tenancies that last six months, would be quite inconvenient to register, from both the Registry's and the tenant's point of view.

   The following types of lease can be registered with their own title:

CROSS REFERENCE

For more on leases, see Chapter 5.

   - leases that, at date of grant, transfer, or creation, have more than seven years to run;
   - leases that take effect more than three months after the date of the grant (sometimes called 'reversionary leases');
   - leases with a discontinuous right to possession ('timeshare leases');
   - property subject to the 'right to buy' provisions of Housing Act 1985.

rentcharge

a charge for the payment of money that is held over freehold land

2. A rentcharge

   A **rentcharge** is a charge for the payment of money over freehold land. Very few new rentcharges can be created and most existing rentcharges are being phased out under the Rentcharges Act 1977.

franchise

a right, conferred by the Crown on a subject, to do something specific on certain land, eg hold a market

3. A franchise

   A **franchise** is the exclusive right to do something on certain land—for example, to hold a market—and most of these are very ancient in origin.

profit à prendre

the right to take natural produce from another person's land

4. A profit à prendre in gross

   A **profit à prendre** is the right to take something from land—for example, firewood—and if it is 'in gross', the benefit of the profit is not attached to any land. It can therefore be registered in its own right.

The rest of the section deals with interests in land to which the title has already been registered. Any interest or charge that either benefits registered land or that is a burden over registered land is subject to the registration provisions. In addition, any disposition of registered land, such as granting a lease over it or selling the freehold to someone else, is subject to the registration provisions. We use the term 'subject to the registration provisions', because some interests, known as overriding interests (see 4.5.6), do not need to be registered.

CROSS REFERENCE

For more on profits à prendre, see Chapter 12, 12.10.

The key point to remember throughout your whole study of land law is that registration must be considered whenever anything happens to registered land: once land is registered, registration affects every interest in it.

4.4 Crown land

As noted earlier, estates in land can be registered—but you will remember that the Crown, uniquely, can own land outright, rather than owning an estate in the land. Indeed, at common law, the Crown could not grant itself an estate at all: it would be like someone being both landlord and tenant—the Crown cannot 'hold' the land of itself. Nonetheless, the Crown wished to be able to register its land, partly because registration now gives better protection against land being taken by squatters.

> **CROSS REFERENCE**
> For more on squatters and adverse possession, see Chapter 6.

LRA 2002, s. 75, gives the Crown power to grant itself a freehold estate out of desmesne land. The Crown can also register a **caution against first registration** of desmesne land—LRA 2002, s. 81. This is an entry made on the register, which means that the Crown will be notified if anyone else tries to register desmesne land—a situation that might arise if someone were claiming adverse possession of that land. This notification would allow the Crown to object to the registration.

> **CROSS REFERENCE**
> For the meaning of desmesne land, see Chapter 2, 2.2.3.

> **caution against first registration** a notice lodged with the Land Registry by any person claiming to have ownership of, or an interest in, unregistered land that obliges the Registry to notify that person of any application for first registration of title to that land

LRA 2002, s. 82, allows an estate that has escheated to the Crown to remain on the register until disposed of by the Crown. This is more convenient than the estate ceasing to exist and then a new estate having to be created by the Crown when the land is disposed of to a new owner.

> **CROSS REFERENCE**
> For the meaning of escheat, see Chapter 2, 2.2.1.

4.5 First registration of title

In this section, we are considering land that is unregistered at the time of a sale, or other relevant event, and which therefore becomes subject to registration on the happening of that event. There was no attempt in 1925 to force everybody to register their land immediately—to do so would have overloaded the system and left the Land Registry unable to cope. Instead, areas of the country were made areas of 'compulsory registration', which meant that any land that was the subject of a 'relevant event', such as a sale, was subject to **first registration of title**. The areas of compulsory registration began with major cities, because there are more separate pieces of land in urban areas.

> **first registration of title**
> the first time that title to an estate in land is registered at the Land Registry and at which point it therefore changes from unregistered land to registered land

Eventually, in 1990, the whole of England and Wales was made an area of compulsory registration. In addition, the number of relevant events was increased by subsequent legislation. These are now set out in LRA 2002, s. 4.

This section requires the first registration of:

- any type of transfer of a 'qualifying estate', whether by sale, gift, inheritance, court order, etc.;
- the grant out of a qualifying estate of leases of more than seven years, plus certain other leases;
- the creation of a protected first legal mortgage of a qualifying estate.

Under LRA 2002, s. 4(2), a 'qualifying estate' is a fee simple absolute in possession (the freehold) or a leasehold estate that has more than seven years to run.

LRA 2002, s. 4, gives the Lord Chancellor power to extend the list of relevant events that will trigger registration. The duty to apply for registration is dealt with in LRA 2002, s. 6, and, broadly speaking, the duty is on the responsible estate owner—the person to whom the estate is transferred when registration is triggered. The estate must be registered within two months of the date on which the relevant event occurs.

The effects of failing to register as required are set out in LRA 2002, s. 7.

 STATUTE

Land Registration Act 2002, s. 7 [Effect of non-compliance with section 6]

(1) If the requirement of registration is not complied with, the transfer, grant or creation becomes void as regards the transfer, grant or creation of a legal estate.

(2) On the application of subsection (1)—

(a) in a case falling within section 4(1)(a) or (b), the title to the legal estate reverts to the transferor who holds it on a bare trust for the transferee, and

(b) in a case falling within section 4(1)(c) to (g), the grant or creation has effect as a contract made for valuable consideration to grant or create the legal estate concerned.

A legal estate that has not been registered within the required time period 'becomes void as regards the transfer, grant or creation of a legal estate': LRA 2002, s. 7(2)(a). This will leave the legal title with the transferor of the estate and he or she will hold it on trust for the transferee. This means that the transferor of the estate will continue to hold the legal title to the land and that the transferee will have only an equitable interest. Any expenses of retransferring the legal estate will fall on the transferee.

If a legal lease or charge was intended, but fails because it is not registered, the transfer operates as if it were a contract to create that interest. This will also result in the transferee having only an equitable interest in the land. Such equitable interests may be unenforceable against a subsequent purchaser of a legal estate in the land. It is therefore essential to register title as required by the Act.

4.5.1 **Cautions against first registration**

Someone who claims an interest in land that is as yet unregistered can lodge a caution against first registration—LRA 2002, s. 15. This means that the Land Registry will let them know if there is any attempt to register the land, giving them a chance to object to the registration.

 EXAMPLE

Bert holds legal title to unregistered land and Anna has a beneficial interest in it under a trust of land. Anna can lodge a caution against first registration against that land, so that she will be notified if Bert applies to register it. That way, she can make sure that any appropriate register entries are made to protect her interest.

CROSS REFERENCE

For more on adverse possession, see Chapter 6.

However, someone who claims to be the owner of a freehold estate or a leasehold estate of which more than seven years are left to run cannot lodge a caution against first registration. Instead, the owner should voluntarily register that estate in the land. This is because lodging a caution should not be used as a substitute for first registration of title to the land. This provision also means that a person claiming to be in adverse possession of unregistered land cannot lodge a caution against first registration, as they will be claiming a freehold or leasehold estate in the land: *Turner v. Chief Land Registrar* [2013] EWHC 1382 (Ch).

4.5.2 Classes of title

The registrar will assign a particular class to each title. The effect of each class of title is set out in LRA 2002, s. 11 [Freeholds], and LRA 2002, s. 12 [Leaseholds].

The vast majority of titles are absolute freehold, absolute leasehold, or good leasehold (see Table 4.1).

Table 4.1 Land Registry classes of title

Class of title	Summary
Absolute freehold/absolute leasehold	The most usual class of title. This means that the Land Registry is satisfied with the title.
Possessory freehold/possessory leasehold	This class of title is granted to squatters who have been on the property long enough to claim the land and to anyone else with no documentary proof of title. It is vulnerable to someone able to prove better title.
Qualified freehold/qualified leasehold	This class of title is very rare and means that the Registry is not completely satisfied with respect to one aspect of the title.
Good leasehold	This class of title means that the Registry is satisfied with the leasehold title, but not necessarily with the estate out of which it has been granted—usually because that estate is not yet registered. In practice, good leasehold is acceptable to purchasers.

4.5.3 The effect of registration with absolute title

Because most titles are absolute, we will concentrate on the legal effect of registration with absolute title.

 STATUTE

Land Registration Act 2002, s. 11 [Freehold estates]

(1) This section is concerned with the registration of a person under this Chapter as the proprietor of a freehold estate.

(2) Registration with absolute title has the effect described in subsections (3) to (5).

(3) The estate is vested in the proprietor together with all interests subsisting for the benefit of the estate.

> (4) The estate is vested in the proprietor subject only to the following interests affecting the estate at the time of registration—
>
>   (a) interests which are the subject of an entry in the register in relation to the estate,
>
>   (b) unregistered interests which fall within any of the paragraphs of Schedule 1, and
>
>   (c) interests acquired under the Limitation Act 1980 (c. 58) of which the proprietor has notice.
>
> (5) If the proprietor is not entitled to the estate for his own benefit, or not entitled solely for his own benefit, then, as between himself and the persons beneficially entitled to the estate, the estate is vested in him subject to such of their interests as he has notice of.
>
> …

▶ CROSS REFERENCE

For more on leasehold title, see Chapter 5.

(LRA 2002, s. 12, contains similar provisions in relation to absolute leasehold title, except that registration is also subject to the terms of the lease—particularly covenants.)

The newly registered proprietor is now the owner of the freehold estate, together with all interests subsisting for its benefit, but subject to the interests listed in the section affecting the estate at the time of registration, as summarized in Table 4.2.

Table 4.2 Interests affecting the first registered proprietor

Section	Interest	Effect
LRA 2002, s. 11(4)(a)	Interests that are the subject of an entry in the register in relation to the estate	This means rights that the registrar enters onto the register—that is, mortgages and any interests protected by notices or restrictions in the register
LRA 2002, s. 11(4)(b)	Unregistered interests that fall within any of the paragraphs of Sch. 1	These are overriding interests— that is, interests that are binding on a transferee without being registered—and include short leaseholds, interests of those who are in 'actual occupation' of the land, unregistered easements and profits, local land charges, and certain other rights—see 4.5.6
LRA 2002, s. 11(4)(c)	Interests acquired under the Limitation Act 1980 (c. 58) of which the proprietor has notice	These are rights of persons who have adversely possessed land and of whom the new registered proprietor has notice. This section is unlikely to apply to many cases.
LRA 2002, s. 11(5)	If the proprietor is not entitled to the estate for his or her own benefit, or not entitled solely for his or her own benefit, then, as between the proprietor and the persons beneficially entitled to the estate, the estate is vested in the proprietor subject to such of their interests of which he or she has notice	This deals with situations in which the proprietor is holding the estate as a trustee. The estate is vested in the proprietor, subject to the rights of the beneficiaries.

LRA 2002, s. 11, makes the registered proprietor the legal owner of the estate, whatever the circumstances of the transfer of the land to him or her. This changes the common law position that no-one can give good title to an estate that he or she does not own.

EXAMPLE

To take an extreme example, if you were to try to sell the Houses of Parliament to Annie, a gullible tourist, she would not become the owner of it, because you have no title to the Houses of Parliament that you can sell!

But if Annie is then *registered* as the proprietor of the Houses of Parliament she *would* become their legal owner, because of LRA 2002, ss. 11 and 58.

You can see a rather more realistic example of this in the case of *Re 139 Deptford High Street* (See 4.7 for more on alteration, rectification, and indemnity.)

CASE CLOSE-UP

Re 139 Deptford High Street [1951] Ch 884

The vendor transferred a shop to the purchaser, together with an annexe. In fact, the annexe did not belong to the vendor, but to someone else. The purchaser was registered as first registered proprietor of the property, including the annexe. Naturally, the true owner of the annexe, once he found out, was keen to get the register altered to correct the mistake.

It was clear that the registered proprietor was the legal owner of the annexe, even though the vendors did not have power to transfer it to him, because they did not own it. If it had not been for registration, he would not have been the owner.

The register was rectified (altered) to exclude the annexe from the registered title.

Re Deptford High Street was decided under the Land Registration Act 1925—but the fact that registration makes the registered proprietor the legal owner of the land is even clearer under LRA 2002, s. 58.

STATUTE

Land Registration Act 2002, s. 58 [Conclusiveness]

(1) If, on the entry of a person in the register as the proprietor of a legal estate, the legal estate would not otherwise be vested in him, it shall be deemed to be vested in him as a result of the registration.

…

Notice that s. 58 mentions only the legal estate. In previous chapters we have seen, however, that the owner of a legal estate need not necessarily be the owner in equity: he or she may be a trustee for someone else, for example. This point is dealt with in LRA 2002, s. 11(5). If the registered proprietor knows the estate is held on trust for someone, that person will still be able to assert the equitable rights of a beneficiary.

CROSS REFERENCE

For more on interests affecting the sole ownership of land, see Chapter 7.

CROSS REFERENCE

For more details on adverse possession, see Chapter 6.

 CROSS REFERENCE

For more on interests gained by squatters, see Chapter 6.

LRA 2002, s. 58, can have strange effects. For example, in *Parshall v. Hackney* [2013] EWCA (Civ) 240, the defendant was wrongly registered as the proprietor of a small piece of land which really belonged to the claimant. The defendant had in fact been in adverse possession of it for some time, but it was held by the Court of Appeal that a person registered as a proprietor of land cannot claim adverse possession, even if registered as proprietor by mistake, and is open to a claim for rectification of the register.

4.5.4 Interests protected by notice on the register

As you can see from LRA 2002, s. 11(4)(a), the registered proprietor is subject to any entries that are protected in the register. Some interests are protected by **notice** on the register.

notice

an entry against a registered title lodged by a person with a specified interest in the land

 STATUTE

Land Registration Act 2002, s. 32 [Nature and effect]

(1) A notice is an entry in the register in respect of the burden of an interest affecting a registered estate or charge.

(2) The entry of a notice is to be made in relation to the registered estate or charge affected by the interest concerned.

(3) The fact that an interest is the subject of a notice does not necessarily mean that the interest is valid, but does mean that the priority of the interest, if valid, is protected for the purposes of sections 29 and 30.

Notices are entered on the charges register section of the register of title. The effect of entering a notice is very different from that of registering title—LRA 2002, s. 32(3). The registrar does not guarantee that the interest is valid, unlike registered estates or charges, but it is vital to register the interest, because registration by notice protects the priority of valid interests. In other words, if a valid interest is registered by notice, it will be binding on a purchaser of the land; if it is not registered, it will not be binding on a purchaser.

The LRA 2002 does not set out what interests can be registered as notices, but s. 33 sets out those that cannot.

 STATUTE

Land Registration Act 2002, s. 33 [Excluded interests]

No notice may be entered in the register in respect of any of the following—

(a) an interest under—

(i) a trust of land, or

(ii) a settlement under the Settled Land Act 1925 (c. 18),

(b) a leasehold estate in land which—

(i) is granted for a term of years of three years or less from the date of the grant, and

(ii) is not required to be registered,

[(ba) an interest under a relevant social housing tenancy,]

(c)   a restrictive covenant made between a lessor and lessee, so far as relating to the de-mised premises,

(d)   an interest which is capable of being registered under the Commons Registration Act 1965 (c. 64) [Part 1 of the Commons Act 2006], and

(e)   an interest in any coal or coal mine, the rights attached to any such interest and the rights of any person under section 38, 49 or 51 of the Coal Industry Act 1994 (c. 21).

he section specifies that interests under trusts cannot be registered by notice. They will appear only s restrictions on the proprietorship register (see 4.5.5). Other excluded interests include most leases f three years or less—unless they are discontinuous, or reversionary leases (see 4.2). Restrictive ovenants in leases are not registrable, because they apply only between the landlord and the enant. The interests in subsections (d) and (e) have their own special registers.

he types of interest that are usually protected by entry of a notice include:

• legal leases for over three years (but not over seven, because longer leases are registrable dispositions);

• equitable leases;

• estate contracts;

• equitable easements and profits à prendre;

• equitable mortgages and charges;

• restrictive covenants in freehold land.

 THINKING POINT

Consider the example register in Form 4.1. What notices can you see?

you look at the charges register, there are three entries. Entries (1) and (3) concern, respectively, n easement of drainage and a legal charge (mortgage), both of which are registrable dispositions nd must therefore be completed by registration under LRA 2002, s. 27. Under LRA 2002, s. 38, owever, the registrar must also note them on the charges register of the estate affected.

ntry (2), however, is a 'noted interest'. It gives notice of restrictive covenants which affect this state. The details of the covenants are contained in the schedule at the end of the register. Note hat restrictive covenants are quite different to 'restrictions', despite the similar name.

here are two types of notice: an **agreed notice** and a **unilateral notice**—LRA 2002, s. 34.

CROSS REFERENCE

For the meaning of restriction, see 4.5.5.

agreed notice a notice on registered land that is either requested or agreed to by the proprietor, or the validity of which satisfies the registrar

unilateral notice

a notice on registered land to which the proprietor will not agree, which consequently represents a disputed interest

STATUTE

Land Registration Act 2002, s. 34 [Entry on application]

(1) A person who claims to be entitled to the benefit of an interest affecting a registered estate or charge may, if the interest is not excluded by section 33, apply to the registrar for the entry in the register of a notice in respect of the interest.

(2) Subject to rules, an application under this section may be for—

   (a) an agreed notice, or

   (b) a unilateral notice.

(3) The registrar may only approve an application for an agreed notice if—

   (a) the applicant is the relevant registered proprietor, or a person entitled to be registered as such proprietor,

   (b) the relevant registered proprietor, or a person entitled to be registered as such proprietor, consents to the entry of the notice, or

   (c) the registrar is satisfied as to the validity of the applicant's claim.

In subsection (3), references to the relevant registered proprietor are to the proprietor of the registered estate or charge affected by the interest to which the application relates.

Agreed notices must satisfy one of the conditions in LRA 2002, s. 34(3): the proprietor asks for the notice to be entered, or the proprietor agrees to the notice, or the registrar is satisfied by the claim giving rise to the notice. This third condition means that agreed notices can be entered even if the registered proprietor objects, provided that the registrar is satisfied that the interest is valid.

EXAMPLE

If an access order has been granted to someone under the Access to Neighbouring Land Act 1992, that right will be registered as an agreed notice, even if the registered proprietor of that land objects.

This is because, despite the proprietor's objection, the Land Registry would be satisfied as to the validity of the notice.

If an agreed notice cannot be entered, a unilateral notice may be entered instead—LRA 2002, s. 35.

STATUTE

Land Registration Act 2002, s. 35 [Unilateral notices]

(1) If the registrar enters a notice in the register in pursuance of an application under section 34(2)(b) ('a unilateral notice'), he must give notice of the entry to—

   (a) the proprietor of the registered estate or charge to which it relates, and

   (b) such other persons as rules may provide.

(2) A unilateral notice must—

    (a) indicate that it is such a notice, and

    (b) identify who is the beneficiary of the notice.

(3) The person shown in the register as the beneficiary of a unilateral notice, or such other person as rules may provide, may apply to the registrar for the removal of the notice from the register.

Because the registrar does not have to be satisfied that the interest claimed is genuine, there is potential for someone to enter a unilateral notice for hostile reasons. This might cause a registered proprietor who is trying to sell the land considerable difficulties, because many purchasers will be put off by the very existence of a unilateral notice, on the basis that it indicates disagreement over rights in the land.

Therefore, the registered proprietor and others interested in the land are informed about the unilateral notice by the registrar. The registered proprietor can then apply for its cancellation. If the beneficiary of the unilateral notice opposes the cancellation, the matter will be referred to the Land Registration division of the Property Chamber First-tier tribunal, which may uphold the notice—turning it into an agreed notice, or ordering registration of the interest in some more appropriate way—or order its cancellation. If the beneficiary of the notice has acted without reasonable cause, the registered proprietor can bring an action against that beneficiary in tort and claim damages for breach of statutory duty.

4.5.5 Interests protected on the register by the entry of a restriction

Restrictions are entries that are placed on the proprietorship part of the register and they restrict the right of the registered proprietor to deal with his or her land. Restrictions are most often used to protect 'family'-type interests, many of which will be overreached on the sale of the land.

> **CROSS REFERENCE**
> For the meaning of overreaching, see Chapter 2, 2.5.3.

restriction a limitation on the right of a registered proprietor to deal with the land or charge in a registered title

 STATUTE

Land Registration Act 2002, s. 40 [Nature]

(1) A restriction is an entry in the register regulating the circumstances in which a disposition of a registered estate or charge may be the subject of an entry in the register.

(2) A restriction may, in particular—

    (a) prohibit the making of an entry in respect of any disposition, or a disposition of a kind specified in the restriction;

    (b) prohibit the making of an entry—

        (i) indefinitely,

        (ii) for a period specified in the restriction, or

        (iii) until the occurrence of an event so specified.

> (3) Without prejudice to the generality of subsection (2)(b)(iii), the events which may be specified include—
>
> (a) the giving of notice,
>
> (b) the obtaining of consent, and
>
> (c) the making of an order by the court or registrar.
>
> The entry of a restriction is to be made in relation to the registered estate or charge to which it relates.

The purpose of a restriction is to ensure that certain conditions are complied with on the transfer of land, because 'no entry in respect of a disposition to which the restriction applies may be made in the register otherwise than in accordance with the terms of the restriction'—LRA 2002, s. 41(1). If, for example, the consent of a certain person is required for the sale of the property, no transfer can be registered without that consent.

Some restrictions will be entered automatically by the registrar under LRA 2002, s. 44.

 STATUTE

Land Registration Act 2002, s. 44 [Obligatory restrictions]

(1) If the registrar enters two or more persons in the register as the proprietor of a registered estate in land, he must also enter in the register such restrictions as rules may provide for the purpose of securing that interests which are capable of being overreached on a disposition of the estate are overreached. …

❯ **CROSS REFERENCE**

For more on the types of restrictions entered in cases of co-ownership, see Chapter 8, 8.7.

Other restrictions may be entered if the registered proprietor applies for them to be entered, or consents to them being entered, or if the person applying for the restriction 'otherwise has a sufficient interest in the making of the entry'—LRA 2002, s. 43(1).

As with notices, if a person applies for a restriction to be entered without reasonable cause, the registered proprietor will be able to sue in tort for any loss caused.

4.5.6 Interests that override first registration

overriding interests

certain rights and interests in land that need not be protected by registration, but which will bind the proprietor and any subsequent purchaser unless overreached

Overriding interests are interests that do not need to be registered, but which are nevertheless binding on a purchaser of the estate. They are an obvious breach of the 'mirror principle' of land registration, because they make it impossible for the register to be a true reflection of all of the interests in the land. Despite this, they were not abolished by the LRA 2002, on the grounds that is not reasonable to expect those with the benefits of such rights to register them. As you study each of the overriding interests below, you might wish to consider this reasoning.

The statute divides overriding interests into those which override the first registration of land (when unregistered land becomes registered land) and those which override subsequent registrable dispositions of land (for example, when registered land is sold).

Those interests that override first registration of land are set out in LRA 2002, Sch. 1, and include:

- leases;
- persons in actual occupation;

- easements and profits;
- customary and public rights;
- local land charges;
- mineral rights;
- (other miscellaneous rights).

4.5.6.1 Leases

STATUTE

Land Registration Act 2002, Sch. 1, para. 1 [Leasehold estates in land]

A leasehold estate in land granted for a term not exceeding seven years from the date of the grant, except for a lease the grant of which falls within section 4(1) (d), (e) or (f).

LRA 2002, Sch. 1, para. 1, provides that short leases are overriding interests. Longer leases (those over seven years) are registrable interests, but shorter leases are not, other than those that are reversionary and certain local authority leases. Shorter leases are protected by being overriding interests. Similar provision is made for relevant social housing tenancies by Sch. 1, para. 1A. These paragraphs apply only to legal leases, because the term used is 'leasehold estate'. A tenant under an equitable lease who actually lives in the property, however, is likely to have an overriding interest under LRA 2002, Sch. 1, para. 2, as a 'person in actual occupation' of the land. It may be argued that it would be pointless and inconvenient to register short leases, as the existence of a tenant occupying the land is normally apparent to a purchaser.

4.5.6.2 Persons in actual occupation

STATUTE

Land Registration Act 2002, Sch. 1, para. 2 [Interests of persons in actual occupation]

An interest belonging to a person in actual occupation, so far as relating to land of which he is in actual occupation, except for an interest under a settlement under the Settled Land Act 1925 (c. 18).

LRA 2002, Sch. 1, para. 2, provides that the interests of persons who are in actual occupation of the land are overriding interests. This is a very important category: it is intended to protect those who live on the land, or who are otherwise in actual occupation of it.

The first, very important, point to grasp is that being in actual occupation is not itself enough to give someone an overriding interest in land: a person must have an interest in land to start with, which is then coupled with his or her actual occupation, to create an overriding interest.

EXAMPLE

1. Clare has just moved in with her boyfriend, Don. She has not paid any money towards the house and Don has not made her any promises about ownership.

Clare will not have an overriding interest in Don's house. Although she is living there and is in actual occupation, she does not have an interest in the house.

2. Eddie has just helped his girlfriend, Fiona, to buy a house. He has paid part of the deposit and has agreed to help her with mortgage payments. Fiona has told him that he should think of himself as part-owner, but Eddie does not want to put his name on the register in case his ex-wife finds out he has more money than he has declared.

Eddie may well have an overriding interest in the house. His payment of part of the deposit, and the agreement between him and Fiona, may have created either a resulting or constructive trust in his favour, which gives him an interest in the house. As long as he lives in the house, he will have both an interest plus actual occupation, which amounts to an overriding interest.

In other words:

interest in land + actual occupation = overriding interest

Interests in land capable of overriding

It is quite clear that the interest in land must be a proprietary right that can bind third parties: if it is not, then the fact of actual occupation will not make it binding on purchasers.

For example, in *National Provincial Bank v. Ainsworth* [1965] AC 1175, the right of a wife to stay in her husband's house after he had left her (the deserted wife's equity) was held not to be a proprietary right and so could not be an overriding interest. The modern statutory equivalent—the spouse's or civil partner's statutory right of occupation—is also incapable of being an overriding interest—Family Law Act 1996, s. 31(1)(b).

▶ CROSS REFERENCE

For more on *National Provincial Bank v. Ainsworth* and proprietary rights, see Chapter 1, 1.1.4.

In addition, if you look back at LRA 2002, Sch. 1, para. 2, you will see that interests under the Settled Land Act 1925 are incapable of being overriding interests. These are successive interests in land, under old law.

▶ CROSS REFERENCE

For more detail on this this case see Chapter 7, 7.3.3.

Q CASE CLOSE-UP

Scott v. Southern Pacific Mortgages Ltd (Re North East Buyers Property Litigation) [2015] AC 385, [2014] UKSC 52

The Supreme Court reiterated that an overriding interest can be founded only on a proprietary right. Mrs Scott had sold her home to a purchaser, relying on a promise that the house would be leased back to her for as long as she wanted to live there. Unknown to her, the purchaser really intended to grant a legal mortgage over the property to SPM and pocket the money. The house was registered in the purchaser's name at the same time as the mortgage granted to SPM, and a short-term lease in breach of the mortgage conditions was granted to Mrs Scott.

The purchaser duly defaulted on the loan repayments, and SPM sought possession of the house. The Supreme Court held that the promise to grant a lease did not take priority over the charge by way of legal mortgage because it was not a proprietary right.

Many different types of proprietary rights can be sufficient for actual occupation to turn them into overriding interests. In *Swift 1st Ltd v. Chief Land Registrar* [2015] EWCA Civ 330, for example, it was held that the right to rectify the register (see 4.6.1) was an interest capable of being an overriding interest.

CROSS REFERENCE
For more on the overreaching of overriding interests, see Chapter 7, 7.3.3.

Most cases on this area of the law, however, concern rights under resulting or constructive trusts of land and it is clear that these rights, even though they are potentially overreachable, can be overriding interests—*Williams & Glyn's v. Boland* [1981] AC 487. Rights that have actually been overreached, however, are no longer interests in land and cannot be overriding—*City of London Building Society v. Flegg* [1988] AC 54.

CROSS REFERENCE
For more on *Williams & Glyn's v. Boland* and *City of London Building Society v. Flegg*, see Chapter 7, 7.3.3.

Actual occupation

As we have already stated, actual occupation without an interest in the land does not give rise to an overriding interest under LRA 2002, Sch. 1, para. 2. The reverse is also true: an interest without actual occupation does not give rise to an overriding interest either. It is important, therefore, to know what is meant by 'actual occupation'.

> **CASE CLOSE-UP**
>
> ***Williams & Glyn's Bank plc v. Boland*** [1981] AC 487
>
> The question had to be decided whether two wives were in actual occupation of their matrimonial homes.
>
> It was argued in favour of the bank that their occupation was merely as a '*shadow*' of their husbands' occupation, or alternatively, that their occupation was not adverse to their husbands and therefore did not amount to actual occupation.
>
> Fortunately, the House of Lords did not accept these arguments. As Lord Wilberforce said, at 504: 'Were the wives here in "actual occupation"? These words are ordinary words of plain English, and should, in my opinion, be interpreted as such.' He went on to hold that their ordinary living in the house was indeed actual occupation.

If the property is a dwelling house, actual occupation has been found in cases in which a person supervises builders—*Lloyds Bank plc v. Rosset* [1989] Ch 350 (although the case was eventually reversed on the grounds that Mrs Rosset did not have an interest in the house—[1991] AC 107).

CROSS REFERENCE
For more on *Lloyds Bank plc v. Rosset*, see Chapter 9, 9.5.2.

If a person is temporarily absent from a house, but usually lives there, this will not prevent that person from being in 'actual occupation' while he or she is away.

> **CASE CLOSE-UP**
>
> ***Chhokar v. Chhokar*** [1984] FLR 313
>
> A wife who had an interest in the family home went into hospital to have a baby. During that time, her husband sold their house at an under-value and left the country with the money.
>
> The Court of Appeal accepted that the wife had an overriding interest in the house; her absence in hospital did not mean that she ceased to be in actual occupation.

Similarly, in *Link Lending Ltd v. Bustard* [2010] EWCA Civ 424, a person who was detained in hospital under the Mental Health Act 1983, but who made regular visits home and who always intended to return there, was held to be in actual occupation of her home.

On the other hand, temporary presence in a house is unlikely to constitute actual occupation: it must be more permanent.

> ### 🔍 CASE CLOSE-UP
>
> ***Abbey National Building Society v. Cann*** [1991] 1 AC 56
>
> A mother tried to claim an overriding interest in her son's house. She needed to prove actual occupation on the day she moved into the house. In fact, she was abroad on that day, but her son and husband moved her property into the house.
>
> It was held by the House of Lords that this did *not* amount to actual occupation. Lord Oliver said that actual occupation did not have to involve physical presence and that a caretaker, for example, could occupy the property on behalf of his employer, but it had to '*involve some degree of permanence and continuity which would rule out mere fleeting presence*' (at 93). Measuring up for curtains or planning decorations before moving in would not amount to actual occupation.

⚫ CROSS REFERENCE

For more on *Abbey National v. Cann*, see Chapter 7, 7.3.3.

If the property is not a dwelling house, actual occupation can be shown by a number of means. In *Kling v. Keston Properties Ltd* (1989) 49 P & CR 212, the parking of a car in a lock-up garage was held to be actual occupation. However, in *Chaudhary v. Yavuz* [2011] EWCA Civ 1314, [2013] Ch 249 (CA (Civ)) (see 4.6.1.2), tenants walking up and down a staircase built on neighbouring land was not enough to show actual occupation of that land.

> ### 🔍 CASE CLOSE-UP
>
> ***Baker and another v. Craggs*** [2016] EWHC 3250 (Ch) [2017] Ch 295
>
> Vendors sold some land including a yard to the defendant. There was a delay in registering the transfer and, during this delay, the vendors sold other land to the claimants, including a right of way over the yard. The second transfer was registered first.
>
> The issue was whether the right of way was valid, as the vendors were still the legal registered proprietor of the yard at the time of the second transfer, but the land belonged to the defendant in equity.
>
> Newell J held that the defendant did have an equitable interest in the property, and that he was in actual occupation of the yard at the time of the second transfer. His occupation was more than fleeting, as he had been working on the barn, and that was accessed through the yard. He therefore had an overriding interest in the land, including the yard.
>
> However, the payment of the purchase money for the second transfer to two trustees overreached the overriding interest, and so the easement was valid.

⚫ CROSS REFERENCE

For more on the registration gap, see 4.6.

If the actual occupation does not extend to the whole of the property, the overriding interest applies to only that part actually occupied 'so far as relating to land of which he is in actual occupation'— LRA 2002, Sch. 1, para. 2. This wording reversed the previous law under Land Registration Act 1925, s. 70(1)(g), as decided in *Wallcite Ltd v. Ferrishurst Ltd* [1999] 1 All ER 977. In that case, a person who had rights in both offices and a garage was held to have an overriding interest in both, despite the fact that only the offices were occupied. Under LRA 2002, this would no longer be the case.

4.5.6.3 **Easements and profits**

STATUTE

Land Registration Act 2002, Sch. 1, para. 3 [Easements and profits à prendre]

3. A legal easement or profit à prendre.

A legal easement (such as a private right of way) or profit à prendre (such as a right to fish in a river) will override first registration of land. Note that this will not apply to equitable easements or profits.

> **CROSS REFERENCE**
> For more on, and the meanings of, easements and profits, see Chapter 12, 12.2.

4.5.6.4 **Customary and public rights**

STATUTE

Land Registration Act 2002, Sch. 1, paras 4–5 [Customary and public rights]

4. A customary right.
5. A public right.

Customary and public rights are enjoyed by the public or some group of people. An example would be the rights of way over a public footpath. These rights are overriding.

> **CROSS REFERENCE**
> For more on customary and public rights, see Chapter 12, 12.2.7, particularly Table 12.1.

4.5.6.5 **Local land charges**

STATUTE

Land Registration Act 2002, Sch. 1, para. 6 [Local land charges]

6. A local land charge.

Local land charges are registered on an independent register originally kept by all local authorities within England and Wales, but now transferred to the Land Registry by the Infrastructure Act 2015, s. 34. They contain such matters as tree preservation orders, outstanding liability for any charges levied by local authorities, etc. Local land charges are overriding interests.

4.5.6.6 **Mineral rights**

STATUTE

Land Registration Act 2002, Sch. 1, paras 7–9 [Mines and minerals]

7. An interest in any coal or coal mine, the rights attached to any such interest and the rights of any person under section 38, 49 or 51 of the Coal Industry Act 1994 (c. 21).
8. In the case of land to which title was registered before 1898, rights to mines and minerals (and incidental rights) created before 1898.
9. In the case of land to which title was registered between 1898 and 1925 inclusive, rights to mines and minerals (and incidental rights) created before the date of registration of the title.

These are mineral rights dating from before 1925 which are not recorded anywhere and which are therefore protected as overriding interests.

4.5.6.7 Miscellaneous rights

There were a number of rights of ancient origin listed in LRA 2002, Sch. 1, paras 10–16 (now repealed), which remained as overriding interests for ten years after the LRA 2002 came into force. This was to allow those who owned them time to register them. They included franchises, manorial rights, and the liability to repair sea walls and church chancels.

They ceased to be overriding on 13 October 2013 and if owners of such interests have not registered them, they will be unenforceable following any registered dispositions after that date.

4.6 Registrable dispositions

Once land is registered, any dealing with it must take registration into account. This section therefore looks at the law applying to land that is already registered. As we have seen in Chapter 3, 3.3, LRA 2002, s. 23, sets out the registered proprietor's powers to deal with the estate. Major dealings with registered land are registrable dispositions—that is, dealings that must be registered if they are to take effect at law.

A **registrable disposition** is a transfer of an estate or interest in land that is already registered. Under LRA 2002, s. 27(2)(a), the estate or interest must be registered in the name of the new proprietor.

> **registrable disposition**
>
> a transfer of an estate or interest in registered land that is to be registered in the name of the new proprietor

 STATUTE

Land Registration Act 2002, s. 27 [Dispositions required to be registered]

If a disposition of a registered estate or registered charge is required to be completed by registration, it does not operate at law until the relevant registration requirements are met.

In the case of a registered estate, the following are the dispositions which are required to be completed by registration—

(a) a transfer,

(b) where the registered estate is an estate in land, the grant of a term of years absolute—

    (i) for a term of more than seven years from the date of the grant,

    (ii) to take effect in possession after the end of the period of three months beginning with the date of the grant,

    (iii) under which the right to possession is discontinuous,

    (iv) in pursuance of Part 5 of the Housing Act 1985 (c. 68) (the right to buy), or

    (v) in circumstances where section 171A of that Act applies (disposal by landlord which leads to a person no longer being a secure tenant),

(c) where the registered estate is a franchise or manor, the grant of a lease,

> (d) the express grant or reservation of an interest of a kind falling within section 1(2)(a) of the Law of Property Act 1925 (c. 20), other than one which is capable of being registered under the Commons Registration Act 1965 (c. 64) [Part 1 of the Commons Act 2006],
>
> (e) the express grant or reservation of an interest of a kind falling within section 1(2)(b) or (e) of the Law of Property Act 1925, and
>
> (f) the grant of a legal charge.
>
> ...

LRA 2002, s. 27, sets out the dealings with registered land that are registrable dispositions and which must therefore be completed by registration if they are to take effect at law. As you can see, they include:

- a transfer of the estate,

- the grant of leases of over seven years (plus certain other leases, including reversionary leases and timeshare leases),

- the grant of interests falling under LPA 1925, s. 1(2). This is the section listing those interests in land that can be legal, rather than equitable. Such interests include legal easements and profits, legal rentcharges, and legal charges, or mortgages.

Until it is registered, the registrable disposition has no effect at law, so the transferee does not become the legal owner until the moment at which the transfer is registered. This means that the transferor remains as the registered proprietor during the time it takes the Land Registry to process the application for registration. The as yet unregistered owner cannot carry out actions which require legal ownership of the land, such as serving a notice to quit to a tenant—see *Stodday Land Ltd v. Pye* [2016] EWHC 2454 (Ch).

The transferor could continue to deal with the land, creating new interests in it, such as easements or leases. However, if the transferor were to do so, it would be a breach of contract and of trust, because the land belongs in equity to the transferee. The transferee would, however, be bound by those dispositions under the terms of LRA 2002, s. 28.

> **CROSS REFERENCE**
>
> For an example of this in practice, see *Baker and another v. Craggs* [2016] EWHC 3250 (Ch) [2017] Ch 295 at 4.5.6.2.

The time between the date of the transfer and the date of registration is known as the **registration gap**. The significance of the registration gap is illustrated by Figure 4.1. It is accepted as a weakness of the land registration system and provisions to eliminate the registration gap were introduced by the LRA 2002. These provisions provide for a system of electronic conveyancing but have not been brought into force.

> **registration gap**
>
> the period of time between the date of the transfer of property and the date of land registration

Figure 4.1 The registration gap

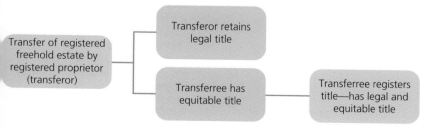

The effect of registering a registrable disposition is set out in LRA 2002, s. 29:

> ### 📖 STATUTE
>
> **Land Registration Act 2002, s. 29 [Effect of registered dispositions: estates]**
>
> (1) If a registrable disposition of a registered estate is made for valuable consideration, completion of the disposition by registration has the effect of postponing to the interest under the disposition any interest affecting the estate immediately before the disposition whose priority is not protected at the time of registration.
>
> (2) For the purposes of subsection (1), the priority of an interest is protected—
>
>   (a) in any case, if the interest—
>
>   (i)　is a registered charge or the subject of a notice in the register,
>
>   (ii)　falls within any of the paragraphs of Schedule 3, or
>
>   (iii)　appears from the register to be excepted from the effect of registration,
>
> ...

---

priority

when an interest in land is binding on its new registered proprietor

---

postponement

when an interest in land is not binding on its new registered proprietor

---

The section uses the terms **priority** and **postponement**. In terms that we have used previously, if an interest in the land *is binding* on the new registered proprietor, it is said to have priority; if it *is not binding* on the new registered proprietor, it is said to have been postponed to his or her estate.

Notice that the section applies only to a disposition made 'for valuable consideration'. Transfers by way of gift, for example, do not give the new registered proprietor priority over any previously created interest in the land, registered or not—LRA 2002, s. 28. Transfers by way of sale, on the other hand, give the new registered proprietor priority over 'any interest affecting the estate immediately before the disposition whose priority is not protected at the time of the disposition'—so any interest in the land not protected in one of the ways listed in s. 29(2) will not be binding on the new proprietor.

The ways in which the priority of an interest can be protected (so that the interest remains binding on the new proprietor) can be summarized as in Table 4.3.

Table 4.3 Interests that have priority over a purchaser of registered land

Section	Definition	Summary
LRA 2002, s. 29(2)(a)(i)	'is a registered charge'	This means a correctly registered mortgage
LRA 2002, s. 29(2)(a)(i)	'or the subject of a notice in the register'	This means interests that are protected on the register by the entry of a notice in the charges register
LRA 2002, s. 29(2)(a)(ii)	'falls within any of the paragraphs of Schedule 3'	This means that it is an overriding interest, which is binding without the need for registration. These include short leaseholds, certain interests of persons in actual occupation of the land, certain legal easements, local land charges, and a number of other rights listed in LRA 2002, Sch. 3.
LRA 2002, s. 29(2)(a)(iii)	'appears from the register to be excepted from the effect of registration'	This will apply only if the estate was registered with a grade of title other than absolute—that is, as either qualified or possessory title

Therefore, if the interest in the land was created before the sale of the property, but was not protected by an entry on the register and is not an overriding interest, then a purchaser of the freehold estate will 'take' (i.e. acquire title) free from it. Figure 4.2 illustrates the effect of LRA 2002, s. 29.

Figure 4.2 The effects of registration

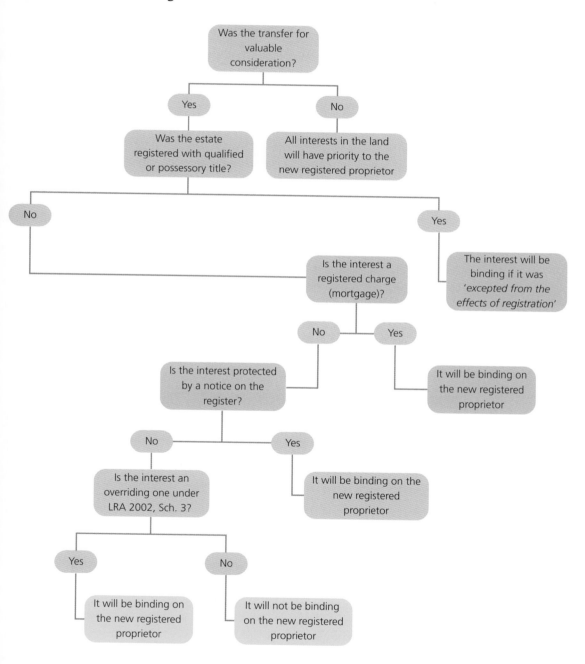

4.6.1 **The protection of those who are registered as a result of a registrable disposition**

When there has been a registrable disposition of land and it has been correctly registered, the **disponee** is protected by LRA 2002, s. 26.

disponee
the person to whom a registrable disposition is made

 STATUTE

Land Registration Act 2002, s. 26 [Protection of disponees]

(1) Subject to subsection (2), a person's right to exercise owner's powers in relation to a registered estate or charge is to be taken to be free from any limitation affecting the validity of a disposition.

(2) Subsection (1) does not apply to a limitation—

(a) reflected by an entry in the register, or

(b) imposed by, or under, this Act.

(3) This section has effect only for the purpose of preventing the title of a disponee being questioned (and so does not affect the lawfulness of a disposition).

Once registered as a result of a registered disposition, the new proprietor is entitled to exercise owner's powers in respect of the estate 'free from any limitation affecting the validity of the disposition', unless that limitation is reflected by an entry in the register or imposed under the LRA 2002. This means that the new proprietor is treated as correctly registered, subject only to entries in the register and other statutory limitations.

Under LRA 2002, s. 26(3), however, if the disposition was actually unlawful in some way, its registration does not make it lawful. This is a complicated concept and you may understand it better if you think about an example.

 EXAMPLE

Davan and Emma are the registered proprietors of Hillcrest Farm. They hold the land on trust for themselves for life and then for their nephew, Freddy, absolutely. The terms of the trust state that Freddy's consent is needed for any sale of Hillcrest Farm—but there is no restriction in the proprietorship register preventing a sale from taking place without Freddy's consent.

Davan and Emma sell the land to their friend, Govan, without getting Freddy's consent. He is devastated and wants to get Hillcrest Farm back.

LRA 2002, s. 26, means that Govan's title is protected because, although the sale was unlawful (it was in breach of trust), that invalidity was not reflected by an entry in the register—there was no restriction entered and it was not affected by any provision in LRA 2002.

Section 26 does *not* actually make the sale itself lawful, however, Davan and Emma can be sued for breach of trust, and they will be liable in damages. In addition, if Freddy can show that Govan knew about the trust, he may be held liable in equity to Freddy for knowing receipt of trust property.

It can be argued that, because the new registered proprietor can still be held personally liable, the protection given by LRA 2002, s. 26, is not as good as it first appears to be. The registered proprietor may well feel unprotected by the legislation.

4.6.1.1 Forged dispositions

The protection of disponees under a disposition of the land that turns out to have been a forgery has been a controversial matter. Under the old law, LRA 1925, in the case of *Malory Enterprises Ltd v. Cheshire Homes (UK) Ltd* [2002] EWCA Civ 151, the Court of Appeal held that a transfer of registered land that was a forgery (it was executed by someone pretending to be the registered proprietor) gave the transferee a legal title to the land, but not the equitable title. In other words, the transferee held the land on a bare trust for the former registered proprietor. This case was followed in *Fitzwilliam v. Richall Holding Services* [2013] EWHC 86 (Ch), a similar case under LRA 2002. This meant that the innocent transferee under a forged transfer did not have the protection of LRA 2002, s. 26.

> CROSS REFERENCE

For more on bare trusts, see Chapter 7, 7.2.2.

It was also unclear whether the transferee could get an indemnity (compensation) from the Land Registry when the land was transferred back to the true owner because the Court in *Malory Enterprises* held that a forged transfer is not a 'disposition'.

However, a recent case has changed this:

🔍 CASE CLOSE-UP

Swift 1st Ltd v. Chief Land Registrar [2015] EWCA Civ 330

Mrs R was the registered proprietor of a house which was her home at all material times. In 2006, someone took out a loan from Swift 1st Ltd, the appellants, and created a forged charge (mortgage) over Mrs R's house as security. The charge was registered on Mrs R's register of title. When the loan was not paid back, the appellants sought to repossess Mrs R's house. She argued that since the charge was a forgery, she was not liable to pay, and that her right to have the register rectified plus her actual occupation was an overriding interest in her home.

The appellants accepted this, but argued for an indemnity from the Land Registry, as they were innocent disponees who had suffered a loss.

The Court of Appeal decided that *Malory* had been decided *per incuriam*, and that they were therefore at liberty to depart from it. A transfer under a forged disposition conveys both the legal and equitable interest in the property to the innocent disponee, who is entitled to an indemnity under LRA 2002, Sch. 8, para. 1(2)(b).

Therefore both the 'bare trust' which was formerly imposed in cases of forgery, and the rule that there was no right to an indemnity were overruled.

4.6.1.2 What happens if the purchaser actually knows about an unregistered interest?

One possible disadvantage of systems of registration is that they enable unscrupulous people, who know that an interest is not registered, to take advantage of that fact. We have seen an example of exactly this sort of thing happening in a case concerning the registration of land charges in unregistered land—*Midland Bank v. Green* [1981] AC 513. (Note that this is not a case concerning registered land, but that we are using it as an example here because its facts illustrate the kind of dilemma to which we are referring.)

> CROSS REFERENCE

For more on *Midland Bank v. Green*, see Chapter 2, 2.5.2.1.

In that case, a father knew that his son's option to buy the family farm was not registered under the Land Charges Act 1972 and, after falling out with his son, the father sold the property at a fraction of its true price to his wife. She knew all about the option, but was held by the House of Lords not to be bound by it, because it was unregistered.

What would the situation be if someone were to undertake the same action in relation to registered land? Would the court stand by and let them do it, or would it apply equitable principles such as 'equity will not allow a statute to be used as an instrument of fraud'?

Under LRA 1925, there was a much-criticized decision in *Peffer v. Rigg* [1977] 1 WLR 285 that seemed to mean that a purchaser who had knowledge of an unregistered interest could be bound by it.

CASE CLOSE-UP

Peffer v. Rigg [1977] 1 WLR 285

Two brothers-in-law bought a house for their mother-in-law to live in. It was registered in Mr Rigg's sole name, but it was actually held on trust by him for himself and Mr Peffer.

No restriction was entered on the register, so Mr Peffer's equitable interest was unregistered. Later, as part of a divorce settlement, Mr Rigg transferred the house to his wife for the sum of £1.

Clearly, this transfer was in breach of trust and Mr Rigg was liable to Mr Peffer for half the value of the house. The issue was, however, whether Mrs Rigg held the house on trust for Mr Peffer, because she knew all about his equitable interest in the house.

Graham J held that Mrs Rigg was a trustee for Mr Peffer. The transfer to Mrs Rigg in circumstances under which she knew of the breach of trust gave rise to a constructive trust in favour of Mr Peffer.

A constructive trust is one that arises because equity imposes it on someone who has acted improperly.

There are other cases in which a constructive trust has been imposed on a purchaser who has behaved improperly.

CASE CLOSE-UP

Jones v. Lipman [1962] 1 WLR 832

The defendant had entered into a contract to sell his land to the claimant. He changed his mind and, to escape the contract, transferred the land instead to a company over which he had control. The agreement to sell the land to the claimant was not registered by notice.

Russell J ordered the company to sell the land to the claimant at the agreed price. As the judge, very colourfully, said:

> The defendant company is the creature of the first defendant, a device and a sham, a mask which he holds before his face in an attempt to avoid recognition by the eye of equity.

In a slightly different set of circumstances, the case of *Lyus v. Prowsa Developments* [1982] 1 WLR 832 recognized that an unregistered contract can be enforced against a purchaser of the land.

CASE CLOSE-UP

Lyus v. Prowsa Developments [1982] 1 WLR 832

The claimants had agreed to buy a plot of land from a building company, with a house built on it to their specifications. They had paid a deposit, but when the house was only part-built, the company became insolvent and a bank became entitled to sell the land as mortgagees.

The bank sold the land to Prowsa Developments subject to, and with the benefit of, the contract to complete the house and sell it to the claimants. Prowsa promised to honour the contract, but failed to do so. The contract was not registered.

Dillon J held that Prowsa was subject to a constructive trust. It not only knew of the contract, but also had expressly agreed to honour it.

The main criticism of these cases, especially of *Peffer v. Rigg*, is that they come close to saying that it is fraud for a purchaser of land to rely on the provisions of an Act of Parliament to escape liability. LRA 2002, s. 26, provides that a disponee can assume that the registered proprietor is free to sell the land without any restrictions unless they are registered, or imposed under the Act—such as overriding interests. If, in fact, a purchaser will be made liable personally as a constructive trustee, this seems to do away with the protection in the Act.

This was considered at para. 4.11 in the Law Commission Report (2001), which introduced the LRA 2002, and it was accepted that a disponee might be personally liable under a constructive trust. However, it appears that knowledge alone will not be held sufficient to impose such a trust, but that other considerations must be present, such as the obvious sham in *Jones v. Lipman* or the express promise in *Lyus v. Prowsa Developments*. This seems to be confirmed by *Chaudhary v. Yavuz*, decided under LRA 2002.

CASE CLOSE-UP

Chaudhary v. Yavuz [2011] EWCA Civ 1314, [2013] Ch 249 (CA (Civ Div))

A first floor flat was accessible only by using an exterior staircase and balcony situated on the neighbouring defendant's land. The staircase had been built by the claimant in 2006, and had been of advantage to both the claimant and his then neighbour, as it allowed the neighbour to demolish an old internal staircase on his own property. However, no right of way was registered by the claimant over the new staircase. When the neighbour's property was sold to the defendant, he demolished the exterior staircase and balcony, rendering the flat inaccessible. The claimant tried to claim that the defendant was bound by his unregistered equitable right of way, as the staircase was plainly visible, and the standard conditions of sale included a term rendering the property subject to incumbrances 'discoverable by inspection of the property before the contract'.

The Court of Appeal did not accept this argument. The defendant had entered into no specific agreement to honour the right of way. Therefore, in the absence of registration, he was not bound by it.

The Court also rejected an argument that the claimant was in actual occupation of the staircase because the tenants had been walking up and down it. This was not sufficient to show occupation, but only use of the staircase as a right of way—which was, as explained earlier, unregistered and unenforceable.

4.6.2 **Interests that override registered dispositions**

Earlier in this chapter (see 4.5.6), we looked at interests that override first registration. There is a similar list of interests that override registered dispositions and this is contained in LRA 2002, Sch. 3.

In many respects, the list in Sch. 3 is the same as that in Sch. 1—but there are two big differences:

- interests of persons in actual occupation—LRA 2002, Sch. 3, para. 2;
- easements and profits à prendre—LRA 2002, Sch. 3, para. 3.

In each case, the Sch. 3 paragraph is much longer than that of Sch. 1 and cuts down the number of interests that will count as overriding interests.

4.6.2.1 **Interests of persons in actual occupation**

 STATUTE

Land Registration Act 2002, Sch. 3, para. 2 [Interests of persons in actual occupation]

An interest belonging at the time of the disposition to a person in actual occupation, so far as relating to land of which he is in actual occupation, except for—

(a) an interest under a settlement under the Settled Land Act 1925 (c. 18);

(b) an interest of a person of whom inquiry was made before the disposition and who failed to disclose the right when he could reasonably have been expected to do so;

(c) an interest—

   (i) which belongs to a person whose occupation would not have been obvious on a reasonably careful inspection of the land at the time of the disposition, and

   (ii) of which the person to whom the disposition is made does not have actual knowledge at that time;

(d) a leasehold estate in land granted to take effect in possession after the end of the period of three months beginning with the date of the grant and which has not taken effect in possession at the time of the disposition.

If you compare this paragraph with the equivalent one under LRA 2002, Sch. 1, you will see that it is much longer and more complex. Certain things do remain the same—the meaning of actual occupation is the same, as is the fact that the overriding interest extends only to the land actually occupied.

It is also vitally important to show that the person claiming the right in the land has a valid proprietary interest in it. Remember that:

interest in land + actual occupation = overriding interest

The differences lie in the number of situations that are excluded from the paragraph—a person is not in actual occupation if:

- the interest claimed is an interest under the Settled Land Act 1925 (this was also in LRA 2002, Sch. 1);
- the occupier did not tell the purchaser about his or her interest in the land when asked about it and 'could reasonably have been expected to do so';

- the interest is one that would not have been obvious on a 'reasonably careful inspection' of the land at the time of the disposition unless the purchaser actually knew of the interest;
- it is an interest under a reversionary lease.

▶ CROSS REFERENCE

This provision is considered in more detail in Chapter 7, 7.3.3.2.

This paragraph is evidence of the policy in the LRA 2002 to reduce the number of overriding interests. It raises certain questions, including when it will be reasonable for a person to disclose his or her interest in the land and what is meant by a 'reasonably careful inspection' of the land. In *Thomas v. Clydesdale Bank plc* [2010] EWHC 2755 (QB) it was held that 'it is the visible signs of occupation which have to be obvious on inspection' (per Ramsey J at [40]). Additionally, the judge held that the 'actual knowledge' required in Sch. 3, para. 2(c)(ii) is 'actual knowledge of the facts giving rise to the interest' rather than actual knowledge of the interest itself.

4.6.2.2 Easements and profits

 STATUTE

Land Registration Act 2002, Sch. 3, para. 3 [Easements and profits à prendre]

(1) A legal easement or profit à prendre, except for an easement, or a profit à prendre which is not registered under the Commons Registration Act 1965 (c. 64) [Part 1 of the Commons Act 2006], which at the time of the disposition—

(a) is not within the actual knowledge of the person to whom the disposition is made, and

(b) would not have been obvious on a reasonably careful inspection of the land over which the easement or profit is exercisable.

(2) The exception in sub-paragraph (1) does not apply if the person entitled to the easement or profit proves that it has been exercised in the period of one year ending with the day of the disposition.

LRA 2002, Sch. 3, para. 3, excludes a number of legal easements and profits from the category of overriding interests.

A legal easement or profit will override a registered disposition only if:

- the purchaser actually knows of it; or
- it is obvious on a reasonably careful inspection of the land over which the easement or profit is exercisable; or
- it has been exercised within the period of one year before the disposition.

▶ CROSS REFERENCE

For more on easements and profits, generally, and for more detailed discussion of LRA 2002, Sch. 3, para. 3, in particular, see Chapter 12, 12.5.1.2.

This paragraph is also intended to cut down the number of legal easements and profits that do not appear on the register, in line with the policy of the LRA 2002 of reducing the number of overriding interests.

4.6.3 Electronic conveyancing (e-conveyancing)

LRA 2002, Pt 8 (ss. 91–95), introduced provisions for a move to **electronic conveyancing or e-conveyancing**. This part of the Act has not been brought into force, however, and in July 2011 the Land Registry announced the suspension of further development of e-charges and e-transfers following a consultation exercise. However, in February 2017, the Land Registry launched a consultation on a change to the Land Registration Rules 2003 to allow for, amongst other reforms, fully

electronic conveyancing, or e-conveyancing

the transfer of land by electronic, rather than paper-based, means digital conveyancing documents with e-signatures. The results of the consultation were published in January 2018, and changes are planned from 6 April 2018.

One major advantage of electronic conveyancing was to be the elimination of the registration gap—the period of time between a person having the land transferred to them and their being registered as the proprietor. If there is a registrable disposition, the legal estate does not pass until registration takes effect and, in the meantime, there can be dealings with the legal title by the previous owner, who remains the registered proprietor. Such dispositions will often not be binding on the purchaser, under LRA 2002, s. 29(1), because they will have arisen at a later time than did the transfer to the purchaser.

If an overriding interest is created before the estate is registered, however, it will be binding on the registered proprietor—and this is what happened in *Barclays Bank plc v. Zaroovabli* [1997] Ch 321, in which a lease was binding on a mortgagee who had not yet registered the mortgage. A similar situation concerning an overriding easement occurred in *Baker and another v. Craggs* [2016] EWHC 3250 (Ch), [2017] Ch 295, but in this case the overriding interest was overreached.

CROSS REFERENCE

For more details on the registration gap, see 4.6.

There have also been cases in which a purchaser has tried to exercise the rights of a registered proprietor, but was unable to do so because he or she was not yet registered. In *Brown and Root Technology Ltd v. Sun Alliance and London Assurance Co. Ltd* [2001] Ch 733, for example, the purchaser of a leasehold estate tried to give notice to bring the lease to an end, but could not do so for this reason. This case has recently been followed in *Stodday Land Ltd v. Pye* [2016] EWHC 2454 (Ch).

4.7 Alteration of the register

CROSS REFERENCE

For a reminder of the three principles of registration of title, see 4.1.

One of the three principles of registration of title is the indemnity principle. This means that the state guarantees registered title and that a registered proprietor should feel secure in the knowledge that he or she is the true owner of the land, and that interests in it are correctly reflected in the register. This does not, however, mean that the register is absolutely free from mistakes or that those mistakes cannot be put right.

Provisions for altering the register are contained in LRA 2002, s. 65, and Sch. 4.

4.7.1 Introduction

STATUTE

Land Registration Act 2002, Sch. 4, para. 1 [Introductory]

In this Schedule, references to rectification, in relation to alteration of the register, are to alteration which—

(a) involves the correction of a mistake, and

(b) prejudicially affects the title of a registered proprietor.

Under LRA 2002, there are two kinds of changes to the register:

- Alteration

An **alteration** is any change to the register.

- Rectification

A **rectification** is an alteration to the register that prejudicially affects the title of the registered proprietor and which is made to correct a mistake. This would be the case if the alteration of the register to correct a mistake made the land less valuable, for example, or removed some of the land from the title.

Not surprisingly, rectification is subject to stricter rules than are other alterations.

> **alteration**
> any change to the register

> **rectification**
> a change to the register that is made to correct a mistake and which prejudicially affects the title of the registered proprietor

4.7.2 **Who can alter the register?**

Any person may apply for alteration of the register; they need not have an estate or interest in the land to have standing to do so: *Paton v. Todd* [2012] EWHC 1248 (Ch).

The register can be altered either by the court or by the registrar. The powers of the court are set out in LRA 2002, Sch. 4, para. 2(1).

📖 STATUTE

Land Registration Act 2002, Sch. 4, para. 2 [Alteration pursuant to a court order]

(1) The court may make an order for alteration of the register for the purpose of—

   (a) correcting a mistake,

   (b) bringing the register up to date, or

   (c) giving effect to any estate, right or interest excepted from the effect of registration.

...

The powers of the registrar are set out in LRA 2002, Sch. 4, para. 5, and are the same as those of the court, except that the registrar also has power to remove superfluous (unneeded) entries from the register.

4.7.3 **The grounds for altering the register**

4.7.3.1 **Correcting a mistake**

There are a number of cases illustrating the kinds of mistake that may occur in transferring land. For example, the same piece of land may be transferred to two different people: generally, this means that the later transfer is a mistake, but if it is registered first, the registered proprietor will become the legal owner. This happened in the case of *Re 139 Deptford High Street* [1951] Ch 884, in which the register was altered to give the land back to the rightful owner. But if the registered proprietor is in possession of the land, this will be a rectification and may not be granted—see, for example, *Epps v. Esso Petroleum* [1973] 1 WLR 1071.

Alternatively, there may be an entry on the register that should not be there. In *Re Dances Way, West Town, Hayling Island* [1962] Ch 490, an easement was mistakenly entered on the register. This entry could be removed.

Transfers of land obtained by fraud may also be reversed under this heading. In *Baxter v. Mannion* [2011] EWCA Civ 120, it was held that Sch. 4, paras 1 and 5 could be used to restore land to its

CROSS REFERENCE

For adverse possession, especially more on this case, see Chapter 6, 6.9.2.2.

rightful owner after a claim for adverse possession had wrongly been allowed. No distinction was to be drawn between fraud and a mistake induced by a wrong application, because in both cases false information had been given to the registrar.

Rectification may change the priority of interests on the register.

🔍 CASE CLOSE-UP

Gold Harp Properties Ltd v. MacLeod [2014] EWCA Civ 1084 (CA (Civ))

In this case the top floor of a building was held on long leases by the respondents. The freehold owners, the Ralphs, engineered a scheme to forfeit the leases then create new leases ultimately in favour of the appellants, Gold Harp Ltd, a company owned and controlled by them. They got the forfeited leases removed from the Register of Title and registered the new lease in favour of Gold Harp. The Court held that the forfeiture had been defective, and that the old leases should not have been removed from the register. The appellants sought alteration of the register under LRA 2002, Sch. 4. They wanted the registers of title of their leases reinstated, and those leases noted on the freehold title. The problem was that the new lease to Gold Harp had now been registered, and might therefore have priority over their leases. LRA, s. 29, gives priority to a registered disposition except where prior interests are registered or overriding. Neither applied here.

It was held by the Court of Appeal that the rectification did change the priorities of the interests, and that the old leases took priority over Gold Harp's lease. The Court held that the case fell within LRA 2002, Sch. 4, para. 8:

> The powers under this Schedule to alter the register, so far as relating to rectification, extend to changing for the future the priority of any interest affecting the registered estate or charge concerned.

4.7.3.2 Bringing the register up to date

CROSS REFERENCE

For easements, generally, and for the meaning of establishing an easement of light by prescription, in particular, see Chapter 12, 12.4.4.5.

Bringing the register up to date involves adding or removing an entry, because the situation has changed or because a right has been established. For example, if someone has established an easement of light by prescription, that should be registered.

This provision also allows the register to be altered if, for example, a transfer which is voidable for fraud is avoided. For example, in *Norwich and Peterborough Building Society v. Steed* [1993] Ch 116, the transfer was effected by the misuse of a **power of attorney** and the original owner was reinstated. This has recently been confirmed in the case of *NRAM v. Evans* [2017] EWCA Civ 1013 in which it was held that if the register is changed as the result of the rescission of a voidable (as opposed to void) transaction, this is not rectification of the register, but 'bringing the register up to date'. The consequence of this is that, since there is no rectification, no indemnity is payable.

power of attorney

a formal instrument by which one person empowers another to act on his or her behalf

4.7.3.3 Giving effect to any estate, right, or interest excepted from the effect of registration

The giving of effect to any estate, right, or interest excepted from the effect of registration is to do with estates registered with possessory or qualified title, and is beyond the scope of this book.

4.7.3.4 Removal of superfluous entries

Removing superfluous entries simply means removing entries that are no longer required, such as a notice about an option that has expired. There is, of course, bound to be some overlap between this ground and that of bringing the register up to date.

4.7.4 Restrictions on altering the register: rectification against a proprietor in possession

Where either the courts or the registrar wish to alter the register, a proprietor in possession has additional protection under LRA 2002, Sch. 4, para. 3.

 STATUTE

Land Registration Act 2002, Sch. 4, para. 3

...

(2) If alteration affects the title of the proprietor of a registered estate in land, no order may be made under paragraph 2 without the proprietor's consent in relation to land in his possession unless—

    (a) he has by fraud or lack of proper care caused or substantially contributed to the mistake, or

    (b) it would for any other reason be unjust for the alteration not to be made.

...

(4) In sub-paragraph (2), the reference to the title of the proprietor of a registered estate in land includes his title to any registered estate which subsists for the benefit of the estate in land.

Firstly, we need to know what is meant by a 'proprietor in possession'. This is defined in LRA 2002, s. 131.

 STATUTE

Land Registration Act 2002, s. 131 ['Proprietor in possession']

(1) For the purposes of this Act, land is in the possession of the proprietor of a registered estate in land if it is physically in his possession, or in that of a person who is entitled to be registered as the proprietor of the registered estate.

(2) In the case of the following relationships, land which is (or is treated as being) in the possession of the second-mentioned person is to be treated for the purposes of sub-section (1) as in the possession of the first-mentioned person—

    (a) landlord and tenant;

    (b) mortgagor and mortgagee;

    (c) licensor and licensee;

    (d) trustee and beneficiary.

...

You can see from this section that a proprietor is in possession if:

- he or she is physically in possession of the land; or
- the land is in the possession of someone entitled to be registered as proprietor (such as a trustee in bankruptcy, for example); or
- it is one of the special relationships in s. 131(2).

LRA 2002, s. 131(2), says, for example, that land in the possession of a tenant is treated as being in the possession of the landlord. This means that the proprietor would still be treated as being in possession if the property was let to tenants. A squatter on land is not treated as being in possession for this purpose—LRA 2002, s. 131(3).

So, once the court or the registrar has established that the alteration of the register is going to affect the title of the registered proprietor prejudicially and that he or she is a proprietor in possession, rectification of the register can be ordered only if:

- the proprietor in possession either caused the mistake or substantially contributed to it by fraud or lack of proper care;
- it would, for any other reason, be unjust for the alteration not to be made.

Fraud or lack of proper care goes beyond submitting a transfer for registration that turns out not to be accurate. In this case, the land may be wrongly described and the buyer simply may not know this. This is a change from the previous law, because older cases, such as *Re 139 Deptford High Street* (see 4.7.3.1), had found that proprietors who put forward an inaccurate conveyance for registration were guilty of contributing to the mistake, even where they were acting completely innocently. Someone who gains possession of land by fraud, however, would clearly not be entitled to argue that he or she should keep it.

Most of the cases have been on the second ground: that of it being unjust not to rectify the register.

 CASE CLOSE-UP

Kingsalton Ltd v. Thames Water [2001] EWCA Civ 20

In this case, a registered proprietor was in possession of a disputed strip of land that had been erroneously conveyed twice.

Rectification was not ordered, but instead an indemnity was paid to the person who should have been the owner (see 4.7.5 for when an indemnity will be paid).

An argument based on human rights was rejected in this case; rectification was held not to be a deprivation of property under the European Convention on Human Rights (ECHR), Protocol 1, Art. 1, because it was a proportionate measure to enhance the security of land, and compensation in the form of an indemnity was paid.

If the registered proprietor has full knowledge of the other party's interest, the register may be rectified, even though the proprietor is in possession.

 CASE CLOSE-UP

Horrill v. Cooper (1998) 1 P & CR 293

Because of a mix-up, a restrictive covenant was not entered on the register. In fact, the registered proprietor in possession knew all about the mix-up and had paid less for the land because of it.

It was held that it was unjust not to rectify the register to give effect to the covenant.

A similar situation occurred in the complicated case of *Sainsbury's Supermarkets v. Olympia Homes Ltd* [2005] EWHC 1235 (Ch). Rectification was ordered to give effect to an unregistered option. The registered proprietor had been registered by mistake and all of the parties had proceeded on the basis that the option was valid; the prices agreed between the parties reflected this. Under these circumstances, it would have been unjust not to rectify.

These two cases show that the courts will look at the parties' behaviour—for example, in terms of agreements about the price of the land—and will use their discretion under this provision to avoid unjust enrichment.

In *Baxter v. Mannion* (see 4.7.3.1) it was unjust not to rectify the register against the new proprietor in possession because he had wrongly claimed to have fulfilled the conditions for adverse possession.

In *Parshall v. Hackney* [2013] EWCA (Civ) 240, it was unjust not to rectify the register where a series of mistakes by the land registry had moved a slip of land from one title to another, even though the (mistakenly) registered proprietor was using the land for parking.

An example of a case in which the discretion was not exercised is *London Borough of Hounslow v. Hare* (1990) 24 HLR 9.

 CASE CLOSE-UP

London Borough of Hounslow v. Hare (1990) 24 HLR 9

In this case, the registered proprietor in possession had exercised her right to buy her council house. It turned out that she should not have had a right to buy, so the sale was *ultra vires* (beyond the powers of) the council.

The Court would not rectify the register because the house was Hare's home.

This case shows why the legislation takes the rights of registered proprietors in possession so seriously.

4.7.5 **Indemnity**

LRA 2002, Sch. 8, provides the rules as to when the Land Registry will pay an indemnity (compensation) to someone suffering loss as a result of a mistake in the register. This right to an indemnity is at the heart of the system of land registration: it is a 'state-guaranteed' system. Those dealing with land are entitled to rely on the register of title and, if the register is wrong, there is a presumption that compensation will be payable. There was increasing concern about fraudsters using the open land register to 'steal' land, or obtain money by fraudulently mortgaging land they do not own. The Land Registry removed certain documents, such as mortgage deeds, from online availability so that signatures cannot be copied and it requires conveyancers to certify the identity of those involved in transactions. If parties are acting in person, they must provide evidence of identity. In 2016–17, the Land Registry paid out £6.9m for 995 claims, compared with £8m for 1,003 claims in 2015–16. However, the largest single claim in 2016–17 was £702,290 for a forged charge, so fraud is still a problem, although increasing numbers of fraudsters are being detected and stopped.

LRA 2002, Sch. 8, para. 1, sets out when an indemnity will be payable.

4.7.5.1 **Loss caused by rectification**

 CASE CLOSE-UP

Land Registration Act 2002, Sch. 8, para. 1 [Entitlement]

(1) A person is entitled to be indemnified by the registrar if he suffers loss by reason of—
rectification of the register,

...

(2) For the purposes of sub-paragraph (13)(a)—

(a) any person who suffers loss by reason of the change of title under section 62 is to
be regarded as having suffered loss by reason of rectification of the register, and

(b) the proprietor of a registered estate or charge claiming in good faith under a
forged disposition is, where the register is rectified, to be regarded as having suffered loss by reason of such rectification as if the disposition had not been forged.

...

It is very important to note that it is essential that the loss is caused by *rectification*, not by any other
type of alteration of the register. Remember, rectification is an alteration to the register that prejudicially affects the title of the registered proprietor and which is made to correct a mistake. Some
changes to the register may appear to affect the title of the registered proprietor prejudicially, but
may not, in fact, do so.

The classic case of this is if the register is altered to give effect to an overriding interest.

 CASE CLOSE-UP

Re Chowood's Registered Land [1933] Ch 574

In this case, no indemnity was payable when the register was altered so as to give effect to the
rights of a squatter who had gained title to part of the land.

The rights of the squatter under the law at that time amounted to an overriding interest, which
was always binding on the registered proprietor, whether he knew about it or not. He had not
suffered any loss, so could not claim an indemnity.

Therefore, not everyone who feels they have suffered a loss will get compensation. This rule makes
perfect sense within the scheme of registration, however, because every registered proprietor takes
the land subject to any overriding interests subsisting in it at the date of registration, even if they do
not always know about them.

See also *NRAM v. Evans* [2017] EWCA Civ 1013 at 4.7.3.2.

The claimant in *Baxter v. Mannion* (see 4.7.3.1) did not receive an indemnity, as the effect of the
decision was that he had never been entitled to the land at all, so no loss was caused by the rectification.

LRA 2002, Sch. 8, para. 1(2)(b), provides that proprietors claiming under a forged disposition should
be able to claim indemnity in the same way as if the disposition had not been forged. This was
considered in *Swift 1st Ltd v. Chief Land Registrar* [2015] EWCA Civ 330 (see 4.6.1.1) and an indemnity was given.

4.7.5.2 **Loss caused by a decision not to rectify**

STATUTE

Land Registration Act 2002, Sch. 8, para. 1 [Entitlement]

(1) A person is entitled to be indemnified by the registrar if he suffers loss by reason of—

...

(b) a mistake whose correction would involve rectification of the register,

...

An indemnity may also be payable if a mistake is not rectified. This is more likely under the modern law, because there is a presumption against rectifying against a proprietor in possession and a less strict definition of what constitutes contributing to a mistake.

4.7.5.3 **Losses caused by other types of mistake**

LRA 2002, Sch. 8, para. 1, goes on to list a number of further 'administrative' types of mistake that are not caused by rectification, in respect of which indemnity can be claimed. Remember that the person claiming the indemnity must show a loss caused by the error before a claim can be made.

STATUTE

Land Registration Act 2002, Sch. 8, para. 1 [Entitlement]

(1) A person is entitled to be indemnified by the registrar if he suffers loss by reason of—

...

(a) a mistake in an official search,

(b) a mistake in an official copy,

(c) a mistake in a document kept by the registrar which is not an original and is referred to in the register,

(d) the loss or destruction of a document lodged at the registry for inspection or safe custody,

(e) a mistake in the cautions register, or

(f) failure by the registrar to perform his duty under section 50.

...

4.7.5.4 **Fraud or lack of proper care**

STATUTE

Land Registration Act 2002, Sch. 8, para. 5 [Claimant's fraud or lack of care]

(1) No indemnity is payable under this Schedule on account of any loss suffered by a claimant—

(a) wholly or partly as a result of his own fraud, or

(b) wholly as a result of his own lack of proper care.

> (2) Where any loss is suffered by a claimant partly as a result of his own lack of proper care, any indemnity payable to him is to be reduced to such extent as is fair having regard to his share in the responsibility for the loss.
>
> ...

Under LRA 2002, Sch. 8, para. 5, if someone causes his or her own loss by fraud, he or she is not entitled to an indemnity in relation to that loss. Even if the fraud were to be only partly the cause of the loss, no indemnity would be payable.

If lack of proper care is the whole cause of the loss, then, similarly, no indemnity is payable; if the loss is only partly caused by lack of proper care, however, then a reduced indemnity will be payable. This is very like the principle of contributory negligence in the law of torts. So, for example, if the person suffering the loss did not check the details of the transaction carefully, or did not check on the identity of the person claiming to transfer the land, he or she may be held partly liable for his or her own loss.

4.7.5.5 The amount of indemnity payable

Indemnity is intended to compensate the person who has suffered the loss. Both losses that arise as a direct result of the mistake—such as the value of the land lost if the register is rectified—and any consequential losses—such as the costs of a sale falling through because of a mistake on the register—may be claimed.

Where an estate, interest, or charge over land has been lost, LRA 2002, Sch. 8, para. 6, sets out the rules for valuation of that interest.

 STATUTE

Land Registration Act 2002, Sch. 8, para. 6 [Valuation of estates etc.]

Where an indemnity is payable in respect of the loss of an estate, interest or charge, the value of the estate, interest or charge for the purposes of the indemnity is to be regarded as not exceeding—

(a) in the case of an indemnity under paragraph 1(1)(a), its value immediately before rectification of the register (but as if there were to be no rectification), and

(b) in the case of an indemnity under paragraph 1(1)(b), its value at the time when the mistake which caused the loss was made.

As you can see, there are two different ways of valuing the indemnity payable:

- If rectification is ordered, the amount payable is the market value of the estate, interest, or charge at the moment before rectification was ordered—that is, at current market value.
- If rectification is *not* ordered, the amount payable is the value of the estate, interest, or charge at the time at which the mistake was made—that is, its value at some time in the past. Because land generally rises in value over time, this will usually be a lesser amount.

This disparity in the two valuations was raised in *Kingsalton Ltd v. Thames Water*, but held not to be in breach of the ECHR.

Summary

1. Land registration is a national system, first introduced in 1925 and now regulated by the Land Registration Act 2002.

2. Different provisions of the Act apply to first registration of land and to registrable dispositions.

3. A person registered as the first proprietor of the land owns the legal estate, even if the person transferring the land to him or her did not have power to do so.

4. The first registered proprietor takes the land subject to entries in the register, interests that override first registration, and rights obtained by adverse possession.

5. Once land is registered, any dealing with it will be subject to registration provisions. Such dealings may be registrable dispositions, registrable by notice or restriction, or interests that override registered dispositions.

6. Someone registered as the result of a registrable disposition—that is, a disponee—is entitled to assume that the seller had power to deal with the land, unless there was a restriction on his or her powers or an overriding interest. The disponee may be held personally liable, however, if he or she assists in a breach of trust by the registered proprietor.

7. Mistakes in the register may be corrected. This is known as an 'alteration', or, if it adversely affects the registered proprietor, a 'rectification' of the register.

8. An indemnity (compensation) may be payable as the result of a claim for rectification.

The bigger picture

- If you want to see how this area of land law fits into the rest of your studies, you can look at Chapter 16. That whole chapter revolves around the understanding of a register of title. Use it to practise identifying the various interests in land. You might also find it helpful to look at the registration sections in other chapters, such as Chapter 12, 12.5 on the registration of easements; Chapter 13, 13.5.2.4 on the registration of covenants; and Chapter 14, 14.5 on priorities of mortgages. Chapter 7, 7.3 contains vital information on the effect of land registration on co-ownership, and there is a lot of material here about overriding interests, particularly rights of persons in actual occupation of the land.

- Additional cases you may wish to look at on the interpretation of LRA 2002 include:

  Blemain Finance Ltd v. Goulding [2013] EWCA Civ 1630, [2014] 1 P & CR DG16 (CA (Civ Div))

  Walker v. Burton [2013] EWCA Civ 1228, [2014] 1 P & CR 9 (CA (Civ Div))

  Cherry Tree Investments Ltd v. Landmain Ltd [2012] EWCA Civ 736, [2013] Ch 305 (CA (Civ Div))

  Gelley v. Shephard [2013] EWCA Civ 1172, [2014] 1 P & CR DG5 (CA (Civ Div))

- The most authoritative work on land registration is *Ruoff and Roper on the Law and Practice of Registered Conveyancing*, London: Sweet & Maxwell, which you may find in your library or as part of a Westlaw subscription. Alternatively, Harpum, C. and Bignall, J. (2002) *Registered Land: The New Law*, Bristol: Jordan Publishing Ltd is a very comprehensive guide to registration under the LRA 2002, but it is rather technical.

? | Questions

Self-test questions

1. Adam is the owner of unregistered freehold land. He transfers it to Bert. Is Bert obliged to register his title to the land? What will happen if he does not do so?

2. Catherine has a legal easement over the land that is now Bert's. There is no mention of the easement on Bert's new register of title. Is Bert bound by the easement?

3. Bert sells his registered estate to Dolly. Catherine still has not registered her legal easement. Is Dolly bound by it?

4. If Dolly is bound by Catherine's easement:

    (a) is Catherine entitled to ask for the register to be altered to show her easement?

    (b) is Dolly entitled to an indemnity if the value of her land with the easement over it is less than it would be without such a burden?

Exam questions

1. 'Because [overriding interests] subsist and operate outside the register, they are an inevitable source of tension within the land registration system. In making proposals for reform there is often a difficult balance to be struck between, on the one hand, the desire to achieve a fair result in individual cases, and on the other, the goal of making conveyancing simpler, quicker and cheaper, which is the justification for title registration.'

(*Law Commission, Land Registration for the 21st Century, Consultative Document*).

Discuss.

2. In 2015, Gerry bought a plot of land from Veronica. It consisted of a small farm and outbuildings with some scrubland. Title to it had not previously been registered, so Gerry applied for and received registration as proprietor with absolute title. Unfortunately, the conveyance of the land mistakenly included a small barn belonging to Tom. Gerry has also discovered that several surrounding landowners have rights to water their animals at the stream running through his land, and there are two rights of way crossing it. This means that it will be difficult to turn the land into a development of holiday cottages, which is what Tom intended. Tom wishes he had never bought the land at all.

Advise Tom and Gerry.

 You will find answers to these questions online at www.oup.com/uk/clarke_directions6e/.

Further reading

Bogusz, B., 'Defining the scope of actual occupation under the LRA 2002: some recent judicial clarification' [2011] Conv 268

This is an article on the interpretation of LRA 2002, Sch. 3, para. 2 (rights of persons in actual occupation) case law.

Dixon, M., 'Rectification and priority: further skirmishes in the land registration war' (2015) 131(Apr) LQR 207–13

This examines the decision in *Gold Harp Properties v. MacLeod* [2014] EWCA Civ 1084.

Griffiths, G., 'An important question of principle—reality and rectification in registered land' [2011] Conv 331

This case note discusses the case of *Baxter v. Mannion* [2011] EWCA Civ 120.

Hopkins, N., 'Priorities and sale and lease back: a wrong question, much ado about nothing and a story of tails and dogs' [2015] 3 Conv 245–53

This discusses *North East Property Buyers Litigation, Re* [2014] UKSC 52, [2015] AC 385 (SC).

Law Commission/HM Land Registry (1998) *Land Registration for the Twenty-First Century: A Consultative Document*, Law Com No. 254, available online at http://www.lawcom.gov.uk/wp-content/uploads/2015/04/lc254.pdf

Law Commission/HM Land Registry (2001) *Land Registration for the Twenty-First Century: A Conveyancing Revolution*, Law Com No. 271, available online at http://www.lawcom.gov.uk/wp-content/uploads/2015/04/Lc271.pdf

These two Law Commission/HM Land Registry reports set out the reasons for the reform of the law in the LRA 2002.

Updating the Land Registration Act 2002 A Consultation Paper, Consultation Paper No. 227: http://www.lawcom.gov.uk/project/land-registration/

The recent consultation paper on reform of the LRA 2002.

Dollar, P. 'Is the Land Registry fit for purpose?' (2017) 1743 EG 63–65

An article looking at many of the new cases on land registration, including *Stodday Land Ltd v. Pye* [2016] EWHC 2454 (Ch), [2016] 4 WLR 168 (Ch D (Manchester)); *Baker v. Craggs* [2016] EWHC 3250 (Ch), [2017] Ch 295 (Ch D); *Wood v. Waddington* [2015] EWCA Civ 538, [2015] 2 P & CR 11 (CA (Civ Div)); *Bennett v. Winterburn* [2015] UKUT 59 (TCC), [2015] 2 P & CR DG9 (UT (Tax)).

The Land Registry publishes online a number of very helpful practitioners' guides to many aspects of registration. They can be found at https://www.gov.uk/topic/land-registration/practice-guides.

Lees, E., Registration make-believe and forgery—*Swift 1st Ltd v. Chief Land Registrar* (2015) 131(Oct) LQR 515–19

This article discusses the problems caused by forgery in land registration.

McFarlane, B., 'Eastenders, Neighbours and Upstairs Downstairs: Chaudhary v Yavuz' [2013] 1 Conv 74

This is a case note on *Chaudhary v. Yavuz* [2011] EWCA Civ 1314.

Willams, P., 'When the experts get it wrong' [2014] 5 Conv 369–74

This short article examines a number of difficulties which have arisen with LRA 2002.

Online Resources

For more advice relating to this chapter, including self-test questions and an interactive glossary, visit www.oup.com/uk/clarke_directions6e/.

5 Leases

LEARNING OBJECTIVES

By the end of this chapter, you will be able to:

- explain what is meant by a 'leasehold estate in land';
- identify the essential requirements of a lease;
- distinguish between a lease and a licence;
- understand how a lease is created and explain the necessary formalities;
- identify some of the usual covenants contained in a lease;
- offer a general overview of the enforceability of leasehold covenants.

Introduction

We have already looked at freehold estates in land (see Chapter 3) and we have seen that they are for an indefinite duration. The other estate in land is the leasehold estate—more commonly referred to as simply a 'lease'. A lease is a more limited estate in land than a freehold, because it is only granted for a specified period of time. In practice, this period can be very short, or very long indeed: sometimes, even thousands of years. You will probably already be quite familiar with some of the aspects of a lease, perhaps through renting accommodation while at university or through buying a leasehold flat. There is a very specific set of sometimes quite complicated legal principles and rules that apply to the leasehold estate, and, in this chapter, we will disentangle them.

5.1 Frequently used terms

Before we start looking at what it means to have a leasehold estate in land, we will have a quick look at some of the most frequently used terms in this area of law. Each of these will be explained in more detail as we go through the chapter, but, at this stage, it will help you to have some understanding of their meaning.

> **term of years absolute** this refers to the leasehold estate
>
> **lease or tenancy** any such term refers to a lease: shorter leases tend to be called tenancies, longer leases tend to be referred to as leases—but often, for all practical purposes, the terms are used interchangeably
>
> **landlord or lessor** the person granting the lease, which is sometimes described as 'letting' the property
>
> **tenant or lessee** the person to whom the lease is granted
>
> **reversion** the interest that the landlord retains in the land after the lease has finished

5.2 Leases in practice: some examples

We will shortly be looking at the legal meaning of a lease, but first, it might be helpful simply to understand how a lease works in practice. Leases can be granted in respect of residential, commercial, and agricultural property—but, for the rest of this chapter, we will concentrate on residential leases. These are the sorts of lease with which you may well already be familiar.

 EXAMPLE

Alex owns a freehold house in London. One day, his employer tells Alex that he is going to be working in New York for two years. Rather than sell his house or leave it empty, Alex decides to let the property: he will rent it out while he is away. He grants a two-year lease to Rav, in return for a monthly rent.

Both parties sign a lease agreement, under which they promise to do various things. Rav agrees to pay rent and not to wreck Alex's house; Alex agrees that Rav can live in the premises without interruption and disturbance, and to keep the house in good repair while Rav is living there.

At the end of two years, Rav moves out and Alex moves back in. Rav's interest in the land has ended with the end of the lease.

Their relationship might be illustrated as in Figure 5.1.

Sometimes, the situation can get more complicated.

Figure 5.1 The landlord–tenant relationship

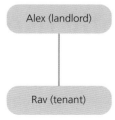

EXAMPLE

Yasmeen owns a freehold house in London. She grants a twenty-five-year lease of the property to Davina. The lease agreement contains a clause allowing Davina to 'sublet' the property with Yasmeen's consent. This means that, if she chooses, Davina can rent the property out to somebody else. She decides to sublet to Pete. She can only sublet the property for a period shorter than her own interest in the land. (This is common sense—she cannot grant a sublease of thirty years if she herself only has an interest in the land for twenty-five years.) She lets the property to Pete.

The relationship of the parties might be illustrated as in Figure 5.2.

Figure 5.2 The landlord–tenant–subtenant relationship

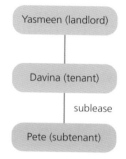

These two examples will give you some idea of how a lease works in everyday situations.

Legally, however, the nature of a lease is quite tricky. On the one hand, it is a contract, as we have seen, because essentially the parties promise each other that they will do, or will not do, certain things; on the other hand, because a lease confers an estate in the land, it gives the tenant a proprietary interest in the land itself—which is why, in our last example, Davina is able to sublet the property. Part of the legal difficulty inherent in leases lies in this dual character: the lease has one foot in contract law and the other in land law.

5.3 Statutory protection

Over the years, the law has provided statutory protection for the tenant, to reduce bad practice by landlords. The kind of protection given to the tenant partly depends on the kind of lease that he or she holds. Detailed consideration of the statutory protection is outside the scope of this book, but we will mention it when we start to examine the essential characteristics of a lease—partly because most of the cases arose in situations in which landlords were trying to avoid their statutory obligations!

5.3.1 **Definition of a lease**

The statutory definition of a lease under Law of Property Act 1925 (LPA 1925), s. 205(xxvii), is a good starting point at which to begin our exploration of leases.

STATUTE

Law of Property Act 1925, s. 205(xxvii)

'Term of years absolute' means a term of years (taking effect either in possession or in reversion whether or not at a rent) … liable to determination by notice … and … includes a term for less than a year, or for a year or years and a fraction of a year or from year to year; …

We have attempted to pick out the most important points in the subsection, because the whole definition is lengthy and somewhat circular.

We can, however, identify some useful information.

The phrase 'term of years' refers to the fact that the lease is granted for a period of time. It can begin immediately (**in possession**) or in the future (**in reversion**), although not more than twenty-one years in the future—LPA 1925, s. 149(3).

> **in possession**
> immediately

> **in reversion**
> at some point in the future

 THINKING POINT

Look at Form 5.1, the sample tenancy agreement.

Try to identify the names of the parties and the length of the lease. Read through the covenants contained within it. It may be helpful to refer back to it as you read through this chapter and then to have a final look at it when you have finished the chapter.

> **determined**
> ended; terminated

It can be ended (**determined**) by one of the parties giving notice.

The duration can be for any length of time, provided that it is certain. It can be for a fixed period, which can be a fraction of a year, less than a year, a year, or more than a year. The lease can also operate as a periodic tenancy (see 5.3.2.2), which may run from year to year.

We will look a little further at these different types of lease and how they are created, and then we will think about the essential elements that are present in every kind of lease.

5.3.2 Types of lease

5.3.2.1 Fixed-term lease

> **fixed-term lease**
> a lease that is entered into for a fixed period of time

The **fixed-term lease** is probably the most common kind of lease. You may well have seen it in practice, if you have rented accommodation yourself. It simply means a lease for a fixed period of time, which can be for as long as the parties want it to be. If you buy a leasehold flat, the lease will often be for over 100 years; if you rent a student flat, it may be for a period of six months or for the duration of the academic year.

The key ingredient with fixed-term leases is that the period is fixed and certain at the time of creation. The lease cannot continue indefinitely.

> **periodic tenancy**
> a lease or tenancy in which rent is payable at fixed intervals and which continues indefinitely from one rent period to the next, until being terminated by notice

5.3.2.2 Periodic tenancy

A **periodic tenancy** may last indefinitely: it is a lease that runs from week to week, from month to month, or from year to year. It can arise by the express agreement of the parties, or by implication, should a tenant move into the property with the permission of the landlord and pay rent, which the landlord accepts.

Effectively, the periodic tenancy is being renewed at the end of each term—that is, at the end of each period for which rent is paid—which prevents the term from being uncertain. So, for example, if the tenancy agreement stipulates a weekly rent, it will be a weekly periodic tenancy; if the payment term is monthly, it will be a monthly periodic tenancy, etc. Even if the tenant actually makes the payment on a different basis, the agreement will set the length of the term.

The term is important in a periodic tenancy because the length of its term determines the notice period should either side wish to terminate the lease. The notice period required to end the tenancy is usually equivalent to a single payment term. The only exception to this is that the termination of an annual tenancy will only require six months' notice.

5.3.2.3 Tenancy at will

The **tenancy at will** is an odd type of tenancy that is seldom seen nowadays, except sometimes in transitional periods—for example, between the end of one lease and the start of another. It is odd because the interest that it confers on the tenant is neither a lease nor a licence, but something in between.

> **tenancy at will**
> a lease or tenancy, which usually arises by implication, that can be terminated by the landlord or tenant at any time

It is essentially a personal agreement between the parties—*Wheeler v. Mercer* [1957] AC 426. The tenant at will has no proprietary interest in the land, so he or she cannot, for example, assign any interest in the property to someone else. The tenant at will can, however, continue to live in the property until either he or she, or the landlord, decides that the arrangement is to end, or until the death of one of the parties. There is no need for either side to give notice, which makes the whole situation rather precarious.

Tenancies at will often arise when a more formal arrangement has come to an end, or if the parties are negotiating the terms for a formal lease, but the tenant moves into the property before the negotiations are finalized.

5.3.2.4 Tenancy at sufferance

The **tenancy at sufferance** arises when a tenant stays on in a property after the end of a fixed-term lease. Unlike a tenancy at will, the landlord does not explicitly consent to this, but he does tolerate—that is, 'suffer'—it.

> **tenancy at sufferance**
> a lease or tenancy that arises when a tenant stays on in a property after a lease is ended, but to which occupation the landlord has not indicated agreement or otherwise

Under the tenancy at sufferance, while the tenant's initial occupation of the premises was lawful, after the end of the fixed-term tenancy, he or she can be removed at any moment. This is not, then, a very comfortable situation for the tenant!

5.3.2.5 Tenancy by estoppel

The **tenancy by estoppel** arises if the person granting the lease does not, in fact, have any estate in the land from which it is possible to make that grant. Despite his or her lack of title, if the agreement reflects all of the essential characteristics of a lease (see 5.5), the court will 'estop'—that is, prevent—the landlord from denying the existence of the lease.

> **tenancy by estoppel**
> a lease or tenancy that exists despite the fact that the person who granted it had no right to do so

An example may make this clearer.

→ **EXAMPLE**

George is in the process of buying a house. Before the purchase is completed, he grants a lease of the property to Nick. Technically, at this stage, George does not have any estate in the land that he is purchasing. But if the agreement confers exclusive possession for a term on Nick, George will be estopped (prevented) from denying the tenancy, because of his lack of title. It will be a tenancy by estoppel.

Note, too, that after completion of the purchase, once George becomes the legal owner of the property, the tenancy by estoppel is automatically converted into a 'proper' tenancy. This is known as 'feeding the estoppel'.

CROSS REFERENCE

For more on adverse possession, look at Chapter 6.

Mitchell v. Watkinson [2014] EWCA Civ 1472 concerned a tenancy by estoppel, where a father entered into a tenancy with a cricket club after he had gifted the relevant land to his son. The implications of this and subsequent events led to a successful claim by the cricket club that they were in adverse possession of the land many years later.

5.4 Creation of a lease

A lease may exist in law—that is, it may be a **legal lease**—or in equity—that is, it may be an **equitable lease**.

legal lease a lease that creates an estate in land for a term of years absolute and with certain formalities

equitable lease a lease that grants an interest in land on terms that correspond to those of a legal lease, but without completion of the legal formalities

5.4.1 **Legal leases**

 STATUTE

Law of Property Act 1925, s. 52(1)

All conveyances of land or of any interest therein are void for the purpose of conveying or creating a legal estate unless made by deed.

CROSS REFERENCE

For more on deeds, see Chapter 3.

Under LPA 1925, s. 52(1), to create a legal lease, as with any legal estate in land, the parties must execute a deed, with all of the formalities that this requires.

5.4.1.1 **Leases of three years or less**

There are some exceptions, however, to this requirement. LPA 1925, s. 52(2)(d), makes an exception for 'leases or tenancies … not required to be made in writing'.

premium (or fine)
a sum that is sometimes charged by a landlord as the 'price' of granting a lease, which is usually seen in commercial or long leases

According to LPA 1925, s. 54(2), leases granted for a period of three years or less, taking effect in possession, with no **premium (or fine)**, and at **market value** do not need to be in writing. Such leases can, then, be legal leases, despite the lack of a deed, or even if made orally by agreement between the parties.

market value
a full rent at current economic rates

For all other leases, if they are to be legal leases, a deed must be executed. If this is not done, the lease will take effect only as an equitable lease for the period stated, or alternatively as a legal periodic tenancy if the tenant moves in and starts paying rent. For example, in *Hutchison v. B&DF Ltd* [2008] EWHC 2286 (Ch), the defendants were allowed into possession of business premises although the lease documents had not been signed. It was held that the oral agreements for leases of less than three years were valid legal leases, and that an oral agreement for a lease of five years took effect as a periodic tenancy.

5.4.1.2 **Registration**

Generally, interests in land will only take effect as legal interests once they have been registered—LRA 2002, ss. 4(1) and 27(1). Leases are no exception to this rule, although there are some additional considerations to bear in mind.

Not all leases need to be registered in order to be legal leases. LRA 2002, ss. 4(2)(b) and 27(2)(b), state that only leases of over seven years in duration must be registered. Most leases for durations of up to seven years can still take effect as legal leases even without registration, provided that the necessary formal requirements have been carried out, as they are overriding interests (see Table 5.1).

Parliament has left open the possibility that, in the future, it may vary the requirement to register only leases exceeding seven years in duration—LRA 2002, s. 118(1)(b). It seems likely that this may one day be extended to become a requirement for all leases of over three years. Under the old LRA 1925, only leases of over twenty-one years had to be registered, but this was widely considered to be insufficient.

Finally, a number of particular kinds of lease must be registered to take effect as legal leases even if they are for less than seven years. The most important of these is a lease that 'takes effect in possession after the end of the period of three months beginning with the date of the grant'—effectively, a lease that does not start immediately—and a lease 'under which the right to possession is discontinuous'—for example, a timeshare. These and the other exceptions can be found in LRA 2002, s. 27(2)(b).

If registration is required and not complied with, the lease will take effect only as an equitable lease.

Remember that each leasehold estate is registered independently, with its own title number. This can mean that one piece of land has a number of different entries in the Land Register.

> **CROSS REFERENCE**
> For more on the registration of legal interests, see Chapter 3.

➡ EXAMPLE

Matthew owns the freehold title to The Grange, a large Victorian property, which is registered land. He decides to divide it up into three flats, and grants two 120-year leases to Greg and Will. He decides to keep one of the flats for himself and rents it out to Tim for a year.

How many separate titles would be registered at the Land Registry?

Three separate titles would appear on the register for the property. Matthew's freehold title would obviously be registered, as would Greg and Will's long leases (they exceed seven years). Tim's lease would not be registered, because it is for less than three years.

5.4.1.3 **Summary**

We therefore have slightly different requirements for leases of different durations, which are summarized in Table 5.1.

> **CROSS REFERENCE**
> For more on the registration of leases, see Chapter 4.

Table 5.1 The requirements for a legal lease

Duration of lease	Formalities (legal lease)	Registration
Three years or less (including periodic tenancies)	Can be oral, or by contract, with no need for a deed	Not yet required—they take effect as overriding interests
Between three and seven years	Deed necessary	Not yet required—they take effect as overriding interests
Over seven years	Deed necessary	Required

Failure to comply with the formalities and registration (where necessary) will result in the creation of an equitable lease for the term specified, or a legal periodic tenancy if the tenant has moved in and is paying rent. Since a periodic tenancy is less than three years (it takes effect from year to year or month to month), this takes effect as an overriding interest.

5.4.2 **Equitable leases**

As we have just seen, many equitable leases arise by accident, as a result of failure to comply with the statutory requirements to create a legal lease. Sometimes, the parties will draft a contract for this lease, but will not get around to executing it as a deed. If it is the kind of lease that needs to be made by deed and a deed is not prepared, then the lease will exist only as an equitable lease.

 CASE CLOSE-UP

Walsh v. Lonsdale (1820) 21 Ch D 9

The landlord tried to grant a seven-year lease of a mill to the tenant. One of the terms of the agreement was that the rent was payable in advance, which meant, in this case, at the start of each year. No deed was executed.

The tenant moved into the mill. He paid his rent in arrears (at the end of the year). A few years later, the landlord claimed that the tenant was behind with his rent and insisted that the agreement was for payment of rent in advance.

The tenant argued that the lease agreement had never been executed as a deed and so was not effective. He said that, because he had been paying and the landlord had been accepting rent, a periodic tenancy had arisen (see earlier) and one of the terms of this tenancy was payment of rent in arrears.

The Court of Appeal said that, in the absence of a deed, an equitable lease had arisen. Underlying the Court's decision was the equitable maxim 'equity treats as done that which ought to be done'. Under the circumstances of the lease contract, the Court would have awarded an order for specific performance, which means that it would have ordered each of the parties to comply with its side of the contract. Equity would therefore treat the agreement as though it had been properly made: it would consider it to be an equitable lease, made on the same terms as originally agreed. The tenant had to pay his rent in advance.

Remember that, for an equitable lease, there must first be a valid contract for the grant of a lease. For leases created after 26 September 1989, this means complying with Law of Property (Miscellaneous Provisions) Act 1989 (LP(MP)A 1989), s. 2(1).

 STATUTE

Law of Property (Miscellaneous Provisions) Act 1989, s. 2(1)

A contract for the sale or other disposition of an interest in land can only be made in writing and only by incorporating all the terms which the parties have expressly agreed in one document, or, where contracts are exchanged, in each.

The contract must also be one for which the court would award specific performance. Specific performance is a discretionary remedy and its grant depends on a number of factors. For example, the court may not award such a remedy if the party asking for the remedy is in breach of covenant.

Although it might seem, looking at *Walsh v. Lonsdale*, that an equitable lease is effectively the same as a legal lease, do not be deceived. All equitable interests are more vulnerable to third parties than are their legal counterparts and there may also be issues when looking at the enforceability of lease-hold covenants in equitable leases, because there will be no privity of estate (see 5.7.1).

> **CROSS REFERENCE**
> For the meaning of specific performance, see Chapter 3.

5.5 Essential characteristics of a lease

In order to identify the characteristics that are common to all leases, we must turn to the leading case of *Street v. Mountford* [1985] AC 809.

Remember throughout that the context for this case, and for many of the cases to which we refer in the subsequent discussion, is that the landlord was trying to avoid the appearance of a lease. If he were found to have granted the tenant a lease, the tenant would be protected by statute—particularly, at that time, the Rent Act 1977, which regulated the rent (among other things). If the landlord had created only a **licence**, then the tenant would have no statutory protection.

In all of these cases, the landlords dressed the lease agreements up as 'licence agreements'. In order to work out whether the agreement was a lease or a licence, it was necessary for the courts to consider the elements that are both essential and common to every lease, but not to the grant of a licence.

licence
a personal arrangement between licensor and licensee under which the licensee may occupy the licensor's property for a specified purpose

---

Q CASE CLOSE-UP

Street v. Mountford [1985] AC 809

Mr Street and Mrs Mountford entered into an agreement whereby Mr Street agreed to allow Mr and Mrs Mountford to occupy furnished rooms for a rent of £37 per week. The agreement was headed 'Licence Agreement' and included a clause stating that Mrs Mountford accepted that the agreement did not confer on her the protection of the Rent Act 1977.

Some time later, Mrs Mountford attempted to invoke the protection of the Rent Act 1977 in respect of a fair rent. Mr Street argued that, because she only had a licence rather than a tenancy, she could not do this. Eventually, the matter worked its way up to the House of Lords, where their Lordships had to decide whether the agreement was, in reality, a tenancy, or a licence, as it was described.

Lord Templeman, firstly, drew the traditional distinction between a lease and a licence. With a lease, the tenant had an estate in the land: she had the right of exclusive possession of the premises and could exclude all others from the property—even the landlord. With a licence, the licensee had no such rights, because she was given no estate in the land. A licensee was allowed occupation of the premises only by permission of the landlord. The essential elements of a lease, according to Lord Templeman, were 'exclusive possession for a term at a rent' (see 5.5.2 for more discussion about whether a rent is necessary).

In deciding that the agreement was a tenancy, despite its appearance, Lord Templeman looked at the factual matrix of the case: whatever the agreement called itself, if the effect of it was to confer exclusive possession of the premises for a term at a rent, then it was a tenancy.

We will now look at each of the three elements identified in *Street v. Mountford*—that is, certain term, rent, and exclusive possession—in turn.

5.5.1 **Certain term**

certain term
a period that has a specified beginning and end

Although a lease can be for any duration, to be valid, it must have a **certain term**—that is, a certain beginning and a certain end. It can be a fixed term or a periodic term (see 5.3.2.1 and 5.3.2.2).

This does not mean, however, that the lease must continue for the full term. Many commercial leases, in particular, have **break clauses**, which allow the parties to end the lease at various intervals during the term. For example, a 21-year lease may have a seven-year break clause allowing the lease to be ended after seven or fourteen years. What matters is that the lease cannot be indefinite, because one of the essential characteristics of a leasehold estate is that it is for a period of time.

break clause
a clause that allows the parties to bring a lease to an end at various specified points in advance of the lease's end

> ### 🔍 CASE CLOSE-UP
>
> ***Lace v. Chantler* [1944] KB 368**
>
> The tenant was granted a tenancy of a house 'for the duration of the war'.
>
> The Court held that this was not a valid fixed lease: the term granted had to be certain from the outset and 'the duration of the war' was not certain.
>
> The decision had a significant impact on many wartime leases and led to the passing of the Validation of War Time Leases Act 1944, which converted all such agreements into ten-year leases, determinable by one month's notice if the war ended before then.

This requirement was affirmed in *Prudential Assurance Co Ltd v. London Residuary Body* [1992] 3 WLR 279.

> ### 🔍 CASE CLOSE-UP
>
> ***Prudential Assurance Co. Ltd v. London Residuary Body* [1992] 3 WLR 279**
>
> The (then) London County Council purchased a strip of land, situated alongside a road, and then rented it back to its original owner. The rent was £30 per annum and the lease was said to continue until the Council needed the land back in order to widen the road. The road was never widened and, some sixty years on, the tenants had a very good deal, because they continued to pay rent at £30 p.a. The matter went to court, with the House of Lords deciding that the original lease was invalid, because the term was not certain, following *Lace v. Chantler*.
>
> Interestingly, however, the House of Lords found that there was in existence a yearly periodic tenancy, because the tenant had paid and the landlord accepted rent on an annual basis (see earlier). This yearly periodic tenancy could be determined by six months' notice.

A rather surprising decision was made by the Supreme Court in the following case where there was potential uncertainty of term in respect of social housing:

CASE CLOSE-UP

Berrisford v. Mexfield Housing Co-operative [2011] UKSC 52

The claimant had been granted an 'occupancy agreement' which entitled her to live in the property 'from month to month until determined'. The agreement could be ended by the claimant on one month's written notice, but could be determined by the defendants only in four specified circumstances, none of which had occurred.

The defendant housing co-operative served one month's notice on the claimant. They argued that the agreement was to be interpreted as a tenancy from month to month, because any agreement to end it on specified grounds only would make it uncertain, as in the *Prudential Assurance* case.

The Supreme Court held that such an agreement, if entered into before 1925, would have been interpreted as a 'lease for life'. These are converted into ninety-year tenancies by LPA 1925, s. 149(6). Therefore the claimant had a lease for ninety years, subject only to determination on the four grounds agreed.

This is rather surprising, as the courts do not seem to have used this section before in such a way. The Court did give weight to the nature of the property—social housing—and held that certainty of tenure must have been intended.

Berrisford v. Mexfield Housing Co-operative was recently distinguished by the High Court in *Southward Housing Co-operative Ltd v. Walker* [2015] EWHC 1615 (Ch). In this case, the defendants were joint tenants of a property owned by a housing co-operative. The agreement specified that the tenancy could only be terminated if certain conditions occurred, one of which was rent arrears. The housing co-operative duly sought possession when the tenants went into rent arrears, but the tenants claimed that the fact that notice to quit could only be served on restricted conditions meant that the lease was for an uncertain term. They argued that, following *Berrisford*, this meant that they had a ninety-year lease under LPA 1925, s. 149(6). However, the Court decided that although the term was uncertain, it did not give rise to a ninety-year lease. In this case, it was clear that the parties had not intended to create a lease for life. Instead, the agreement should be construed as a contractual licence, which was brought to an end by the notice to quit. This is an interesting development, not least because it demonstrates the importance that the court attaches to the intention of the parties in reaching its decision.

Note, finally, that although we have said that the beginning of the term must be certain, the lease does not need to be expressed as starting on a particular date. It has been held that an agreement to grant a lease based on an uncertain event—for example, the outbreak of war—is sufficiently certain—*Swift v. MacBean* [1942] KB 375.

5.5.2 **Rent**

Although Lord Templeman, in *Street v. Mountford*, implied that rent is an essential requirement for a valid lease, the courts have subsequently decided that this is not the case—*Ashburn Anstalt v. Arnold* [1989] Ch 1.

 THINKING POINT

Can you think why this might be? Have a look again at the statutory definition of a lease at 5.3.1.

The definition clearly states 'whether or not at a rent': the courts could not fly in the face of statute.

Despite this undoubtedly correct judicial reasoning, it seems that payment of rent is likely to be evidence at least indicative of the existence of a lease, even if it is not conclusive.

5.5.3 **Exclusive possession**

A person occupying residential property with the permission of the owner will either be a tenant or a licensee, depending on whether or not he or she has **exclusive possession** of the premises.

> **exclusive possession**
> possession of a property to the exclusion of all others, including the landlord

The concept of exclusive possession is central to the grant of a lease. It means essentially that the tenant can exclude anyone else from the premises, even the landlord. The landlord who reserves the right to enter the property to maintain it from time to time does not negate exclusive possession—*Street v. Mountford*—nor does it matter that the landlord keeps a set of keys—*Aslan v. Murphy* [1990] 1 WLR 767.

It is, however, a concept with which the courts have sometimes struggled, as we shall see. It means that the tenant can effectively control the property: he or she has the right to decide who comes into it and who he or she wants to keep out.

> **exclusive occupation**
> sole occupation of all, or part, of a property

This can be contrasted with the right of a licensee. A licensee occupies the property only by permission of its owner: the licensee has no proprietary right in the property itself. He or she may have **exclusive occupation** of it, but this is different from exclusive possession. The licensee's interest will not be binding on third parties, unlike the interest of a tenant in the land—*Ashburn Anstalt v. Arnold*. All exclusive occupation means is that the occupier has sole or exclusive use of the property, or part of it.

In the 1970s, 1980s, and early 1990s, there was a succession of cases in which the courts grappled with the concept of exclusive possession. In most of these cases, the landlord wanted to avoid creating a lease, because that would confer statutory protection on the tenant. The best way in which to avoid the court construing an agreement as a lease was to ensure that the agreement did not confer the right of exclusive possession on the occupier—and landlords went to extreme lengths to avoid the appearance of exclusive possession, as we shall see!

Our starting point will be a case before *Street v. Mountford* which marked a high point for landlords, although the courts soon redressed the balance between landlord and tenant.

Q   CASE CLOSE-UP

Somma v. Hazelhurst [1978] 1 WLR 1014

A young unmarried couple wanted to rent a bedsit to share together. They each entered into a separate agreement with the owner of the property. The unusual agreement stated that the owner could, if she wished, move in with the couple—or even move a stranger in with them!

Let us pause for a moment here.

   THINKING POINT

Why do you think that the agreement contained these odd suggestions?

The owner was trying to avoid conferring exclusive possession on the occupiers. If they were found to have exclusive possession, the agreement would have been a lease and the Rent Acts would have protected the tenants.

CASE CLOSE-UP

Somma v. Hazelhurst [1978] 1 WLR 1014

The Court found that there was only a licence agreement. Exclusive possession had not been conferred on the occupiers.

When *Street v. Mountford* was decided a number of years later, the Court criticized the decision in *Somma v. Hazelhurst*. Although the starting point for determining whether a lease or licence exists is always the agreement itself, Lord Templeman warned that the courts would be careful to detect 'sham devices and artificial transactions' inserted into the agreement to prevent the grant of exclusive possession. The clause in *Somma v. Hazelhurst* allowing the owner to move in with the occupiers was clearly such a sham.

Subsequent to *Street v. Mountford*, the courts would look at the whole factual matrix of the situation and examine the substance of what was actually happening at the premises, in order to decide whether exclusive possession had, in fact, been conferred. This was applied many times by the courts in the years after *Street v. Mountford*.

CASE CLOSE-UP

Aslan v. Murphy [1990] 1 WLR 767; **Crancour Ltd v. Da Silvesa** [1986] 1 EGLR 80

In both of these cases, the owner had inserted a clause apparently requiring the occupier to vacate the premises for an hour and a half each day. In *Aslan v. Murphy*, there was a further clause that the occupier might be required to share the room (measuring 4 ft 3 in x 12 ft 6 in) with another person.

The Court found, in both cases, that these were sham clauses, designed to negate the grant of exclusive possession. When the Court looked at what was actually happening at the premises, it found that the occupiers, as a matter of fact, had exclusive possession and thus both had a lease rather than a licence.

Street v. Mountford said that the title and wording of the agreement (in terms of lease or licence) was not relevant in deciding whether the document conferred a lease or a licence. In *National Car Parks Ltd v. Trinity Development Co. (Banbury) Ltd* [2001] EWCA Civ 1686, however, the Court of Appeal said that the title and wording should be used as a pointer by the courts when ascertaining the nature of the agreement. This decision reflects the fact that, sometimes, the parties do genuinely intend only to confer a licence and that the real intention of the parties should be considered by the courts. The importance of the real intention of the parties has been emphasized by a recent Court of Appeal case.

CASE CLOSE-UP

Watts v. Stewart [2016] EWCA Civ 1247

The appellant, Ms Watts, lived in an almshouse, which is housing provided by a charity for people who have very little money. The trustees of the charity wanted to evict Ms Watts because she had acted in an anti-social manner both to contractors working at the almshouse and also to her neighbour. The charity sought a possession order from the court. Ms Watts claimed that she was a tenant of the almshouse, despite various clauses in the appointment letter which had been sent to her before she began occupying the property, which said, amongst other things, that she would not be a tenant of the charity, and that she could, if necessary, be moved to another property or asked to leave. She also raised some issues relating to charity law and human rights law which we will not consider here: the interest in the case for us relates to whether or not Ms Watts was a tenant of the property.

CROSS REFERENCE

For more on periodic tenancies, see 5.3.2.2 and for tenancies at will see 5.3.2.3.

At first instance, the judge held that Ms Watts was not a tenant: that she occupied the property as 'an appointee' of the trustees, and had only a licence to occupy as a beneficiary of the charity's trustees. Ms Watts appealed to the Court of Appeal: again, we will focus on her main argument, which was that she was a tenant of the charity by virtue of a periodic tenancy.

Ms Watts argued that she had exclusive possession of the property; that she had entered the property as a tenant at will and that this had been converted into a periodic tenancy when she began to pay rent. Her counsel ran a rather brave argument which said that Lord Templeman had been wrong in *Street v. Mountford* when he said that the object of a charity may well not be a tenant, even if that person enjoyed exclusive possession of the property. Her counsel argued that if an owner of a property allowed someone exclusive possession of that property, then the person with exclusive possession became a tenant.

Unsurprisingly, the Court of Appeal disagreed with this assertion, noting that the argument and criticism of Lord Templeman's speech was 'bold, not least because [Ms Watt's counsel] was unable to refer us to any authority or scholarly commentary in support of his criticism' (at [30]). The Court drew the traditional distinction between a *legal* right of exclusive *possession* and a *personal* right of exclusive *occupation*:

> Legal exclusive possession entitles the occupier to exclude all others, including the legal owner, from the property. Exclusive occupation may, or may not, amount to legal possession. If it does, the occupier is a tenant. If it does not, the occupier is not a tenant and occupies in some different capacity (at [31]).

The Court looked at the language of the letter of appointment to Ms Watts from the charity, which included a reference to a tenancy at one point in the document, but said that the 'labels' or language used by the parties did not determine whether something was a licence or tenancy. The Court's focus was on the intention of the parties, having regard to all of the admissible evidence. In the Court's view, Ms Watts was granted a personal licence to occupy the property by the charity, and was not a tenant. The appeal was dismissed.

5.5.4 **Lodgers**

In *Street v. Mountford*, Lord Templeman made it clear that, should someone be a lodger, he or she will be a licensee rather than a tenant. An example of a lodger might be a student renting a room in a family house during term time. Clearly, in this situation, the lodger cannot exclude the homeowner from his or her own home. Lord Templeman said (at 818) that a 'lodger is entitled to live in the premises but cannot call the place his own'.

5.5.5 **Multiple occupiers**

Some interesting issues arise in circumstances under which a number of people share the same premises.

There are a number of possibilities with shared property:

- the occupiers may be joint tenants of the whole property and so may have a lease together;
- the occupiers might be tenants of a particular part of the property, such as their own bedrooms;
- the occupiers may simply be licensees.

Whether the occupiers are deemed to have been granted a lease or a licence will depend on the circumstances of their sharing arrangements.

Q CASE CLOSE-UP

AG Securities v. Vaughan [1990] 1 AC 417

This case was heard at the same time as *Antoniades v. Villiers* [1990] 1 AC 417. The two cases make an interesting contrast.

Four people moved into a four-bedroom flat. Each signed a separate 'licence' agreement with the owner, which allowed him or her to occupy the flat with the other licensees. It also expressly negated any right to exclusive possession. The agreements were all made at different times; some were for differing rents and for different periods. Each of the occupiers had replaced other occupiers when vacancies occurred over a three-year period.

The House of Lords decided that the occupiers were licensees. The four unities required for a joint tenancy (time, interest, possession, title) were not present.

Lord Templeman explained that, if the occupiers had been joint tenants and one of them had died, the remaining three occupiers would have been entitled to exclusive possession of the flat (by the operation of survivorship).

In this situation, however, it was clear that, if one of the occupiers had died, the owner of the property would have had the right to replace him and the existing occupiers could not have prevented him from doing this. They did not, therefore, have exclusive possession of the property and so had a licence.

❯ CROSS REFERENCE
For more on survivorship, see Chapter 8.

Compare this with the case of *Antoniades v. Villiers*.

Q CASE CLOSE-UP

Antoniades v. Villiers [1990] 1 AC 417

A couple lived together in a one-bedroom flat, by themselves. They had each signed a separate 'licence' agreement and had each agreed to pay half the rent. The agreement provided that the owner could move into the accommodation at any time or even arrange for someone else to do so!

The House of Lords decided that this was a lease. The couple had a joint tenancy of the flat. The agreements, although made separately, were interdependent: neither would have signed without the other. The couple had exclusive possession of the property and the clause suggesting that someone else could move in with them was a sham.

5.5.6 **Business premises**

Exclusive possession is also relevant in deciding whether an occupier holds business premises on a lease or licence—*Shell-Mex and BP Ltd v. Manchester Garages Ltd* [1971] 1 All ER 841.

5.5.7 **Exceptional cases**

There are some situations in which, even though all of the essential characteristics of a lease are present, a lease will not exist. Lord Templeman, in *Street v. Mountford*, identified three different categories of case in which this would happen:

1. those in which there is no intention to create a legal relationship;
2. those in which there is only a service occupancy;
3. those in which the landlord had no power to grant a tenancy.

5.5.7.1 **No intention to create a legal relationship**

When the parties enter into a lease, they are entering into a binding contract, intending to be bound by it. Lord Templeman recognized that there may be occasions—particularly in a family context—on which the parties may unintentionally create a lease by satisfying the essential elements. For example, in *Cobb v. Lane* [1952] 1 All ER 1199, a woman allowed her brother to live in her bungalow rent free. This was held to be a licence, rather than a lease, because the woman had no intention to create legal relations: she was simply helping out her brother.

This exception also stretches to acts of friendship or generosity. In *Booker v. Palmer* [1942] 2 All ER 674, a wartime case, evacuees whose home had been bombed were allowed to live in a cottage as a favour. They later claimed (rather ungratefully!) that they had a lease, but the Court of Appeal held that there had been no intention to create legal relations and so there was no lease.

5.5.7.2 **Service occupancy**

There will also be no tenancy if the occupier is living in the premises because he or she is required to do so for his or her job. For example, a school caretaker will often live in the grounds of a school, so that he or she can be on site when needed to repair and maintain the school property. In these circumstances, the caretaker will be a licensee, unless the parties clearly intended otherwise (*Hertfordshire CC v. Davies* [2017] EWHC 1488 (Ch)).

The test to establish whether someone has a service occupancy is to ask whether he or she is 'genuinely required to occupy the premises for the better performance of his duties'—*per* Woolf LJ in *Norris v. Checksfield* [1991] 1 WLR 1241. If he or she is living on the premises simply for convenience, or as some kind of fringe benefit, then the agreement may well result in a tenancy being created.

5.5.7.3 **No power to grant a tenancy**

It has long been thought that a person cannot grant a lease if he or she does not have either a freehold or leasehold interest in the land. This seems to be common sense: if someone only has a licence to occupy a property, how could they possibly grant another person a lease, which would be a greater estate in the land than their own?

This sensible supposition has been shaken slightly by a House of Lords' decision that has had both academics and property lawyers scratching their heads in disbelief.

The following unusual case needs to be considered on its own, before we think about whether it changes anything that we have already said about leases.

Q CASE CLOSE-UP

Bruton v. London and Quadrant Housing Trust [2000] 1 AC 406

London and Quadrant Housing Trust (LQHT) was a charitable organization that provided accommodation for the homeless. For this reason, Lambeth Borough Council gave LQHT a licence to use a block of flats that Lambeth owned. In the agreement between LQHT and Lambeth, it was made clear that no proprietary interest was to be conferred on LQHT. Indeed, it would have been *ultra vires* for Lambeth to make such a grant. The housing was to be used to provide temporary accommodation for the homeless.

As part of this worthy scheme, LQHT offered Mr Bruton a flat, under a weekly licence agreement.

The case came to court because Mr Bruton claimed that LQHT was in breach of a repairing obligation under Landlord and Tenant Act 1985, s. 11. LQHT maintained that, because there was no lease, it was not liable under this section. The Court then had to decide whether Mr Bruton had been granted a lease or a licence.

The Court of Appeal had no difficulty in deciding that Mr Bruton was a licensee.

The House of Lords, however, disagreed. Lord Hoffmann decided that the agreement had all the necessary hallmarks of a tenancy, according to *Street v. Mountford*—that is, exclusive possession for a term at a rent. He also held that, although LQHT had no estate from which to grant a lease, the term 'lease' described the relationship between the parties and did not need to grant a proprietary right or interest in the land.

This is a very strange judgment. If a lease does not have to confer a proprietary right, but is only a contract between the parties, then it starts to look very much like a licence—in which case, are tenants under such contractual leases afforded the statutory protection that tenants under conventional (proprietary) leases enjoy?

In *Bruton*, the implications for the charity providing housing for the homeless are significant: LQHT was suddenly burdened with a duty to repair, despite the fact that it had no proprietary interest in the property!

We suggest that, although you should think about (and hopefully read) the case of *Bruton*—it is, after all, still good law and has not yet been overruled—you should concentrate your efforts on grasping the conventional *Street v. Mountford* principles.

> **CROSS REFERENCE**
> For help in incorporating *Bruton* into an exam question on this topic, see Chapter 16.

5.6 Leasehold covenants

As we have already recognized, a lease is essentially a contract between landlord and tenant. As with any contract, the parties can agree to include any term or clause that they choose. The clauses in a lease are referred to as 'covenants'—but a **leasehold covenant** should not be confused with a freehold covenant.

> **leasehold covenant**
> a clause in a lease, specifying certain obligations on the part of either party

❯ CROSS REFERENCE

For more on freehold
covenants, see Chapter 13.

The phrase 'leasehold covenants' simply refers to the terms included in the lease. These can be expressly stated in the agreement (**express covenants**) or implied by law into the agreement (**implied covenants**). They can be separated into the duties imposed on the landlord (**landlord's covenants**) and the duties imposed upon the tenant (**tenant's covenants**).

> **express covenants** terms that are expressly stated in a lease
>
> **implied covenants** terms that are implied into a lease by law
>
> **landlord's covenants** clauses in a lease specifying the obligations of the landlord under the lease
>
> **tenant's covenants** clauses in a lease specifying the obligations of the tenant under the lease

We will look firstly at some of the usual covenants, and then we will consider briefly the slightly tricky question about whether leasehold covenants can bind landlords and tenants who acquire their title from the original contracting parties.

5.6.1 **The landlord's covenants**

5.6.1.1 **Quiet enjoyment**

The lease agreement will usually contain a term entitling the tenant to 'quiet enjoyment' of the leased premises. If no such express provision is made, then the law will imply such a term into the lease.

'Quiet enjoyment' implies fundamentally that the landlord should allow the tenant to enjoy his or her occupation of the premises without disturbance from the landlord, or their agent, or anyone else claiming title from the landlord (for example, another of their tenants)—*Sanderson v. Berwick-upon-Tweed Corporation* (1884) 13 QBD 547.

Many of the cases involving the breach of this covenant arise in circumstances under which the landlord is trying to evict the tenant from the premises, so the actions taken by the landlord are often somewhat extreme. For example, in *Lavender v. Betts* [1942] 2 All ER 72, the court (not unreasonably) decided that, by removing the doors and windows from the leased premises, the landlord had breached the covenant to quiet enjoyment. Intimidation or threatening behaviour towards the tenant can also breach this covenant—*Kenny v. Preen* [1963] 1 QB 499—and it can also breach statutory protection that is in place for the tenant under Protection from Eviction Act 1977, s. 1(3).

These are quite obvious forms of interference. However, the House of Lords has held that, for a breach to occur, there need not always be direct, physical interference: it potentially includes anything that might interfere with a tenant's occupation of his or her property, such as 'regular excessive noise'—*Southwark Borough Council v. Mills* [1999] 4 All ER 449, 455.

The tenant's right to quiet enjoyment is prospective, which means that it arises from the date on which the tenancy began. This means that, if the breach of covenant is caused by a condition that existed before his or her tenancy began, the tenant will have no redress against the landlord.

> **Q | CASE CLOSE-UP**
>
> ***Southwark Borough Council v. Mills*** [1999] 4 All ER 449
>
> The House of Lords considered a conjoined appeal from two tenants of local authorities who were living in old buildings with no soundproofing. The women complained that they could hear excessive noise from the flats around them. These flats were occupied by other council tenants (who therefore claimed their title from the local authority landlords).

The noise was simply the noise of everyday living, but because of the structure of the flats, it really bothered the women who had to suffer it. The women argued that this was a breach of the covenant to quiet enjoyment of their property.

The House of Lords, firstly, reviewed the history of the covenant and Lord Millett explained (at 467) that there would be a breach where:

> the landlord or someone claiming under him does anything that substantially interferes with the tenant's title or possession of the demised premises, or with his ordinary and lawful enjoyment of the demised premises.

In this case, however, there had been no breach of covenant. The covenant was prospective, which meant that it only took effect from the start of the tenancy: '[t]he covenant does not apply to things done before the grant of the tenancy, even though they may have continuing consequences for the tenant' (per Lord Hoffmann at 455). Unfortunately for the tenants, the problems arising from lack of soundproofing had existed for many years before their tenancy commenced. They had no remedy against their landlords.

The tenant's remedies for breach of this covenant may be an injunction, to stop the landlord from committing further breaches, or damages, to compensate the tenant for any loss suffered.

5.6.1.2 Non-derogation from grant

The somewhat grand-sounding covenant of 'non-derogation from grant' simply means that, having granted the tenancy, the landlord cannot then undermine it in any way. It is implied into the lease agreement.

In *Southwark Borough Council v. Mills*, Lord Millett said that the covenants of non-derogation from grant and of quiet enjoyment were in effect, very similar: '[t]he principle is the same in each case: a man may not give with one hand and take away with the other'.

Q | CASE CLOSE-UP

Harmer v. Jumbil (Nigeria) Tin Areas Ltd [1920] All ER 113

The landlord granted a lease expressly allowing the tenant to use the land to store explosives. In order to do this, the tenant had to obtain a licence under the Explosives Act 1875, which imposed certain restrictions on him. The landlord was aware that some restrictions would be necessary. The landlord retained land adjoining the tenant's property. The licence provided that, if buildings were erected on the landlord's land within a specified distance of the tenant's property, the licence would be withdrawn.

Some years later, the landlord granted a lease of the adjoining land to another tenant. This tenant built in the restricted area and also began reopening old mine shafts—not altogether wise, given the explosives stored next door!

The first tenant brought an action to stop the mining works and remove the buildings, claiming that this amounted to a derogation of the landlord's grant.

The Court of Appeal agreed that the landlord had effectively breached his covenant. If the buildings were allowed to remain, the licence would be withdrawn and the effect, according to Younger LJ, would be to 'completely sterilize the property in his tenant's hands'.

To be in breach of this covenant, the landlord must have known at the time of the grant what the tenant intended to do with the land—*Robinson v. Kilvert* (1889) 41 Ch 88.

If the tenant establishes a breach, he or she may obtain an injunction, stopping the landlord breaching the covenant, and/or damages, to compensate the tenant for the loss suffered.

5.6.1.3 **Covenant to repair**

As you might expect, the landlord will also be subject to certain obligations to maintain the leased premises. Both the common law and statute imply a number of covenants to repair into the lease.

At common law

- Fitness for human habitation

  If the property is let with furniture already in it—that is, if it is furnished—then the law implies a covenant that it is let 'fit for human habitation'. This basically means that it must be suitable for people to live in. Usually, it is fairly easy to work out when a property is *not* fit for human habitation:

  > The meaning of the phrase must vary with the circumstances to which it is applied. In the case of unclean furniture or defective drains or a nuisance by vermin the matter is not, as a rule, one of difficulty. The eye or the nostrils can detect the fault and measure its extent.
  >
  > (*Collins v. Hopkins* [1923] 2 KB 617, 620–1, *per* McCardie J)

  Note, however, that the covenant only says that the property must be fit for human habitation at the beginning of the tenancy: there is no continuing obligation *during* the tenancy—*Sarson v. Roberts* [1895] 2 QB 395.

  The covenant does not apply to unfurnished premises.

- Maintenance of means of access

  A covenant for the 'maintenance of means of access' would apply if a landlord were to own a building divided into a number of rented units—perhaps a block of flats. In this situation, the law will imply a covenant for the landlord to take reasonable steps to keep the 'common parts' of the building in good repair—*Liverpool City Council v. Irwin* [1977] AC 239. The common parts are those parts of the building used by all the tenants—for example, staircases and landings, or corridors between the individual flats.

- Correlative obligations

  Sometimes, in order to make the lease work sensibly, the law will imply a correlative obligation on the landlord. This might be necessary, for example, if the lease expressly imposes a duty on the tenant to repair the *inside* of the leased premises, but does not mention who is responsible for maintaining the *outside* of the premises—*Barrett v. Lounova* [1989] 1 All ER 351. The court would recognize that somebody must be responsible for maintaining the exterior of the premises—otherwise the building might eventually fall down! In these circumstances, then, it may well impose a duty on the landlord to repair the outside, because this would be matched by—that is, it would 'correlate' to—the duty of the tenant to maintain the inside.

Under Statute

- Fitness for human habitation

  In a number of exceptional cases, Landlord and Tenant Act 1985 (LTA 1985), s. 8, imposes a statutory duty on the landlord to keep the property fit for human habitation *during* the tenancy. This only applies to low-rent properties—that is, a tenancy granted after 6 July 1957, for a rent not exceeding £80 p.a. in London and £57 p.a. elsewhere in the country. Those of you paying rent will appreciate how few tenancies will actually meet these criteria!

- Repairing obligations

  LTA 1985, s. 13(1), also imposes repairing obligations on landlords if the lease is for a dwelling house and was granted after 24 October 1961 for less than seven years. Under LTA 1985, s. 11, the landlord has to keep the structure and exterior of the building in repair, as well as the various installations in the house that provide the tenant with gas, electricity, and water. The court will take into account the age and character of the property, and its locality, when considering the extent of the landlord's obligation to repair—LTA 1985, s. 11(3).

If the landlord has breached any of the repairing covenants, the tenant may be able to obtain an order for specific performance, to ensure that the necessary repairs are done. If the tenant, in desperation, has completed the repairs him- or herself, he or she may be entitled to offset the cost of those repairs against future rent payments. The tenant may also be able to recover damages.

> ### 🔍 CASE CLOSE-UP
>
> **Edwards v. Kumarasamy [2016] UKSC 40**
>
> In *Edwards v. Kumarasamy* [2015] EWCA Civ 20, the Court of Appeal considered the extent of a landlord's liability for a defect outside the rented premises. In this case the landlord, Mr Kumarasamy, held a long lease from the freeholder of a second-floor flat. He granted an assured shorthold tenancy to his own tenant, Mr Edwards. When taking some rubbish out, Mr Edwards tripped and injured himself on a defective paving stone which led to the communal bins and car park. He sued Mr Kumarasamy for damages, on the grounds that Mr Kumarasamy had breached his covenant to keep the premises in good repair.
>
> Section 11, LTA 1985 provides that, in addition to the landlord's duty to maintain the structure and exterior of the building, he or she must also keep in good repair any area in which he or she (the landlord) holds an estate or interest. Although Mr Kumarasamy did not own the relevant area—that was owned by the freeholder—he did have a legal easement over it, which permitted him (and therefore his tenant, Mr Edwards) to walk across it. The Court of Appeal said that this meant that Mr Kumarasamy did have an obligation to maintain this area in good repair.
>
> Before this case, case law suggested that the landlord had to be notified that an area had fallen into disrepair before he became liable. There was also a clause in the head lease (between Mr Kumarasamy and the freeholder) that provided that notice of a defect was necessary, so that the freeholder had the opportunity to remedy the defect, before the freeholder was liable. Mr Edwards had not notified Mr Kumarasamy of the defect, and Mr Kumarasamy had not notified the freeholder of the defect.
>
> However, in this case, the Court of Appeal said that the area was external to the property and therefore accessible and visible to the landlord—he should have ensured that it was kept in good repair. It was not necessary for the tenant to give notice of the defect to the landlord in order for the landlord to become liable for any breach. This decision caused some concern to landlords who suddenly seem to have a more onerous obligation in respect of repair to the exterior of the rented property. Mr Kumarasamy appealed to the Supreme Court.
>
> The Supreme Court allowed the appeal, confirming the orthodox position of the law. Their Lordships said that the path did not form part of the exterior of the property, but was instead a means of accessing the property. Mr Kumarasamy was not, therefore, in breach of s.11 of the Act. In addition, although he did have an interest in the relevant area, because of his legal easement, Mr Kumarasamy could not be held liable for a breach of a repairing covenant unless and until he had been notified that a repair was needed. Landlords undoubtedly breathed a sigh of relief after this sensible decision.

5.6.2 The tenant's covenants

5.6.2.1 Rent

Although we have seen that a tenant does not have to pay rent for a lease to exist (see 5.5.2), in the vast majority of cases, an express term requiring payment of rent will be contained in the lease agreement. The agreement will usually state how much rent is to be paid, when it is due, and whether it is to be paid in advance or in arrears.

THINKING POINT

Carl moved into a rented flat on 1 October 2007. His rent is £350 per month in advance. When will October's rent payment be due?

It is due on 1 October—that is, in advance of the coming month.

THINKING POINT

What if Carl's lease had said that his rent was due monthly in arrears?

If the rent were due in arrears, his rent would be due on 31 October—at the end of the month during which he had occupied the property.

Sometimes—particularly in longer leases—the lease will also contain a clause allowing the landlord to review and raise the rent at certain intervals. Different types of tenancy have different levels of protection in terms of the landlord charging a fair rent. Interesting though the statutory framework of such protection is, however, its consideration is outside the scope of this book.

5.6.2.2 **Repair**

Unlike the landlord, the tenant will not be subject to any implied obligation to repair the leased premises. In practice, the lease usually includes a clause requiring the tenant to keep the premises in 'good tenantable repair' or something similar. Most landlords accept that everyday wear and tear is inevitable. The court will interpret the tenant's repairing obligation in the context of the particular premises—*Brew Brothers Ltd v. Snax (Ross) Ltd* [1970] 1 QB 612—for example, taking its age and character into account.

5.6.2.3 **Waste**

waste

any permanent alteration of tenanted property that is caused by the tenant's action or neglect

Lease agreements will often contain a clause prohibiting a tenant from committing **waste**. An obligation is also implied into the agreement.

In this context, the term 'waste' has nothing to do with rubbish: it simply means that the tenant cannot do, or fail to do, anything that would result in the premises being permanently changed in any way. **Voluntary waste** involves the positive act of the tenant changing the nature of the premises. **Permissive waste** occurs if the tenant fails to do something and if that omission leads to a permanent change to the property. This might include, for example, failing to clear out a ditch, resulting in the foundations of the property rotting through—*Powys v. Belgrave* (1854).

voluntary waste waste that is caused by a voluntary action of the tenant

permissive waste waste that is caused by the tenant's neglect

In either case, the tenant is under an implied obligation to use the premises in a 'tenant-like' manner. He or she must, in the words of Lord Denning in *Warren v. Keen* [1953] 2 All ER 1118, 'do the little jobs about the place which a reasonable tenant would do'.

5.6.2.4 **Assignment or subletting**

Assignment occurs if the tenant transfers the whole of his or her remaining interest in the property to someone else (the assignee).

> **assignment**
> the transfer of the whole of the remainder of the term of a lease

> ➡ **EXAMPLE**
>
> If Leanne has a fifteen-year lease on a property and, after five years, she transfers the lease for the whole of the remaining ten years to Tracy, she has assigned her interest. This relationship might be illustrated as in Figure 5.3.

Figure 5.3 **The landlord–tenant–assignee relationship**

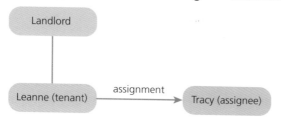

Subletting, meanwhile, occurs if the tenant grants a lease to someone else for a lesser period than his or her own.

> **subletting** the granting of a sublease by someone who is himself or herself a tenant, for a period shorter than that of his or her own (head) lease

> ➡ **EXAMPLE**
>
> Liam has a ten-year lease on the property and he grants a sublease for five years to Debbie. This is a sublease because, at the end of the five years, Liam still has an interest in the property.
>
> This relationship might be illustrated as in Figure 5.4.

Figure 5.4 **The landlord–tenant–subtenant relationship**

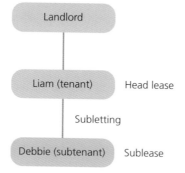

There is often a clause in the lease agreement prohibiting the tenant from assigning or subletting the property to someone else. The reason for this is that most landlords like to know who their tenants are, and to make sure that they are responsible and trustworthy. Sometimes, rather than forbidding the tenant to sublet, the lease will permit it, provided that the tenant obtains the consent of the landlord.

5.6.2.5 Breach of the tenant's covenants

If the tenant breaches one of the covenants in the lease, the landlord has various remedies against him or her.

❯ CROSS REFERENCE

For more on forfeiture, see Chapter 3.

Under certain circumstances, the landlord can forfeit the lease. This means that he or she can decide that the lease is at an end before the end of the term and re-enter the premises. This is obviously an extreme remedy and, in a legal lease, the right of re-entry and forfeiture must be expressly stated: it will not be implied. The exercise of the landlord's right of forfeiture is strictly controlled by statute and the courts.

Less draconian alternatives for the landlord include damages for breach of covenant (other than a covenant for payment of rent) and/or an injunction or order of specific performance.

> **distress**
>
> the seizure of goods as security for the performance of an obligation

At present, the landlord can resort to the ancient remedy of **distress**, which allows him or her to enter the premises and seize the tenant's goods to the value of the outstanding rent. This remedy dates back to the Norman Conquest and some of the legal principles are wonderfully quaint, bringing to mind old black-and-white films of the wicked landlord casting out the poor family from the premises into the night, with no mercy. The Tribunals, Courts and Enforcement Act 2007 contained provisions to abolish the remedy of distress and create a statutory recovery scheme for arrears in respect of commercial premises. One of the parts of this Act established a new scheme called Commercial Rent Arrears Recovery (CRAR). This came into force in 2014. Note though that CRAR only applies to commercial premises, and not to those properties either let or occupied as a dwelling (ie residential property).

5.7 Assignment and the running of covenants

We have seen that leasehold covenants are essentially clauses in a contract (a deed) between landlord and tenant. If either side breaches a covenant, then the wronged party can bring proceedings to remedy the breach. The original parties have **privity of contract**.

> **privity of contract**
>
> the relationship that exists between parties to a contract that allows each to sue, or be sued, under the contract

Problems may arise, however, when either the landlord assigns his or her reversion, or the tenant assigns his or her lease. Remember that 999-year leases are not uncommon: there may be many assignments over the course of a millennium! Suddenly, the parties to the contract are different: what we need to establish is whether the new parties are still bound by the terms of the original agreement.

❯ CROSS REFERENCE

For more on freehold covenants, see Chapter 13.

We will work through an example in stages, to illustrate the process of assignment and to help you to appreciate its implications. We will then look at the law relating to the enforceability of leasehold covenants: firstly, for leases created after 1995 and, then, for those arising before 1996. The reason for this is that the Landlord and Tenant (Covenants) Act 1995 (LTCA 1995) introduced a new statutory regime to simplify the rules about enforceability of leasehold covenants. It only applies to new leases, which means, in broad terms, those created after 31 December 1995—LTCA 1995, s. 1(1).

Remember, throughout that leasehold, covenants operate under different rules from those of freehold covenants.

Thankfully, leasehold covenants are now (relatively) straightforward. The following represents an overview of this substantial topic—but, should you need a more detailed consideration of the subject, please consult the further reading that is listed at the end of the chapter.

➡ **EXAMPLE**

Step 1

Laura owns the freehold of a property. She grants a fifty-year lease to Tilly. Their relationship might be illustrated as in Figure 5.5.

Figure 5.5 Laura grants a fifty-year lease to Tilly

➡ **EXAMPLE**

Step 2

Suppose that Laura assigns her reversionary interest to Leo. The relationships might now look as illustrated in Figure 5.6.

Figure 5.6 Laura assigns her reversionary interest to Leo

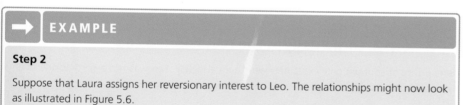

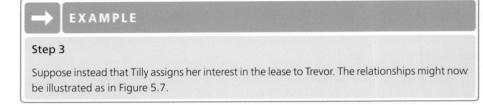

Step 3

Suppose instead that Tilly assigns her interest in the lease to Trevor. The relationships might now be illustrated as in Figure 5.7.

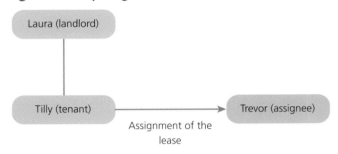

Figure 5.7 Tilly assigns her interest in the lease to Trevor

5.7.1 **Step 1: Laura and Tilly**

privity of estate

the relationship that exists between landlord and tenant under the same lease that allows each to enforce his or her obligations against the other

Between Laura and Tilly there is privity of contract, meaning that, if either party breaches a covenant, the wronged party can sue. There is also **privity of estate**. Privity of estate again refers to a relationship between the parties, but this time it relates to the nature of the relationship between landlord and tenant. Both parties have an estate in the land: Laura has a freehold estate and she has granted Tilly a leasehold estate. Between any landlord and any tenant there will always be privity of estate, as we shall see.

5.7.2 **Step 2: Laura assigns the reversion to Leo**

Here, privity of contract only exists between Laura and Tilly: Leo was not a party to the original contract (Figure 5.8).

THINKING POINT

Who now has privity of estate?

Leo and Tilly: they are in a landlord–tenant relationship.

See Figure 5.8 for an illustration of the relationship as it now stands.

Figure 5.8 Privity of contract and privity of estate at Step 2

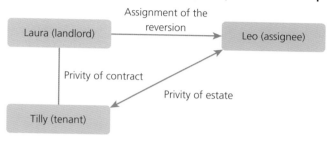

5.7.3 Step 3: Tilly assigns her lease to Trevor

Once again, at this step, privity of contract exists only between Laura and Tilly. There is no privity of contract between Laura and Trevor. There is, however, privity of estate between Laura and Trevor, because they are in a landlord–tenant relationship.

The relationships as they now stand are illustrated in Figure 5.9.

Figure 5.9 Privity of contract and privity of estate at Step 3

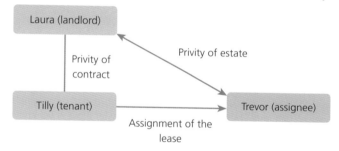

You will have noticed by now that the main difficulty, after the reversion or lease has been transferred, is that privity of contract continues to exist between the original parties. It is not destroyed by the transfer; neither does the transfer create any privity of contract between the new parties. This means that, without the legal mechanisms we are to discuss next, the old parties would remain forever liable for any breaches of covenant by the new parties and the new parties would be unable to sue for any breach of covenant.

We will now consider the legal positions of the parties after Steps 2 and 3.

5.7.4 After Step 2: assignment of the reversion

5.7.4.1 Leases granted after 1995

In our example, Laura assigns the reversion to Leo. LTCA 1995, s. 3(1), first annexes the leasehold covenants to the land itself, which has the effect of transferring to the new landlord the covenants in the original lease, unless those covenants are personal in nature.

In our example, if the lease were to have been granted after 1995, Leo would then automatically be bound by the landlord's covenants in the lease and would have the benefit of the tenant's (Tilly's) covenants. This right only arises from the date of transfer of the reversion. So for example, if Tilly were to owe Laura rent, Leo would not be able to sue her to recover it, because the breach of covenant took place before Leo acquired his interest in the land.

So far so good—but the other problem with leasehold covenants is that, as we have seen, privity of contract continues to exist between the original parties. In our example, this would mean that, if Leo were to breach his landlord's covenant to repair, Tilly could sue Laura if Leo were to refuse to comply!

LTCA 1995, s. 6(2), offers landlords in Laura's position an escape from this continuing obligation. Under this subsection, the original landlord can, with the permission of the tenant, be released from the covenants, and, once released, he or she is free from both burden and benefits. The landlord is also released if the tenant simply fails to respond to the landlord's request for release—LTCA 1995, s. 8(2)(a).

 EXAMPLE

Laura and Tilly's lease was created in 1997. In 2000, Laura assigns her reversion to Leo. In accordance with LTCA 1995, s. 8(1), Laura writes to her tenant, Tilly, to serve notice of the transfer of the reversion and to ask for permission to be released from the covenant. Tilly does not respond to the notice.

Four weeks after the date on which the notice was served and with no response from Tilly, Laura is automatically released from the covenants under LTCA 1995, s. 8(2)(a).

Some time later, Leo breaches his covenant to repair. Because of the LTCA 1995 provisions, Tilly has no redress at all from Laura—she must pursue only Leo for a remedy. Without the provisions, she would have been able to pursue both Leo and Laura.

5.7.4.2 Leases granted before 1996

As we have seen, there is privity of estate between the original tenant, Tilly, and the new landlord, Leo. LPA 1925, ss. 141(1) and 142(1), transfer the benefit and burden of the original covenants from the original to the new landlord—but they only appear to transfer those covenants that 'touch and concern' the land. The meaning of this phrase was the main difficulty under the old law, for leases granted before 1996.

The other difficulty was that the original landlord—Laura—remained liable to the original tenant—Tilly—for any breaches of covenant by the new landlord—Leo. This meant that, in order to protect him- or herself, the original landlord had to obtain an indemnity from the new landlord, which would allow the original landlord to recover from the new landlord any money paid to the tenant if the original landlord were to be sued.

This is not always as useful as it sounds, as the following example demonstrates.

 EXAMPLE

Imagine the same parties as in the previous example, but that, this time, the lease was created before 1996.

Laura transfers the reversion to Leo, with an indemnity clause. Leo breaches his covenant to repair. Tilly discovers that Leo has become insolvent. She decides to sue Laura instead. Laura is forced to pay the cost of repairs. She tries to rely on her indemnity to recover the cost of this from Leo. What do you think will be the problem?

The problem is that Leo will not be able to repay Laura: she will have to bear the cost herself.

5.7.5 **After Step 3: assignment of the tenancy**

5.7.5.1 **Leases granted after 1995**

In our example, the original tenant, Tilly, transfers the tenancy to Trevor. If the lease were to have been granted after 1995, Trevor would have privity of estate, but not privity of contract with the landlord, Laura. Tilly would still have privity of contract with Laura.

On assignment, however, LTCA 1995, s. 5, automatically releases the original tenant from the covenants of the lease. This means that, on assignment, Tilly can walk away from the property with no fear of liability for Trevor's breaches and no right to sue Laura for any of her future breaches under the lease.

 EXAMPLE

Laura and Tilly's lease is created in 1997. In 2000, Tilly assigns her interest to Trevor. Some years later, Trevor does not pay his rent.

LTCA 1995, s. 5, operates to release Tilly from all of the covenants of the lease. Laura cannot sue Tilly for Trevor's unpaid rent.

5.7.5.2 **Leases granted before 1996**

If the lease were to have been granted before 1996, however, Trevor would have privity of estate with the landlord, Laura. This means that he would be able to sue, or be sued, if either party committed any breaches of covenants that 'touch and concern' the land. There would, however, still be privity of contract between Tilly and Laura, the original parties to the lease.

An example will show what this might mean to Tilly.

 EXAMPLE

Laura and Tilly's lease is granted in 1990. In 2000, Tilly transfers the tenancy to Trevor. Some years later, Trevor does not pay his rent.

In this case, because there is privity of contract between Tilly and Laura, Laura can sue Tilly for Trevor's unpaid rent.

Once again, the original tenant can obtain an indemnity, but this will serve little purpose if the new tenant is insolvent. The law before LTCA 1995 obviously exposed the original tenant to great financial risks, because he or she might be sued for a breach occurring many years after assignment.

5.8 Putting it all together

Before we finish thinking about leases, it might be useful actually to look at a real tenancy agreement and to see how it all fits together. The sample agreement in Form 5.1 is one that is actually used in practice. Read right through it and try to identify the various parts of the lease that we have discussed in this chapter. (The thinking points will help to guide you through it step by step.)

Form 5.1 A tenancy agreement

TENANCY AGREEMENT

DATE 17th September 2010

PARTIES 1. **THE** Landlord   BRIAN SMITH

2. **THE** Tenant   TREVOR HOOD

PROPERTY Flat 4, The Warren
Maryfield
Greenfordshire

And any fixtures and land held with the Property

TERM A fixed term of 10 (ten) years months/year(s)
from   17 September 2010   (start date)
until   16 September 2020   (end date)
And thereafter from   month to month
(e.g., month to month)

RENT £ 1,000   per month   (period)

PAYABLE in advance by equal monthly payments on the 17th
day of each month

FIRST PAYMENT to be made on 17th September 2010   (date)

1. **SUBJECT** to clause 7 of this Agreement where it applies, the Landlord lets the Property to the Tenant for the Term at the Rent payable as set out above.

2. **THE** Tenant agrees with the Landlord -

    (1) To pay the Rent as set out above

    (2) (a) To pay any council tax which the Tenant is obliged to pay under the Local Government Finance Act 1992 or any regulations under that Act

    (b) To pay to the Landlord the amount of any council tax which, while the tenancy continues, the Landlord becomes obliged to pay under that Act or those regulations for any part of the period of the tenancy because the Tenant ceases to live at the Property

    (c) To pay all other charges of any kind which are now or later come to be charged to the occupier of the Property as such by any body acting under statutory authority in making such a charge

    (3) To pay for all gas, electricity, water and sewerage services supplied to the Property during the tenancy and to pay all charges for the use of any telephone at the Property during the tenancy. Where necessary, the sums demanded by the service provider will be apportioned according to the duration of the tenancy. The sums covered by this clause include standing charges or other similar charges and VAT as well as charges for actual consumption

(4)   To keep the interior of the Property, the internal decorations and the fixtures, fittings and appliances in the Property in good repair and condition (except for damage caused by accidental fire and except for anything which the Landlord is liable to repair under this Agreement or by law). This clause does not oblige the Tenant to put the Property into better repair than it was in at the beginning of the tenancy

(5)   To allow the Landlord or anyone with the Landlord's written authority to enter the Property at reasonable times of the day to inspect its condition and state of repair, if the Landlord has given 24 hours' written notice beforehand

(6)   To use the Property as   residential only

(7)   Not to alter or add to the Property or do or allow anyone else to do anything on the Property which the Tenant might reasonably foresee would increase the risk of fire

(8)   Not to do or allow anyone else to do anything on the Property which may be a nuisance to, or cause damage or annoyance to, the tenants or occupiers of any adjoining premises or which may adversely affect the energy efficiency rating or the environmental impact rating of the Property for the purposes of an energy performance certificate

(9)   Not to assign or sublet the Property and not to part with possession of the Property in any other way without the Landlord's consent (but the Landlord will not unreasonably refuse or delay dealing with a request for consent to an assignment or subletting). If the Property is not residential property and the Landlord agrees that the Tenant may assign it, the Landlord's agreement may be given subject to the condition that the Tenant will enter into an authorised guarantee agreement within the meaning of the Landlord and Tenant (Covenants) Act 1995

(10)   To give the Landlord a copy of any notice given under the Party Wall etc. Act 1996 within seven days of receiving it and not to do anything as a result of the notice unless required to do so by the Landlord

(11)   To ensure that all smoke and carbon monoxide alarms at the Property are in good working order at all times and in the event of any failure of such devices to notify the Landlord as soon as reasonably practicable

(**Note:** In England the Landlord is responsible for ensuring that appropriate smoke and carbon monoxide alarms are installed in the property and for checking them on the first day of the tenancy.)

(12)   At the end of the Term or earlier if the tenancy comes to an end more quickly to deliver the Property up to the Landlord in the condition it should be in if the Tenant has performed the Tenant's obligations under this Agreement

(13)   During the last twenty-eight days of the tenancy to allow the Landlord or the Landlord's agents to put up a notice that the Property is to be let and to enter and view the Property with prospective tenants at reasonable times of the day if the Landlord has given 24 hours' written notice beforehand

(14)   Not without the prior written consent of the Landlord to permit any person aged 18 or over who is not named in this Agreement to occupy the Property, such consent not to be unreasonably withheld or delayed

(15)   Not to permit any person aged 18 or over to continue to occupy the Property (whether or not named in this Agreement) if that person becomes disqualified as a result of his or her immigration status for the purposes of the Immigration Act 2014

(16)   To do anything reasonably required by the Landlord to enable the Landlord or the Landlord's agent to perform the Landlord's obligations and to comply with any prescribed requirements under the Immigration Act 2014.

3.   **IF** the Tenant -

(1) is at least fourteen days late in paying the Rent or any part of it, whether or not the Rent has been formally demanded, or

(2) has broken any of the terms of this Agreement

then, subject to any statutory provisions, the Landlord may recover possession of the Property and the tenancy will come to an end. Any other rights or remedies the Landlord may have will remain in force.

(**Note:** If the Property is residential, the Landlord may not be able to recover possession without an order of the court under the Housing Act 1988. In some cases set out in the Act the court must make a possession order. In other cases, the court has a discretion whether or not to make an order and is likely to take account of whether unpaid rent has later been paid or a breach of the terms of the tenancy has been made good

Note: If the Landlord wishes to recover possession under section 21 of the Housing Act 1988, the Landlord must give the Tenant notice before the right to recover possession can be exercised. The Landlord should check what statutory requirements, if any, apply to the form of notice and when it can be served.

Note: This clause does not affect any rights of the Tenant under the Protection from Eviction Act 1977.)

4.   **THE** Landlord agrees with the Tenant that the Tenant has the right to possess and enjoy the Property during the tenancy without any interruption from the Landlord or any person claiming through or in trust for the Landlord. But:

(1) this clause does not limit any of the rights under this Agreement which the Tenant has agreed to allow the Landlord to exercise;

(2) this clause does not prevent the Landlord from taking lawful steps to enforce his rights against the Tenant if the Tenant breaks any of the terms of this Agreement.

AGREE1/3

5. **IF** section 11 of the Landlord and Tenant Act 1985 applies to the tenancy, the Tenant's obligations are subject to the effect of that section.

(**Note:** As a general rule, section 11 applies to tenancies of a dwelling-house for a term of less than seven years. It requires the landlord to keep in repair the structure and exterior of the dwelling-house including drains, gutters and external pipes; and to keep in repair and proper working order the installations for the supply of water, gas and electricity, for sanitation (including basins, sinks, baths and sanitary conveniences) and for space heating and heating water. The landlord is not obliged to repair until the tenant has given notice of the defect, and the tenant is obliged to take proper care of the Property and to do small jobs which a reasonable tenant would do.)

6. **IF** the Property is damaged to such an extent that the Tenant cannot live in it, the Rent will cease to be payable until the Property is rebuilt or repaired so that the Tenant can live there again unless

   (1) the cause of the damage is something which the Tenant did or failed to do as a result of which the Landlord's insurance policy relating to the Property has become void; and

   (2) the Landlord had given the Tenant notice of what the policy required.

   Any dispute about whether this clause applies must be submitted to arbitration under Part I of the Arbitration Act 1996 if both parties agree to that in writing after the dispute has arisen.

7. **IF** this Agreement is signed before the Landlord or the Landlord's agent has fully complied with all relevant prescribed requirements under the Immigration Act 2014, the grant in clause 1 above is conditional upon the Landlord or the Landlord's agent being satisfied on reasonable grounds after completion of the prescribed requirements that the grant of the rights given by this Agreement would not give rise to a contravention of the provisions of that Act.

8. **WHERE** the context permits –

   (1) "The Landlord" includes the successors to the original landlord

   (2) "The Tenant" includes the successors to the original tenant

   (3) "The Property" includes any part of the Property.

NOTICE OF LANDLORD'S ADDRESS

The Landlord notifies the Tenant that the Tenant may serve notices (including notices in proceedings) on the Landlord at the following address:

Flat 1, The Warren
Maryfield,
Greenfordshire

(This notice is given under section 48 of the Landlord and Tenant Act 1987, if applicable. The address must be in England or Wales.)

AS WITNESS the hands of the parties on the date specified above

SIGNED by the above-named

   BRIAN SMITH

(the Landlord) in the presence of

Paul Jones
Flat 2, The Warren

SIGNED by the above-named

   TREVOR HOOD

(the Tenant) in the presence of

Fenella Jones
Flat 2, The Warren

DATED   17 September 2010

BRIAN SMITH

and

TREVOR HOOD

Tenancy Agreement
for letting

Rent £ 1,000 per month

THINKING POINT

What kind of a document is this?

This is clearly a tenancy agreement—a contract between the parties, Brian Smith and Trevor Hood. Remember that the terms 'lease' and 'tenancy' are often used interchangeably. If the property being let is residential, it is usually called a tenancy, as in this case. The term 'lease' is more often used in commercial agreements. It is also a deed: it is a formal document that is independently witnessed and signed as a deed.

THINKING POINT

Who is the landlord?

Who is the tenant?

The landlord is Brian Smith and the tenant is Trevor Hood. The names and addresses of the parties are referred to as the 'preliminaries', contained in the 'premises' part of the agreement.

THINKING POINT

Which property is Brian letting to Trevor?

Brian is letting Flat 4, The Warren, to Trevor.

THINKING POINT

What is the term of the tenancy—that is for how long is the tenancy to be held?

The tenancy is for a term of ten years. The term is fixed, in that it has a certain start date and a certain end date. Note that, after the tenancy has come to an end, there is a provision for a monthly periodic tenancy. Remember that certainty of term is one of the essential requirements of a tenancy (see 5.5.1).

THINKING POINT

How much is the rent and when is it payable?

The rent is £1,000 per month, payable in advance—that is, at the beginning of each payment period—on the 17th of every month.

THINKING POINT

Can you see the tenant's covenants?

The tenant's covenants (see 5.6.2) begin at clause 2: 'THE tenant agrees with the landlord ...'

These covenants are fairly standard. They include provision that the tenant (Trevor) will pay rent (clause 2(1)), Council Tax (clause 2(2)(a)), gas and electricity bills (clause 2(3)), etc. They also provide that Trevor will keep the interior of the property in good condition, but that he does not have to leave the property in a better condition at the end of the tenancy than that in which it was at the beginning (clause 2(4)).

The tenant's covenants also include giving the landlord permission to enter and inspect the premises at reasonable times, and with appropriate notice (clause 2(5)).

There are also some things that Trevor cannot do with the property. For example, he cannot sublet it—that is, let it out to another tenant—without the landlord's permission (clause 2(9)), nor can he do anything that may be a nuisance to his neighbours (clause 2(8)).

In this tenancy, the covenants are contained in the body of the agreement. Sometimes—particularly in more complicated, or commercial, tenancies—the covenants are set out in schedules that are attached to the tenancy.

THINKING POINT

Can you see the landlord's covenants?

The landlord's covenants (see 5.6.1) begin at clause 4: 'THE Landlord agrees with the tenant ...'

These covenants are fairly short in this tenancy agreement, but include the provision that the tenant may enjoy the property with quiet enjoyment—that is, without interruption (disturbance) from the landlord. The tenancy also confers exclusive possession of the tenanted premises on Trevor—another essential element of a tenancy (see 5.5.3).

Remember as well that the law implies certain covenants into a tenancy agreement (see 5.6).

THINKING POINT

Is there anything in the tenancy that provides for what will happen if the tenant breaches a covenant—for example, if Trevor does not pay his rent?

Clause 3 says that, if Trevor is at least fourteen days late with his rent or breaks any of the other covenants, then Brian can repossess the property and the tenancy will come to an end. This is called a forfeiture clause.

THINKING POINT

Does this tenancy need to be registered?

Because this is a tenancy for more than seven years, it must be registered whether or not the landlord's estate is registered—LRA 2002, ss. 4(2)(b) and 27(2)(b). Once it has been registered and because it has been made by deed, it will be a legal tenancy, complying with LPA 1925, s. 52(1).

5.9 Ending a lease

Once the lease has ended, the tenant ceases to have any interest in the leased property: it reverts back to the landlord in its entirety. If the tenant stays on in the property without the landlord's permission, the landlord can take legal steps to remove (evict) the ex-tenant from the property. In these circumstances, the most likely and safest course of action for the landlord is to seek an order for possession of the property through the courts before evicting the tenant. Attempting to re-enter a residential property without a court order may result in the landlord facing criminal charges, particularly if he or she threatens or uses violence to do so. Considerable statutory provision protects tenants of residential properties, and landlords will follow the appropriate procedures for seeking possession according to the various types of tenancy. The landlord can also seek a possession order from the court if the tenant has breached some of the covenants in the lease, or is in rent arrears.

Eviction can cause considerable distress and hardship for the tenant. Equally, a landlord unable to evict a tenant who has stopped paying rent can face considerable distress and financial difficulties him- or herself. Parliament has tried to balance the rights of both landlord and tenant in the different forms of legislation. A recent Supreme Court case addressed the important issue of whether the court had to consider the proportionality of an eviction when deciding whether or not to make an order for possession in a private residential tenancy.

Q CASE CLOSE-UP

McDonald v. McDonald [2016] UKSC 28

Mr and Mrs McDonald purchased a property for their adult daughter, Fiona, to live in. Fiona had significant mental health issues, and was unable to work. She had twice before been evicted from public sector tenancies. Her parents bought the property with the assistance of a mortgage, and intended to pay the mortgage repayments with the housing benefit which would pay Fiona's rent for the property, as they had granted her a series of assured shorthold tenancies.

This worked well for a while, until Mr and Mrs McDonald had some business difficulties. They fell behind in their repayments of the mortgage and eventually the lender appointed Receivers to take possession of the property and sell it to recover the outstanding mortgage debt.

The Receivers applied for an order of possession of the property at the county court, to evict Fiona. (For technical reasons, the Receivers were required to do this in the name of Fiona's parents—hence *McDonald v. McDonald.*) At the hearing, expert evidence was given as to the implications of an eviction on Fiona's mental health. The Court heard that it would impact significantly on her, and that as she was unlikely to find alternative accommodation, it was likely that she would become homeless. There was a possibility that she would harm herself or others, or that she would commit suicide. The judge found that an order for possession should

> ❯ CROSS REFERENCE
>
> For more on mortgages, see Chapter 14, especially 14.3.3 on the lender's remedies.

be made, subject to the possibility that Fiona's rights may be protected by Article 8 of the European Convention on Human Rights.

When he considered the applicability of Article 8, he held that the Court could not be asked to consider the issue of proportionality, because Fiona was a residential tenant of a private landlord, and it was that private landlord who was seeking possession. He therefore granted the order for possession.

However, the judge went on to say that if the landlord had been a public authority, then the issue of proportionality would need to be considered by the court, and if that had been the case, the judge said that the circumstances were so exceptional that he would have dismissed the application for possession of the property. Fiona appealed to the Court of Appeal, who dismissed the appeal, and also said that it disagreed with the judge's suggestion that the circumstances were so exceptional that if he had been able to, he would have refused the possession order. Fiona then appealed to the Supreme Court.

The Supreme Court identified three issues before it:

1. Whether a court considering an application for an order for possession against a residential occupier of a private landlord should be required to consider the issue of proportionality under s. 6 of the Human Rights Act 1998 and Article 8 of the European Convention on Human Rights;

2. If the answer to that question is 'yes', could the relevant legislation be read to comply with that conclusion;

3. If the answer to questions 1 and 2 was 'yes', whether the trial judge would have been entitled to dismiss the claim for possession as he suggested that he would have done.

After careful consideration of government policy since 1977 and particularly the nature of assured shorthold tenancies (the type of tenancy that Fiona had), their Lordships reviewed the relevant UK housing legislation and case law precedent. The Court referred to earlier housing cases such as *Manchester City Council v. Pinnock* [2010] UKSC 45, which clearly established that in highly exceptional cases, where a local authority (or other public authority) is seeking possession of a person's home, it would be appropriate for the court to consider the proportionality argument. However, in *Pinnock* the Court had made it very clear that this did not apply to the court's consideration of claims for possession orders by private landlords.

After considering Fiona's arguments, the Court decided '[i]n the absence of any clear and authoritative guidance from the Strasbourg Court to the contrary' (at 40), that although Article 8 may well be engaged when a private landlord brings a possession claim against a residential tenant, it was not open to the tenant to suggest that Article 8 could justify the court making an order which would be contrary to the contractual terms into which the parties had entered. The existing UK legislation had already performed the balancing exercise between the rights of landlord and tenant, and reflected Parliament's conclusion as to the appropriate balance.

If the Supreme Court had decided otherwise, then it would have meant that the rights under the European Convention on Human Rights would have been directly enforceable between private citizens (and so would have 'horizontal effect')—when the Convention was intended to protect the rights of citizens from interference by the state.

It would also mean that the Convention rights of the landlord might be compromised: for example, if the court postponed a possession order for a significant time using the Article 8 argument, then the landlord may well suffer significant financial loss, without compensation. The Court raised the unwelcome possibility of landlords being effectively incentivized to take the law into their own hands in relation to evicting tenants, rather than through the court process, if an additional requirement of proportionality were to be imposed. Their Lordships concluded:

> In the field of proprietary rights between parties neither of whom is a public authority, the state should be allowed to lay down rules which are of general application, with a view to ensuring consistency of application and certainty of outcome. Those are two essential ingredients of the rule of law, and accepting the appellant's argument in this case would involve diluting those rules in relation to possession actions in the private rented sector. (at 43)

Although their Lordships' decision on the first issue meant that it was unnecessary for them to consider the second and third issues, given the potential importance of those issues, they went on to consider them. In respect of the second issue, the Court held that the relevant section was not incompatible with Convention rights. In relation to the third, it held that Fiona's circumstances, although undoubtedly unfortunate, were not so exceptional as to justify an indefinite postponement to possession, and that if it had been open to the Court to order such a postponement after a proportionality assessment, it was likely to be for a period of around six weeks. Consequently, their Lordships dismissed the appeal.

This is an important decision for private landlords, who may otherwise have been significantly disadvantaged in possession proceedings.

Some fixed-period leases simply end with the passing of time. When the period for which the lease has been granted reaches an end, it automatically terminates. Many leases, however, require notice to be given, in accordance with the terms of the lease agreement. This is true of private, residential leases, which are now fairly heavily regulated by statute.

We have also seen that, if a fixed lease ends and the tenant stays on with the landlord's permission, a periodic tenancy is created. This continues until one or the other side gives notice that he or she intends to terminate the tenancy. As discussed at 5.3.2.2, the notice period will be defined by the intervals at which rent has been agreed to be paid.

The tenant can bring the lease to an end either by express or implied **surrender**, which effectively means that he gives the property back to the landlord. The tenant usually achieves this by vacating the property and the landlord has to accept the surrender.

> **surrender**
> the giving up of a tenant's interest in a property to his or her landlord, which might be in the form of a deed (express) or as a consequence of the actions of both parties (implied)

Finally, remembering that a lease has its roots in contract law, it appears that a lease may also be terminated according to contractual principles. This can be achieved by **repudiation** of the lease agreement—that is, if one of the fundamental terms of the contract is to be breached. In *Hussein v. Mehlman* [1992] 2 EGLR 87, the Court held that a landlord's continuing breach of his covenant to repair the premises allowed the tenant to repudiate the contract.

> **repudiation** an indication that a breach of contract will occur in the future, leading to the end of that contract

It also appears that a lease can be terminated by the doctrine of **frustration**—[1981] AC 675.

> **frustration** the termination of a contract as a result of an event that renders its performance impossible or illegal, or otherwise prevents its fulfilment

5.10 Commonhold

commonhold

a way of owning property that features shared areas, for which ownership needs to remain in central ownership and maintenance

Commonhold is a relatively new development in land law. It is aimed at those people who own long leases of properties in a building in which there are a number of such leasehold properties, such as an old house that is subdivided into flats, which are held on long leases, or a block of leasehold flats or offices.

Before the Commonhold and Leasehold Reform Act 2002 (CLRA 2002), the leaseholders of the individual units of property had no choice other than to pay ground rent to the freeholder who still owned the property as a whole. They would also have to pay a service charge to repair and maintain the property, but often would have little say in how their money was spent.

The legislation gives leaseholders in this situation the opportunity to obtain the freehold of their individual property and, collectively, to buy the freehold of the property as a whole. This gives them the opportunity to have a say in how the common parts of the property are maintained and so gives them more control over how their money is spent.

We will now look at the legislative detail of the scheme.

CLRA 2002, s. 1(1), sets out three requirements that must be met for the land to be commonhold.

 STATUTE

Commonhold and Leasehold Reform Act 2002, s. 1(1)

Land is commonhold land if—

   (a) the freehold estate in the land is registered as a freehold estate in commonhold land,

   (b) the land is specified in the memorandum of association of a commonhold association as the land in relation to which the association is to exercise functions, and

   (c) a commonhold community statement makes provision for rights and duties of the commonhold association and unit-holders (whether or not the statement has come into force).

The land, as a whole, must therefore be registered land. The leaseholders then need to set up a **commonhold association**.

commonhold association

the formal body that commonhold leaseholders must establish to manage the common parts of the property so held

This is effectively the group that will manage the common parts of the property. It operates as a management company and must be formally set up, which means that it must be limited by guarantee and registered at Companies House—CLRA 2002, s. 34.

This company is responsible for establishing a reserve fund to maintain the property. To do this, the individual leaseholders will pay service charges, much as they did before—but now they will have more control over how their money is spent. The association must also produce a commonhold community statement, the form of which is governed by CLRA 2002, s. 31. It must fundamentally define the land to be managed by the association, and set out its rights and duties.

If the leaseholders comply with these requirements, they can apply to the Land Registrar to register their commonhold as 'a freehold estate in commonhold land'—CLRA 2002, s. 2(1). In order to register the title, the leaseholders must obtain the consent of the registered proprietor of the freehold of the land (or part of it), the registered proprietors of any leaseholds of over twenty-one years in length, anyone with a charge over the land (so, for example, a mortgagee), and other classes of person that may be prescribed.

If all of the necessary formal requirements have been carried out, the commonhold estate will be registered, both in its own right and on the register entries of the individual proprietors of the property.

As you will see in Chapter 13, there are difficulties involved in enforcing freehold covenants on subsequent owners of land. One of the key advantages of the new scheme is that, when an individual property is sold, any of the rights and duties imposed on the original commonhold owner will be automatically transferred to the new commonhold owner, making life a lot easier for all involved. It should be noted, however, that at the time of writing, very few commonholds have been adopted, and the scheme is widely considered to be unsuccessful.

Summary

1. A lease confers an estate in the land, for a certain period.

2. A lease is a hybrid of contract and proprietary interest.

3. A lease can be legal or equitable, depending on its method of creation.

4. There are various different types of lease, but they all share the same essential characteristics: that the tenant receives exclusive possession for a certain term.

5. Rent is not an essential element, although it is usually present and is indicative of a lease.

6. Even though all of the essential elements of a lease are present, it may still be a licence if there is no intention to create legal relations, or if there is a service occupancy, or—possibly—if the grantor lacks the estate to grant a lease.

7. Leases contain covenants, which impose various obligations on both landlord and tenant.

8. There are rules governing the enforcement of covenants for which the original landlord has assigned his reversionary interest or the original tenant has assigned his tenancy. The rules differ depending on whether the lease came into being before or from 1 January 1996.

9. A lease can be terminated by the passing of time, giving appropriate notice, surrender by the tenant, and the contractual principles of repudiation and frustration.

10. Commonhold is a new kind of landholding that allows owners of leasehold property to obtain the freehold of their individual property and (collectively) of the whole property.

11. Commonhold assists with the transfer of covenants to subsequent owners.

The bigger picture

- If you want to see how this area of land law fits into the rest of your studies, you can look at Chapter 15, especially 15.4.

- For some guidance on what sort of exam questions come up in this area, see Chapter 16, 16.7.

- The Mortgage Repossessions (Protection of Tenants etc.) Act 2010 offers some protection to the tenant in situations where a homeowner (mortgagor) has let the property to the tenant without the permission of the bank who is the mortgagee of the property, and the bank is trying to repossess the property.

- Read more about this at: http://www.communities.gov.uk/publications/housing/mortgagerepossessionguidance.

- Read more about mortgages in Chapter 14.

? Questions

Self-test questions

1. How is a valid legal lease created? What happens if the formal requirements are not carried out?

2. Sasha and Michael move into a one-bedroom flat together. They are a little concerned about two clauses in their 'licence agreement': that the owner of the property reserves the right to move in with them at any time and that they must vacate their premises between 10.30 a.m. and noon each day. Advise Sasha and Michael.

3. Halle has just moved into a new rented flat. She is a little confused about some of the clauses in the lease. Explain to Halle the meaning of the terms 'quiet enjoyment' and 'waste'. If she assigns her interest to Brendan, will he also be bound by the covenants?

Exam question

1. What are the essential characteristics of a lease? If all of these are present, will a lease always be created?

 You will find answers to these questions online at www.oup.com/uk/clarke_directions6e/.

≡ Further Reading

Baker, A., 'Bruton, licensees in possession and a fiction of title' [2014] 6 Conv 495

A thoughtful re-interpretation of Bruton, based on the premise that consensual possession is a root of title.

Bright, S., 'Avoiding tenancy legislation: sham and contracting out revisited' (2002) 61(1) CLJ 146

A look at the courts' approach to the attempts of landlords to avoid creating tenancies.

Clarke, D., 'The enactment of commonhold: problems, principles and perspectives' [2002] July/Aug Conv 349

An analysis of the CLRA 2002.

Lower, M., 'The Bruton Tenancy' [2010] 1 Conv 38

This article looks at the idea of the non-proprietary lease, particularly in Bruton and its application in subsequent cases.

Pascoe, S., 'The end of the road for human rights in private landowners' disputes?' [2017] 4 Conv 269

A thoughtful discussion of the role of human rights law in private landlord cases, following the Supreme Court decision of *McDonald v. McDonald* [2016] UKSC 28.

Smith, P., 'The purity of commonholds' [2004] May/Jun Conv 194

This article examines the relationship between leases and commonholds.

Street v. Mountford [1985] AC 809

It really is worth reading this case in its entirety.

 ## Online Resources

For more advice relating to this chapter, including self-test questions and an interactive glossary, visit www.oup.com/uk/clarke_directions6e/.

6 Adverse possession

LEARNING OBJECTIVES

By the end of this chapter, you will be able to:

- explain what is meant by 'adverse possession';
- understand the rationale for adverse possession;
- distinguish between the old law and the new law in this area;
- understand the law under the Land Registration Act 2002.

Introduction

To see how controversial and important the law on adverse possession has been in the recent past, you need look no further than the leading case in the area: *J. A. Pye (Oxford) Ltd and Others v. Graham and Another* [2002] UKHL 30 *(Pye v. Graham)*. The Grahams, who were farmers, had been using land belonging to a development company (Pye Ltd) to graze their cattle for many years. When Pye Ltd finally wanted to build on the land, the Grahams refused to leave. Pye Ltd sued them in the High Court, but lost, so they appealed to the Court of Appeal, and won. The Grahams then appealed to the House of Lords—and they won! The land, now worth some £10m, belonged to the Grahams, who had used it without paying rent for years, and who now owned it outright. Dismayed, Pye Ltd took its case to the European Court of Human Rights (*J. A. Pye v. United Kingdom*, Application No. 44302/02, 15 November 2005 *(Pye v. United Kingdom)*), where it was held that its human rights had been breached. This did not entitle Pye Ltd to get the land back, but it looked forward to compensation from the UK government. Unfortunately for Pye Ltd, the government appealed to the Grand Chamber, which reversed the previous decision (*J. A. Pye v. United Kingdom,* Application No. 44302/02, 30 August 2007 *(Pye v. United Kingdom)*). Pye Ltd, once the owner of a valuable piece of development land, was left with no land and no compensation—as well as a huge legal bill. How could such a case come about?

This remarkable (and expensive) litigation arose because of the law of adverse possession, which essentially deals with what most people refer to as 'squatters' rights'. It is about squatters taking possession of land without the consent of the owner, which may ultimately lead to the loss of the estate in land from the paper owner to the squatter.

The whole concept of adverse possession seems very strange to most people. In effect, it makes lawful the 'stealing' of land by someone who has no documentary title to it. This raises the question of why the law should allow a squatter in possession of land to claim ownership of it.

The situation described here is extreme: most adverse possession is on a smaller scale and, indeed, it is not always a hostile act. Small areas of land often 'move' between owners when boundary fences are replaced or realigned, and this may happen by mistake rather than by design. The rules of adverse possession are very old and were originally developed under the common law, but the current law can now be found mainly in the Limitation Act 1980 and the Land Registration Act 2002. In this chapter we will first look at why the law permits adverse possession and then at the detailed rules. Because the law changed in 2003, we will need to look at both the old and the new laws. Suffice to say, it has become more difficult to obtain property by adverse possession and, for squatters like the Grahams, the days of acquiring valuable development land for nothing are probably over.

6.1 Reasons for allowing adverse possession

One argument in favour of **adverse possession** is that there has to be a cut-off point in any legal action. You may remember from studying contract law that a person cannot sue on a contract after six years, because at that point the claim becomes stale. In the same way, there has to be some point at which a landowner is too late to claim land back from someone who has been in possession of it for a long time.

Most people would agree that, if someone has been peacefully in possession of a piece of land for many years, it would be too late for someone else to wave a piece of paper claiming title and get the land back. In fact, the **limitation period** for reclaiming land is currently usually twelve years for unregistered land and registered land adversely possessed before 13 October 2003 (see 6.9.2). For registered land adversely possessed after that date, there is no period of limitation as such (see 6.9.2), but the **squatter** may apply to be registered after ten years of adverse possession.

Another argument is that land is a finite resource. If a landowner has not even noticed for many years that someone else is occupying his or her land, why should that person not make better use of it? The squatter might even have wanted to ask permission to use the land, but may not have known for sure who the **paper owner** was. Adverse possession provides a way for abandoned land to be brought into economic use again.

Everybody has heard the maxim 'possession is nine-tenths of the law' and, traditionally, English land law has paid great attention to possession. Any person in peaceful possession of land is treated as having good title to it unless someone else can show a better title—*Harrow London Borough Council v. Qazi* [2003] UKHL 43, [2004] 1 AC 983.

---

adverse possession

the possession of land by someone other than the registered proprietor or unregistered owner, without that proprietor or owner's consent

---

limitation period

statutory time limit after which no action to reclaim land under adverse possession can be started

---

squatter

a person in adverse possession of land

---

paper owner

the person who holds the documentary title—the 'papers'—to the land

---

→ **EXAMPLE**

Arif has been squatting on land for five years. Barbara tries to evict him from the land, claiming that he has no right to be there, because he is not the registered owner.

Barbara is not entitled to succeed unless she can show a better claim to the land than Arif: for example, if she is the registered proprietor, or if she inherited the land under the will of the registered proprietor, or she has been granted a lease by the registered proprietor. Barbara may even win if she shows that she adversely possessed the land in the past, by possessing it for twelve years.

It is not enough, however, for Barbara simply to show that Arif himself has no title. He is entitled to stay there until someone with a better right to possession comes along.

relativity of title

the doctrine that all rights to land are relative and that the person with the best title will be entitled to the land

This aspect of the common law is sometimes called **relativity of title**. The courts looked at all rights to land as relative and would declare the person with the best title to be entitled to the land.

Adverse possession also plays a vital role in relation to unregistered land, in that peaceful possession will eventually cure any defects in title to land. As there is no definitive proof of title in unregistered land, a good root of title going back at least fifteen years is accepted as proof. If the current owner and any predecessors can show peaceful possession for at least twelve years under that title, the law of adverse possession means that the title can be regarded as safe.

> **CROSS REFERENCE**
> For more on establishing title in unregistered land, see Chapter 3, 3.3.3.1.

6.2 Arguments against allowing adverse possession

Despite the long-standing common law protection of possession, there are convincing arguments against adverse possession in modern times.

The vast majority of titles to land are now registered and it is the fact of registration that confers legal title upon the landowner. This makes any argument that is based on relativity of title less convincing, because the register guarantees title.

A squatter can easily look up the proprietor in the register, which is now available online, and negotiate to buy, or lease, apparently unwanted land. Only if the registered proprietor has disappeared without trace is there much justification for a squatter gaining title simply by moving in.

These concerns about adverse possession in modern times were well expressed by Lord Bingham in *Pye v. Graham*.

🔍 CASE CLOSE-UP

Pye v. Graham [2002] UKHL 30

This case (discussed in more detail at 6.5.2.1) concerned the Grahams, farmers who adversely possessed grazing land belonging to an investment company, Pye Ltd.

In giving judgment for the Grahams, Lord Bingham criticized the law of adverse possession as it applied to registered land. He pointed out that the Grahams had been using the land for many years without paying any rent and now had become the owners of very valuable land—worth £10m—without having paid a penny for it, or having to compensate the paper owner in any way.

This does seem unfair. In registered land, if there is no doubt about who actually owns the land, there seems to be very little justification for such a result.

There have also been concerns about squatters moving into empty property such as houses awaiting renovation, or the homes of persons who have died. It can take the paper owners of such properties time and trouble to evict squatters, and the property may be damaged.

6.3 Changes to the law

In their joint report of 1998, the Law Commission and the Land Registry recognized the concerns about the justice of acquiring land by adverse possession in modern times, particularly when that land is registered. The reasons for adverse possession are discussed at paras 10.1–10.19 of the report and it was concluded that the law of adverse possession as it applies to registered land should be reformed. This was a major change in policy, because previously the law relating to registered and unregistered land had been kept as similar as possible. The Land Registration Act 2002 (LRA 2002) changed completely the way in which title to registered land can be acquired by adverse possession.

Even more recently, the Legal Aid, Sentencing and Punishment of Offenders Act 2012 (LASPOA 2012), s. 144, made squatting in residential property a criminal act. This has an effect on gaining title to such land by adverse possession, which we will look at later (see 6.7).

Table 6.1 represents a summary of the relevant dates and provisions.

Table 6.1 A summary of the law of adverse possession

Type of land	Completion of limitation period	Relevant law
Unregistered	Since 1980	Limitation Act 1980
Registered	By 12 October 2003	Limitation Act 1980 and LRA 1925, s.75
Registered	From 13 October 2003	LRA 2002
Registered and unregistered residential buildings	From 1 September 2012	LASPOA 2012, s.144

6.4 The main statutory provisions

6.4.1 The Limitation Act 1980

The Limitation Act 1980 (LA 1980) applies to unregistered land whatever the date of adverse possession; it also applies to registered land if the required period of adverse possession was completed before 13 October 2003—the date on which LRA 2002 came into force.

The LA 1980 works by preventing the paper owner from bringing an action to recover the land once the limitation period has passed. The Act was applied to registered land by the Land Registration Act 1925 (LRA 1925), s. 75 (see 6.9.2).

The main limitation periods are detailed in Table 6.2.

Table 6.2 The main limitation periods

Land	Length of adverse possession required	Authority
Most land	12 years from moment of adverse possession by squatter	LA 1980, s. 15
Land owned by Crown (see, for example, *Roberts v. Swangrove Estates* [2008] EWCA Civ 98)	30 years, but 60 years if the land is foreshore	LA 1980, Sch.1, para. 11
Land held by a tenant under a lease	12 years as against tenant, but a further 12 years as against freeholder when lease comes to an end	*Chung Ping Kwang v. Lam Island Co. Ltd* [1997] AC 38

After the end of the limitation period, the paper owner can no longer go to court to recover the land, which means that the squatter can no longer be evicted.

Note that the time does not stop running even when the squatter transfers the land to someone else, or a different squatter comes into possession, as long as there is no gap between the periods of adverse possession.

 EXAMPLE

Carrie goes into adverse possession of Dave's house.

Four years later, Carrie transfers such rights as she has in the house to Egon. Nine years later, Dave brings an action to evict Egon.

He will be too late, because Egon can add his period of adverse possession to that of Carrie. Egon will be entitled to Dave's land.

The statutory provisions setting out what is required in order to prove adverse possession are in LA 1980, Sch. 1, which establishes the time at which the limitation period starts to run. These provisions are explained at 6.5.

 STATUTE

Limitation Act 1980, Sch. 1, para. 1

Where the person bringing an action to recover land, or some person through whom he claims, has been in possession of the land, and has while entitled to the land been dispossessed or discontinued his possession, the right of action shall be treated as having accrued on the date of the dispossession or discontinuance.

STATUTE

Limitation Act 1980, Sch. 1, para. 8(1)

No right of action to recover land shall be treated as accruing unless the land is in the possession of some person in whose favour the period of limitation can run (referred to below in this paragraph as 'adverse possession'); and where under the preceding provisions of this Schedule any such right of action is treated as accruing on a certain date and no person is in adverse possession on that date, the right of action shall not be treated as accruing unless and until adverse possession is taken of the land.

Adverse possession under the LA 1980 extinguishes the title of the paper owner under s. 17.

 STATUTE

Limitation Act 1980, s. 17 [Extinction of title to land after expiration of time limit]

Subject to—

(a) section 18 of this Act; and

…

at the expiration of the period prescribed by this Act for any person to bring an action to recover land (including a redemption action) the title of that person to the land shall be extinguished.

This means that the squatter becomes the owner of the land, but with no conveyance of land by the paper owner to the squatter. (The full effects of this are explained at 6.8.)

6.4.2 The Land Registration Act 1925

The main purpose of LRA 1925, s. 75, was to apply the LA 1980 to registered land. It now applies only when the period of limitation was already complete before 13 October 2003—the date on which the LRA 2002 came into force.

Where title to the adversely possessed land was registered, the extinguishing effect of LA 1980, s. 17, presented some problems. The title of the paper owner could not simply vanish, because it was still on the register. Once adverse possession had been established, the squatter could apply to be registered as a proprietor; but what happened in the meantime, after the limitation period had been completed and before the squatter had been registered as proprietor? How were the conflicting titles of the registered proprietor and the squatter to be resolved?

The answer was provided by LRA 1925, s. 75.

 STATUTE

Land Registration Act 1925, s. 75 [Acquisition of title by possession]

(1) The Limitation Acts shall apply to registered land in the same manner and to the same extent as those Acts apply to land not registered, except that where, if the

> land were not registered, the estate of the person registered as proprietor would be
> extinguished, such estate shall not be extinguished but shall be deemed to be held
> by the proprietor for the time being on trust for the person who, by virtue of the said
> Acts, has acquired title against any proprietor, but without prejudice to the estates
> and interests of any other person interested in the land whose estate or interest is not
> extinguished by those Acts.
>
> (2) Any person claiming to have acquired a title under the Limitation Acts may apply to
> be registered as proprietor thereof.
>
> …

As can be seen from this section, the paper owner's title was not extinguished, but was instead held on trust for the squatter. (The full effects of this are explained at 6.9.2.1.)

6.4.3 **The Land Registration Act 2002**

LRA 2002, ss. 96–98, apply to registered land when the limitation period under the LA 1980 has not been completed before 13 October 2003. In other words, unless there were twelve years of adverse possession before that date, the new law applies to registered land.

 STATUTE

Land Registration Act 2002, s. 96 [Disapplication of periods of limitation]

(1) No period of limitation under section 15 of the Limitation Act 1980 (c. 58) (time limits in relation to recovery of land) shall run against any person, other than a chargee, in relation to an estate in land or rentcharge the title to which is registered.

(2) No period of limitation under section 16 of that Act (time limits in relation to redemption of land) shall run against any person in relation to such an estate in land or rentcharge.

(3) Accordingly, section 17 of that Act (extinction of title on expiry of time limit) does not operate to extinguish the title of any person where, by virtue of this section, a period of limitation does not run against him.

The most fundamental change made by this section is that there is no longer an automatic barring of title by adverse possession. This means that adverse possession, of itself, does not bar the registered proprietor's title; instead, after being in adverse possession for ten years, the squatter can apply to be registered as the proprietor. Until such an application is made, the squatter has no rights in the land and can usually be evicted by the registered proprietor. (More details are set out at 6.9.2.2.)

6.4.4 **The Legal Aid, Sentencing and Punishment of Offenders Act 2012**

LASPOA 2012, s. 144, makes squatting in residential premises a criminal offence. This does not prevent the squatter from claiming adverse possession *(Best v. Chief Land Registrar* [2015] EWCA Civ 17) but naturally it will act as a deterrent. (For more details see 6.7.)

6.5 WHAT DOES A SQUATTER NEED TO SHOW TO MAKE A CLAIM TO THE LAND?

175

6.5 What does a squatter need to show to make a claim to the land?

No matter which set of legislation applies, there are certain points that must be established before a person can be said to be in adverse possession of someone else's land. They apply equally to registered and unregistered land and to both the old regime under the LA 1980 and the new regime under the LRA 2002—see LRA 2002, Sch. 6, para. 1.

6.5.1 Discontinuance or dispossession

Under LA 1980, Sch. 1, para. 1, time starts to run when the paper owner is dispossessed or when the paper owner discontinues his or her possession.

In most cases, there will be a **dispossession** rather than a **discontinuance**, because the courts accept that even very slight acts by the paper owner will negate any claim of discontinuance. For example, in *Powell v. MacFarlane* (1979) 38 P & CR 452, there was no discontinuance when the paper owner drove to the land and looked at it from a car.

> **dispossession** the act of being dispossessed—that is, of another person assuming ordinary possession of the land
>
> **discontinuance** the act of giving up possession, often an act of simply abandoning the land

Dispossession was defined by Slade J in *Powell v. MacFarlane*, as taking of possession from another without the other's licence or consent. Before 1833, dispossession had to be an 'ouster' by the squatter—an old word that means a forcible ejection of the true owner.

The modern law was clarified in *Pye v. Graham* (see 6.5.2.1), in which Lord Browne-Wilkinson said (at [38]) that there will be dispossession where the squatter 'assumes possession in the ordinary sense of the word'. Therefore, all that is required is that the squatter goes into ordinary possession of the land, because the paper owner cannot be in possession at the same time as the squatter. By definition, if the squatter is in possession, the paper owner has been dispossessed by the squatter.

6.5.2 Adverse possession

As well as there being a discontinuance or dispossession, another person (the squatter) must have gone into adverse possession—LA 1980, Sch. 1, para. 8(1). If the land simply remains unoccupied, the limitation period will not start to run.

It is therefore important to define 'adverse possession', so that both the start and end of the limitation period can be established. This is essential to knowing when title is extinguished under the LA 1980, or when the squatter is entitled to apply to be registered as proprietor under the LRA 2002.

LA 1980, Sch. 1, para. 1, defines adverse possession as when 'the land is in the possession of some person in whose favour the period of limitation can run'. Possession itself is not defined in the Act, but has been considered by case law. The leading case is the decision of the House of Lords in *Pye v. Graham*, in which Lord Browne-Wilkinson expressly approved the judgment of Slade J in *Powell v. MacFarlane* and adopted the definition of possession as set out in that case.

CASE CLOSE-UP

Powell v. MacFarlane (1979) 38 P & CR 452

The land in question was rough land bought originally to grow Christmas trees. The owner went abroad and, apart from occasional brief visits, did nothing with the land from 1956 to 1973.

The claimant, who was aged 14 at the time, started to use the land to graze his cow, go shooting, store trees prior to taking them to timber mills, and clearing and fencing work.

Slade J identified three main elements to adverse possession:

- the required degree of exclusive physical possession (occupation or control) of the land; and
- an intention to possess the land to the exclusion of all others, including the paper owner, sometimes referred to as *animus possidendi*; and
- an absence of consent by the paper owner (the paper owner did not give permission for the squatter to be on the land).

It was held that the claimant was not in adverse possession, because, although he had physical possession of the land without the consent of the owner, he lacked the *animus possidendi*— the necessary intention to possess.

Each of these three elements will now be considered in more depth.

6.5.2.1 Physical possession

physical possession
actual occupation or control of land

Physical possession of land is a question of degree, and the necessary degree will be determined partly by the nature of the land.

The degree of occupation and control that will be necessary to show possession of a residential property will be very different to that required to show possession of a tract of open moorland.

CASE CLOSE-UP

Red House Farms (Thorndon) Ltd v. Catchpole [1977] 2 EGLR 125

The land in question was marshland. The only sensible use anyone could suggest for it was shooting over it. The defendant, Mrs Catchpole, used it for that purpose and, at all material times, the only access to the land in question was through her land.

This was held by the Court of Appeal to be a high enough degree of exclusive physical control.

CASE CLOSE-UP

Tecbild Ltd v. Chamberlain (1969) 20 P & CR 633

In contrast, allowing children to play on undeveloped land, and tethering and exercising ponies there, were held to be insufficient to establish adverse possession.

The Court of Appeal described them as 'trivial acts of trespass', which did not suffice for adverse possession.

6.5 WHAT DOES A SQUATTER NEED TO SHOW TO MAKE A CLAIM TO THE LAND?

177

In *Prudential Assurance v. Waterloo* (1999) 17 EG 131, the land in question was one face of a wall: decorating the wall, and attaching lights and an entryphone system established its possession.

In *Buckinghamshire County Council v. Moran* [1990] Ch 623 (see 6.5.2.2), the defendant incorporated into his garden a piece of land that had been acquired by the council for road widening. He maintained fences, locked gates, and cultivated the land. This was held by the Court of Appeal to be a sufficient degree of physical control to amount to possession.

Physical possession also means treating the land exactly as an owner would treat it. This was held in the leading case of *Pye v. Graham*.

🔍 CASE CLOSE-UP

Pye v. Graham [2002] UKHL 30

The grazing land in question had been bought by Pye Ltd, a property investment company. It did not have an immediate use for the land, which had been bought in the expectation that it could eventually be used for housing. In the meantime, Pye Ltd initially granted grazing licences to the Grahams, who farmed the adjoining land.

In December 1983, the last of these licences came to an end and was not renewed. The Grahams continued to graze cattle on the land.

The last contact between the Grahams and Pye Ltd was in August 1984. From September 1984, the Grahams grazed cattle on the land, took crops of hay, manured the land, maintained hedges and ditches, and generally farmed the land as they had before. They had the only key to the gate, so Pye Ltd could not have obtained access without the Grahams' cooperation.

The House of Lords, reversing the Court of Appeal's decision, held that the Grahams *had* adversely possessed the land, so that Pye Ltd could not reclaim it when it started possession proceedings in April 1998.

Lord Browne-Wilkinson made it clear that there does not need to be any special type of possession to make it *'adverse'*. He said (at [36]):

> The question is simply whether the defendant squatter has dispossessed the paper owner by going into ordinary possession of the land for the requisite period without the consent of the owner.

Fencing is usually good evidence of physical control. In both *Pye v. Graham* and *Buckinghamshire County Council v. Moran*, the land was fenced off from others.

In *George Wimpey and Co. Ltd v. Sohn* [1967] Ch 487, Russell LJ said that it was in exceptional cases only that enclosure (fencing) of the land would not indicate adverse possession. In that particular case, it did not, because an easement to use the fenced land as a garden was established and that explained the fencing. If others are allowed to come and go freely through the land, there is unlikely to be the required degree of physical control—*Battersea v. Wandsworth* (2001) 19 EG 148. However, the land does not need to be fully enclosed; an unlocked gate will not be fatal to a claim of adverse possession if there is otherwise a sufficient degree of control: *Greenmanor Ltd v. Pilford* [2012] EWCA Civ 756.

Other actions that have been held to indicate exclusive physical control include controlling who may squat in a dwelling house, changing the locks, putting up 'no trespassing' signs, erecting buildings or fixtures on the land, and paying council tax. It is impossible to give a complete list: the important thing is to look for a sufficient degree of physical occupation and control, the nature of which will vary with the type of land in question.

6.5.2.2 **Intention to possess (*animus possidendi*)**

animus possidendi
an intention to possess
the land to the exclusion
of all others

The squatter must have ***animus possidendi***: intention to possess the land to the exclusion of all others, including the paper owner.

> ### 🔍 CASE CLOSE-UP
>
> ***Powell v. MacFarlane*** (1979) 38 P & CR 452
>
> Slade J described *animus possidendi* as follows (at 471):
>
> > *animus possidendi* involves the intention, in one's own name and on one's own behalf, to exclude the world at large, including the owner with the paper title if he be not himself the possessor, so far as is reasonably practicable and so far as the processes of the law will allow.
>
> The claimant was unable to establish the relevant intention to possess when he first entered the disputed land. He was only 14 years old at the time and Slade J found that he did not intend to possess the land, but simply to use it for grazing his family's cows. Such use may give rise to an easement or profit à prendre in the right circumstances, but it is not a sufficient intention for adverse possession.

❯ CROSS REFERENCE

For more on easements and profits à prendre, see Chapter 12.

It is clear that intention is a separate requirement from that of physical control of the land. Lord Browne-Wilkinson reiterated this point in *Pye v. Graham*, at [40]. He compared a friend staying overnight in a house, looking after a house while the owner is away, with a squatter staying overnight in the house: both are in possession of the house, but the friend has the intention to take care of the house, not to take adverse possession of it.

Despite the fact that they are separate requirements, however, intention is proven primarily by what the squatter does on the land, rather than by his or her declared intentions. It is clear from the case law that evidence of exclusive physical control of land also goes to show evidence of intention to possess the land.

> ### 🔍 CASE CLOSE-UP
>
> ***Buckinghamshire County Council v. Moran*** [1990] 1 Ch 623
>
> The claimant council was the paper owner of a strip of land bought many years before for road widening. The defendant's predecessor in title had incorporated the land into his garden in 1967 and the house was sold to the defendant with such rights as they had acquired over the extra land.
>
> The defendant bought the house in 1971 and padlocked the gate leading from the road to the extra land, so that the only access to the land was though his garden. He cultivated the land, mowing the lawn, laying flowerbeds, etc.
>
> In 1976, the council became aware of his use of the land and there was some correspondence, in which the defendant claimed the right to use the land until it was needed for widening and stated that he was consulting his lawyers. The council responded by saying that the defendant had no right to use the land, to which he replied claiming adverse possession. Nothing further happened until 1985, when the council began possession proceedings. The Court of Appeal held that this was too late, and that the land had been adversely possessed by the defendant.

The Court's reasons were that the defendant had acquired complete physical possession of the land and annexed it to his own land by October 1973. His actions unequivocally showed his intention to possess the land. The defendant had enclosed the land fully, so that access was only via his garden, and he had locked the gate that kept out everyone, including the council.

The Court also considered whether the required intention was to own the land, or simply to possess it for as long as possible. They made it quite clear that intention to possess is required, not intention to own. As Slade LJ said (at 643), the required intention is 'an intention for the time being to possess the land to the exclusion of all other persons, including the owner with the paper title'.

It was also held that knowledge of the paper owner's future use of the land (in this case, the road widening) will not prevent the trespasser forming an intention to possess it.

 THINKING POINT

What do you think showed the defendant's intention to possess? What had he done to the land to indicate his intention?

As can be seen from the *Moran* case, the same acts that show physical possession often show intention to possess as well. For example, fencing is usually good evidence of intention to possess—but, if a different explanation for fencing can be found, it may negative that finding. In *Inglewood Investment Co. Ltd v. Baker* [2003] 2 P & CR 23, for example, it was found that the fence was to keep in sheep rather than to establish possession.

In *Pye v. Graham* the House of Lords considered whether the Grahams' willingness to have paid for a new grazing licence, if one had been offered, negated an intention to possess. It was held that it did not. This decision supports the fact that the squatter needs only to show an intention to keep possession for as long as the law allows. If the paper owner takes action within the limitation period, the squatter will have no option other than to pay for the use of the land, or to leave. In *Alston v. BOCM Pauls Ltd* [2008] EWHC 3310 (Ch), the squatter farmed the land in question. He did not think much about whether he had any right to be there, but he intended to stay there as long as he could and would not have left unless compelled to do so. This was held to be sufficient intention to possess.

6.5.2.3 **Without consent**

Possession cannot be adverse if the claimant is on the land with the consent of the landowner.

The Court of Appeal in *Parshall v. Hackney* [2013] EWCA Civ 240 held that a person who is the registered proprietor of land cannot maintain a claim for adverse possession of it, even if his registration as proprietor was made in error. This may be related to the idea that adverse possession must be 'adverse' in the sense of 'without consent'.

There are a number of particular situations in which someone is on land with consent and the problem is usually to try to spot when that consent comes to an end, so that adverse possession can start.

Tenancies

Anyone occupying land as a tenant cannot be in adverse possession. A tenant cannot adversely possess land that is the subject of the tenancy, because that would be to deny his or her landlord's

CROSS REFERENCE

For more on leases and tenancies, see Chapter 5.

title, which the tenant cannot do. Once the lease has ended, however, the tenant who stays in possession of the land can be in adverse possession of it.

In the case of an oral or implied periodic tenancy (one that has been created without writing, or one implied by law through the payment of rent) LA 1980, Sch. 1, para. 5(1) and (2), provides that time starts to run from the end of the first year or other period, or, if rent is received after that date, from the date of the last receipt of rent.

 EXAMPLE

Gerald moves into Hill House, which is owned by Jack. There is no written lease, but Gerald pays Jack £100 per month. Jack goes away on an extended holiday, so Gerald decides to stop paying the rent.

Clearly, while Gerald is paying rent to Jack, he is not in adverse possession of Hill House and the limitation period cannot start to run. Once Gerald stops paying rent, however, the limitation period will begin on the date of the last receipt of rent by Jack.

A former tenant who is given permission to stay on at the end of a tenancy will not be in adverse possession, because he or she has the consent of the landlord to be there.

Interestingly, however, if the tenant goes into possession of other land near to the leased land, whether it belongs to the landlord or someone else, there will be a presumption that the land is being acquired for the landlord, rather than for the tenant.

 CASE CLOSE-UP

London Borough of Tower Hamlets v. Barrett [2005] EWCA Civ 923

In this case, a piece of wasteland next to a pub was adversely possessed by the tenant of the pub.

It was held that the tenant acquired it on behalf of his landlord, the freeholder. The landlord transferred the freehold of the pub to the tenant and this operated to transfer the adversely possessed land as well. The council, the paper owner of the wasteland, was unable to reclaim it.

The presumption is rebuttable: if the land is a long way away from the demised (tenanted) land, it is more likely that the tenant will be held to have acquired it on his own behalf.

Trustees

A trustee cannot acquire title by adverse possession against a beneficiary—LA 1980, s. 22(2). This will also mean that one co-owner of property cannot acquire title against the other by adverse possession.

❱ CROSS REFERENCE

For more on co-ownership, see Chapter 8.

Licences

❱ CROSS REFERENCE

For a comparison of licences with leases, see Chapter 5, 5.5.

It is quite clear that if someone is in possession of someone else's land with their permission, then their possession is not adverse. Such permission is referred to as a licence. There are a number of different situations in which a licence can arise.

Vendor and purchaser licences

The standard conditions of sale under which most land is sold provide that a purchaser who is allowed into possession before the transfer has taken place is there as a licensee of the vendor. Clearly, such a licensee cannot claim adverse possession against the vendor if the land is never transferred as intended. However, there are cases in which this term of the contract is absent or varied, and in these cases a different answer may be reached. See the online resources for more details.

Express licences

An express licence is one that is deliberately created by a landowner in favour of some other person. Since licences are not proprietary interests and can be created without formality, it can be quite difficult to be sure when a licence has been granted and whether or not it has been revoked.

In *Pye v. Graham*, the Grahams originally occupied the land under a series of licences. These licences were in writing and were expressly limited to eleven months. It was therefore easy to establish that the last licence came to an end on a certain date and that possession after that date could be regarded as adverse. This, however, will not necessarily be the case if an open-ended licence is given.

> **CROSS REFERENCE**
>
> For more on licences, see Chapter 5, 5.5.

Q | CASE CLOSE-UP

Trustees of Grantham Christian Fellowship v. Scouts Association [2005] EWHC 209 (Ch)

There were two pieces of adjoining land: one owned by the Scouts and one by a church. The church left its land undeveloped and granted a licence to the Scouts to use it, provided that they kept it tidy. The Scouts occupied it from 1959 until 2002, using it for recreation. They also built a rockery and a shed on it. There were changes in the Scout leaders during that time and the original licence was all but forgotten. When the Scouts tried to claim ownership of the land by adverse possession, however, Blackburne J held that the licence had never been revoked, so that their possession was never adverse.

The licence was not like the one in *Pye v. Graham*: it did not require the payment of rent and it did not have a fixed end date. Therefore, it could be held to be still in existence despite many years passing.

The grant of a licence means that the possession is not adverse, so the question arises whether the paper owner can unilaterally grant a licence to a squatter in order to prevent or stop the limitation period from running.

Q | CASE CLOSE-UP

BP Properties v. Buckler [1987] 2 EGLR 168

A licence was granted without rent to a disabled woman who would not leave the property despite a possession order against her. She did not reply to the offer of licence, but continued to live in the house with her son. After her death, her son claimed the house by adverse possession.

It was held that Mrs Buckler had been a licensee, even though she had not formally accepted the licence. Therefore, the claim to adverse possession failed.

The decision in *BP Properties v. Buckler* is surprising, because it means that if a paper owner offers a squatter a licence, the onus is on the squatter to reject it in order to stay in adverse possession. However, the case has recently been followed by the Privy Council in the case of *Smith v. Molyneaux* [2016] UKPC 35.

CASE CLOSE-UP

Smith v. Molyneaux [2016] UKPC 35

A sharecropper was told orally that he could stay on the land until it was needed for develop-ment. When asked to leave, he refused on the grounds that he had been in adverse possession of the land for the required period. The Privy Council held that the oral permission had created a licence, so the defendant was a licensee and not in adverse possession.

Implied licences

An implied licence is one which is not expressly granted, but which was implied by the law because the actions of the squatter were not inconsistent with the future plans of the owner: *Leigh v. Jack* (1879) 5 Ex D 264. It was held that uses of land that do not interfere, and are consistent, with the uses to which the paper owner wants to put the land are not acts of dispossession and do not pro-vide evidence of discontinuance of possession by the paper owner.

For example, in *Wallis's Cayton Bay Holiday Camp v. Shell-Mex* [1975] QB 94, it was held that using land as part of the frontage to a holiday camp was by implied licence of the paper owner as it did not conflict with their future intended use of the land.

As you can appreciate, this would make it very difficult to claim adverse possession unless the squatter were to do something radical to the land, such as building on it.

This doctrine of implied licence was expressly overruled in LA 1980, Sch. 1, para. 8(4).

STATUTE

Limitation Act 1980, Sch. 1, para. 8(4)

For the purpose of determining whether a person occupying any land is in adverse possession of the land it shall not be assumed by implication of law that his occupation is by permission of the person entitled to the land merely by virtue of the fact that his occupation is not incon-sistent with the latter's present or future enjoyment of the land.

This provision shall not be taken as prejudicing a finding to the effect that a person's occupation of any land is by implied permission of the person entitled to the land in any case where such a finding is justified on the actual facts of the case.

In *Buckinghamshire County Council v. Moran* (see 6.5.2.2) the Court of Appeal held that the inten-tions of the future owner were irrelevant in deciding whether the squatter's possession of the land was adverse. The House of Lords further endorsed this decision in *Pye v. Graham*, in which the reasoning in *Leigh v. Jack* was expressly overruled and the future intentions of the paper owner were held to be irrelevant to adverse possession.

At this point, it seemed very clear that the doctrine of implied licence played no part in the law—but there were further developments, based on the Human Rights Act 1998 (HRA 1998), which brought this doctrine briefly back into play again.

6.6 Human rights

or a more detailed discussion of the law in this area, see the online resources.

he brief revival of the doctrine of implied licence was directly due to the influence of human rights aw on adverse possession and in particular European Convention on Human Rights (ECHR), Protocol , Art. 1.

STATUTE

European Convention on Human Rights, Protocol 1, Art. 1

Every natural or legal person is entitled to the peaceful enjoyment of his possessions except in the public interest and subject to the conditions provided for by law and by the general principles of international law.

The preceding provisions shall not, however, in any way impair the right of a State to enforce such laws as it deems necessary to control the use of property in accordance with the general interest or to secure the payment of taxes or other contributions or penalties.

he issue was raised before the House of Lords in *Pye v. Graham*, but because that case was decided efore the HRA 1998 came into effect (2 October 2000), the House of Lords could not consider the oint. When Pye Ltd eventually lost its land to the Grahams, however, it took its case to the European Court of Human Rights (ECtHR) in Strasbourg, to try to get compensation from the UK government or its loss.

n the meantime, *Beaulane Properties v. Palmer* [2005] EWHC 1071 (Ch) held that the law on adverse possession under the LA 1980 as it applied to registered land was contrary to ECHR, Protocol , Art. 1. Nicholas Strauss QC held that the correct course of action was to interpret the law so as o accord with human rights, as he had the power to do under HRA 1998, s. 3. He concluded that e should reintroduce the idea of implied licence, by reading the LA 1980 as if Sch. 1, para. 8(4), ad not been enacted. This essentially resurrected the rule in *Leigh v. Jack* for cases in which adverse ossession of registered land occurred between 2 October 2000 (when the HRA 1998 came into orce) and 12 October 2003 (when the LRA 2002 came into force).

he first decision of the ECtHR in *Pye v. United Kingdom*, Application No. 44302/02, 15 November 005 partially vindicated the decision of Nicholas Strauss QC in *Beaulane*, because the Court ecided that the LA 1980 and LRA 1925, s. 75, were indeed incompatible with ECHR, Protocol 1, rt. 1.

owever, the UK government referred the decision to the Grand Chamber of the ECtHR (*Pye v. nited Kingdom*, Application No. 44302/02, 30 August 2007)—in effect, appealing the decision f the original Chamber. The Grand Chamber found, by a majority of ten judges to seven, that he law of adverse possession as it had applied in *Pye v. Graham* was *not* a breach of Protocol 1, rt. 1.

ince Pye Ltd eventually lost its case, it did not get any compensation and was faced with a huge bill or legal costs. However, the decision of the Grand Chamber could not and did not overrule the ecision in *Beaulane Properties v. Palmer*. This left the law in a rather confused state, but this has ince been effectively resolved by the Court of Appeal in the case of *Ofulue v. Bossert* [2008] EWCA iv 7, [2008] 3 WLR 1253.

> **Q**   **CASE CLOSE-UP**
>
> ***Ofulue v. Bossert*** [2008] EWCA Civ 7, [2008] 3 WLR 1253
>
> A house was registered in the name of Mr Ofulue in 1976. He let the house to tenants, and moved to Nigeria. In 1981 the former tenants left and allowed the Bosserts into the property. At that time the property was in very poor condition. The Bosserts did a number of repairs and paid the rates, but did not pay any rent. The twelve-year limitation period was held by the trial judge to have ended in 1999, and was therefore before the HRA 1998 came into force. However, the Court of Appeal considered, *obiter dicta*, whether it should follow *Pye v. United Kingdom* and Arden LJ, in the only substantive judgment, held that the court was bound to do so. However, since the point was not strictly raised by the case, *Beaulane* was not expressly overruled.
>
> (Note that the Court of Appeal's decision was upheld by the House of Lords at [2009] UKHL 16, after an appeal on a point not relevant to this discussion.)

This has effectively ended claims that the operation of the law of adverse possession, as it applied to registered land before the LRA 2002 came into force, is in breach of human rights law. The doctrine of licences implied by law can once more be consigned to history, and this is reinforced by *Terence Chambers v. Havering LBC* [2011] EWCA Civ 1576, in which the doctrine in *Leigh v. Jack* was said to be 'heretical and wrong'.

⟩ CROSS REFERENCE

See 6.5.2.3.

It must be remembered, however, that a licence can be granted orally and informally, and without requiring a response from the licensee—*BP Properties v. Buckler* [1987] 2 EGLR 168 and *Smith v. Molyneaux* [2016] UKPC 35.

6.7 Offence of squatting in a residential building

There is now a criminal offence of squatting in a residential building:

>   **STATUTE**
>
> **Legal Aid, Sentencing and Punishment of Offenders Act 2012**
>
> **144 Offence of squatting in a residential building**
>
> (1) A person commits an offence if—
>
>   (a) the person is in a residential building as a trespasser having entered it as a trespasser,
>
>   (b) the person knows or ought to know that he or she is a trespasser, and
>
>   (c) the person is living in the building or intends to live there for any period.
>
> (2) The offence is not committed by a person holding over after the end of a lease or licence (even if the person leaves and re-enters the building).

(3) For the purposes of this section—

    (a) 'building' includes any structure or part of a structure (including a temporary or moveable structure), and

    (d) a building is 'residential' if it is designed or adapted, before the time of entry, for use as a place to live.

(4) For the purposes of this section the fact that a person derives title from a trespasser, or has the permission of a trespasser, does not prevent the person from being a trespasser.

...

(7) For the purposes of subsection (1)(a) it is irrelevant whether the person entered the building as a trespasser before or after the commencement of this section.

This provision has the effect of criminalizing the act of entering into a residential building as a trespasser and living there or intending to live there for any period. The offence is committed whether the entry as a trespasser occurs before or after 1 September 2012 when the section came into force.

The Land Registry at first took the view that a breach of this section prevented the acquisition of a dwelling house by adverse possession. However, the Court of Appeal in *Best v. Land Chief Registrar* [2015] EWCA Civ 17 held that it does not have this effect. The squatter may be committing an offence but can still gain title by adverse possession.

6.8 Stopping the clock

There are a number of ways in which the limitation period can be stopped from running. If that happens, the squatter will have to start the period again from the beginning.

6.8.1 **Successful action for possession within limitation period**

Clearly, the most obvious way of stopping the clock is to bring a successful action for possession before the period of twelve years is up or, in the case of the new regime under the LRA 2002, before the squatter has applied for registration following at least ten years of possession.

It is essential to bring an action for possession promptly. In *Buckinghamshire County Council v. Moran* [1990] 1 Ch 623, for example, the council became aware of the annexation of its land by Mr Moran in 1976, but it did not begin possession proceedings until 1985, at which point it was too late and the council lost the land.

The proceedings must be commenced, by the service of a writ, before the twelve years have passed, and must be pursued to a conclusion—in *Ofulue v. Bossert* [2008] EWCA Civ 7, [2008] 3 WLR 1253 the original possession proceedings were discontinued and therefore did not stop time running.

6.8.2 **Regaining physical possession**

If the paper owner regains physical possession of the land, this will interrupt the period of adverse possession. However, the action taken must be such as to deprive the squatter of physical possession in a meaningful way: *Zarb v. Parry* [2012] 1 WLR 1240. Simply going onto the land and declaring you are taking possession, or putting up a notice, or planting a flagpole, were said not to be effective.

6.8.3 **Acknowledgement of the paper owner's title by the squatter**

A formal acknowledgement of the paper owner's title by the squatter will stop time running—LA 1980, s. 29. This acknowledgement must be in writing and signed by the person making it—LA 1980, s. 30—so a mere oral acknowledgement will not be sufficient.

 CASE CLOSE-UP

Archangel v. Lambeth (2000) EGCS 148

A letter signed by the squatter referring to the disputed land as '*Lambeth's property*' was held to have stopped time running.

 CASE CLOSE-UP

Bigden v. Lambeth (2000) ECGS 147

A petition addressed to the council against the sale of the block of flats in question to a housing association was held to be a sufficient acknowledgement of title. This is a good example of an implicit acknowledgement of title. The squatters did not specifically state that the property belonged to Lambeth, but they did not question the power of the council to sell the property or to assert a better title to it.

Other kinds of implicit acknowledgement of title include offering to buy or to rent the land from the paper owner.

In *Colchester Borough Council v. Smith* [1992] Ch 421, an agreement to rent the land (a garden allotment) seems to have occurred after the limitation period had expired. It was held, nevertheless, to be an effective acknowledgement of title, because it was a bona fide compromise of the dispute over the ownership of the land, and the defendant was therefore estopped from going behind it and reopening the original dispute.

In *London Borough of Tower Hamlets v. Barrett* [2005] EWCA Civ 923, it was held that acknowledgement of title by the landlord will not prevent a tenant from acquiring land by adverse possession. This seems rather odd, in view of the fact that the tenant is generally deemed to have acquired the land on behalf of his or her landlord (see 6.5.2.3).

It is important to remember that the squatter does not have to believe that he or she is the true owner of the land. As we saw in *Pye v. Graham*, the Grahams did not think of themselves as owners of the grazing land and would have paid rent if they had been asked for it. A willingness to pay rent if demanded is not a formal acknowledgement of title and did not bar them from successfully claiming adverse possession.

6.8.4 **Payment of rent by the squatter**

As we saw earlier, if the squatter pays rent, he or she cannot be in adverse possession—LA 1980, ss. 29–30.

6.8.5 **The grant of a licence**

As discussed earlier, a squatter who is on the land by permission of the paper owner cannot be in adverse possession. In *BP Properties v. Buckler* [1987] 2 EGLR 168, the unilateral grant of a licence by the paper owner that was not acknowledged by the squatter was held to be effective in stopping time running, and this has been followed in *Smith v. Molyneaux* [2016] UKPC 35. Therefore a paper owner who writes or speaks to the squatter granting permission to stay on the land will stop time running, even if there is no reply. This seems very strange, because any acknowledgement of title must be in writing (see 6.8.3), so it is unclear why silence should be enough to constitute acceptance of a licence to occupy.

6.8.6 Letter threatening action

In *Buckinghamshire County Council v. Moran*, letters demanding the land back were held to be ineffective to stop time running, although earlier cases such as *Wallis's Cayton Bay Holiday Camp v. Shell-Mex* had suggested to the contrary. Since *Buckinghamshire County Council v. Moran* was approved in *Pye v. Graham*, the true law appears to be that letters by themselves will not stop time running; the paper owner must bring possession proceedings.

6.8.7 Fraud, concealment, or mistake

LA 1980, s. 32, provides that the running of the limitation period will be postponed if the action is based upon the fraud of the defendant, if any fact relevant to the claimant's right of action has been concealed by the defendant, or if the action is based upon a mistake. The limitation period does not begin until the fraud, concealment, or mistake has been discovered, or could, with reasonable diligence, have been discovered.

6.9 The effect of adverse possession

Adverse possession under the LA 1980 extinguishes the title of paper owner, as we saw at 6.4.1. This means that the squatter now becomes the owner of the land.

Because the title of the previous owner ceases to exist under LA 1980, s. 17, there should be no possibility of the previous title to the land being revived, even if there is a subsequent acknowledgement of title by the squatter. As we saw at 6.8.3, however, in *Colchester Borough Council v. Smith* [1992] Ch 421 such an acknowledgement was held to be effective as a genuine compromise of a dispute about the land.

There is no conveyance of land to the squatter. The squatter takes the land subject to all proprietary obligations, even if they are unregistered, because he or she is not a purchaser—*Re Nisbet and Potts' Contract* (1906) 1 Ch 386. The squatter's title will not, however, be subject to a mortgage taken out after adverse possession commenced; but if the mortgage was taken out before adverse possession commenced, the squatter will be bound by it, unless no payments were made under the mortgage for the limitation period—LA 1980, s. 29(3).

6.9.1 Unregistered land

6.9.1.1 Freehold land

The squatter will have no paper title to the land. In order to sell the land, he or she would have to make a declaration of adverse possession in respect of it, because there would be no title deeds available. In practice, the squatter will register the land at the Land Registry with possessory title, which can be upgraded twelve years later to absolute title.

⮞ CROSS REFERENCE

For more on different classes of title, see Chapter 4, 4.5.2.

▶ CROSS REFERENCE

For more on indemnities in registered land, see 4.7.5.

 CASE CLOSE-UP

Diep v. Land Registry [2010] EWHC 3315 (Admin)

The claimant challenged the decision of the Land Registrar to register land he had acquired by adverse possession with possessory title only. Mitting J upheld the registrar's decision, and the policy of the Land Registry, because an absolute title would give rise to a claim for indemnity if the paper owner turned up later and made a successful claim. Public funds were therefore at risk, so a cautious approach was wholly justified.

A possessory title can be sold, but a purchaser will expect to pay less for it. Usually, title insurance is taken out to compensate the purchaser if there is any subsequent challenge to the title.

6.9.1.2 **Leasehold land**

If there is adverse possession against a tenant, the squatter extinguishes the tenant's estate after twelve years; the landlord's estate is not extinguished until twelve years after the landlord has the right to possession against the tenant. In the meantime, the squatter has a freehold title, but one that is liable to be determined by the landlord once the lease comes to an end. The squatter never becomes a tenant of the landlord.

 EXAMPLE

Henry has been in adverse possession of a piece of unregistered land at the end of his garden for twelve years. He has discovered that Isabel owns the freehold of the land, but that the land has been leased to Jack until 2030.

Henry has extinguished Jack's title, because he has been in adverse possession for twelve years.

He will not extinguish Isabel's title until 2042 (twelve years after the lease ends).

The dispossessed tenant remains a tenant of the landlord, so the landlord can forfeit the lease for breach of covenant during its term. This will bring forward the landlord's right to eject the squatter. Therefore, it is in the squatter's interest to ensure that all of the covenants are complied with—otherwise the land may be reclaimed by the landlord.

The dispossessed tenant also remains in a contractual relationship with the landlord. This raises the question of whether the tenant can deliberately bring an end to that contract by surrendering the lease to the landlord, thus bringing the tenant's estate to a premature end and entitling the landlord to possession. The landlord could then evict the squatter. This occurred in *Fairweather v. St Marylebone Property* [1963] AC 510, in which the House of Lords held by a majority that the tenant could surrender the lease and that the landlord was entitled to evict the squatter.

 EXAMPLE

In the previous example, Jack might surrender his lease to Isabel. She could then evict Henry, because her freehold title has not been extinguished and will not be extinguished for twelve years.

6.9.2 **Registered land**

6.9.2.1 **Periods of limitation completed by 12 October 2003**

Freehold land

As we saw earlier, title to registered land cannot simply be extinguished. Therefore, some mechanism for applying the LA 1980 had to be found. This was provided by LRA 1925, s. 75.

 STATUTE

Land Registration Act 1925, s. 75 [Acquisition of title by possession]

(1) The Limitation Acts shall apply to registered land in the same manner and to the same extent as those Acts apply to land not registered, except that where, if the land were not registered, the estate of the person registered as proprietor would be extinguished, such estate shall not be extinguished but shall be deemed to be held by the proprietor for the time being on trust for the person who, by virtue of the said Acts, has acquired title against any proprietor, but without prejudice to the estates and interests of any other person interested in the land whose estate or interest is not extinguished by those Acts.

(2) Any person claiming to have acquired a title under the Limitation Acts may apply to be registered as proprietor thereof.

...

Instead of being extinguished, the squatter's title is held on trust by the registered proprietor. This is a rather odd trust, because the registered proprietor is obliged to act as trustee for someone who effectively may have 'stolen' the land. Until it is registered in the squatter's name, the registered proprietor (paper owner) continues to hold the legal title to the land, but the squatter has the beneficial (equitable) title.

This equitable title was originally protected as an overriding interest under LRA 1925, s. 70(1)(f), but is now protected as an overriding interest only if the squatter remains in actual occupation under LRA 2002, Sch. 3, para. 2.

The trust comes to an end when the squatter is registered as proprietor in place of the paper owner.

Leasehold land

The imposition of a trust under LRA 1925, s. 75(1), means that there were different results if a leasehold estate in registered land was adversely possessed. The dispossessed tenant could not bring forward the landlord's right to evict the tenant by surrendering the lease, as can be done with un-registered land, because the tenant is obliged to act as trustee for the squatter.

 CASE CLOSE-UP

Spectrum Investment Co. v. Holmes [1981] 1 WLR 221

In this case, the tenant tried to surrender the lease after the squatter had been registered with an absolute freehold title in respect of the tenant's estate.

It was held that, although this case was indistinguishable from *Fairweather v. St Marylebone Property* except that the land was registered, the tenant had no estate left to surrender.

Therefore, the squatter was entitled to keep the land until the lease expired.

That case expressly left open the position before the squatter is registered as proprietor—the time during which the registered proprietor is holding on trust for the squatter. This point was raised in *Central London Estates v. Kato Kagaku* [1998] 4 All ER 948.

 CASE CLOSE-UP

Central London Estates v. Kato Kagaku [1998] 4 All ER 948

It was held that the same result applied where the squatter had not yet registered the adversely possessed leasehold estate. LRA 1925, s. 75, meant that the tenant held the leasehold estate on trust for the squatter.

When the tenant surrendered the lease to his landlord, the trusteeship passed to the landlord, so that it could not evict the squatter.

The result was that the squatter maintained valuable rights to a courtyard in central London, on which he was running a car park, until the end of the leasehold estate in 2028. The landlord could not evict the squatter until that date.

EXAMPLE

Look back at the previous examples.

Suppose that Henry had completed twelve years of adverse possession of registered land before 12 October 2003. The land was leased to Jack until 2030. Jack would hold his estate on trust for Henry unless, and until, Henry was registered as proprietor.

Unlike the previous example, Jack cannot surrender the lease to Isabel either before, or after, Henry is registered as proprietor. Once Henry is registered, Jack has no estate to surrender; before Henry is registered, Jack holds on trust for him and cannot act in breach of trust. If he were to try to do so, Isabel would hold the land on trust for Henry until 2030.

These two cases clearly indicated that adverse possession could not work in exactly the same way in registered and unregistered land even before the reforms of 2002—and, in this way, they paved the way for the realization that different considerations apply to registered land.

6.9.2.2 Limitation periods completed from 13 October 2003

LRA 2002, ss. 96–98, apply to registered land for which the limitation period under the LA 1980 has not been completed before 13 October 2003.

The most fundamental difference between the LA 1980 rules and those under the LRA 2002 is that there is no longer an automatic barring of title by adverse possession. Under the LA 1980 rules, once the twelve years was up, the paper owner could not do anything about the squatter—it was too late!

Now, adverse possession alone does not bar the registered proprietor's title—LRA 2002, s. 96. Instead, after being in adverse possession for ten years, the squatter has the right to apply to the Land Registry to be registered as the proprietor of the land that he or she has adversely possessed. Note that the period has been reduced to ten years—but you would be wrong to think that this makes adverse possession under the LRA 2002 easier: the reverse is actually true.

The squatter has no rights in the land until an application to be registered is made, and can defend an action for possession only if one of the grounds in LRA 2002, Sch. 6, para. 5, (discussed later) can be made out. In the vast majority of cases, a squatter can be evicted however long he or she has been on the land.

The squatter must be in possession of the land when the application to be registered is made—that is, the ten years' adverse possession relied upon must immediately precede the date of the application.

> ## EXAMPLE
>
> 1. Karen has been in adverse possession of a house since 1 January 2000, and is still living there. Since 2 January 2010 she has been able to apply to the Land Registry to be registered as proprietor. However, the registered proprietor, Linda, can bring an action for possession against Karen at any time before she applies, and will succeed unless Karen can show one of the limited grounds in LRA 2002, Sch. 6, para. 5.
> 2. Manvir was in adverse possession of grazing land adjoining his garden for ten years ending in March 2010. Since then, however, he has stopped using the land. He cannot now make an application to be registered as proprietor, because he is not in possession of the land.

Note that it is for the Land Registry to determine initially whether someone is in adverse possession of the land under LRA 2002, not the courts: *Swan Housing Association v. Gill* [2012] EWHC 3129 (QB). It is only after the Land Registry has made its decision under the procedure outlined below that the court can consider the matter.

When the Land Registry receives the application, it will firstly decide if the squatter has an arguable case. If so, the Land Registry will notify certain people interested in the land:

- the registered proprietor;
- any registered chargee (mortgagee);
- if the estate is leasehold, the registered proprietor of any superior registered estate (for example, the freehold);
- certain other people interested in the land—LRA 2002, Sch. 6, paras 1 and 2.

These people have 65 days within which to object to the registration. As you can see, this is very different to the LA 1980, under which the registered proprietor got no warning at all that someone else was claiming the land.

▶ CROSS REFERENCE

For more on rectification and indemnity, see Chapter 4, 4.7.

If the registered proprietor does not respond at all, the land is presumed to have been abandoned and the squatter is entitled to be registered as the new proprietor. There is no provision to extend the time limits for replying, even in cases of hardship. However, a claim for rectification can be made if there are grounds for doing so.

> ## CASE CLOSE-UP
>
> **Baxter v. Mannion** [2011] EWCA Civ 120
>
> It was held that a registered proprietor who did not object in time, but who had valid grounds for disproving adverse possession, could apply for rectification of the register. A person who did not have adequate grounds for claiming adverse possession was not entitled to be registered as registered proprietor of the land; this was implicit in LRA 2002, Sch. 6, para. 1. The registration had therefore been obtained by a mistake, which could be put right under LRA 2002, Sch. 4, paras 1 and 5.

If an objection is received in time, the squatter will not be registered as the proprietor unless the case falls within one of the exceptions in LRA 2002, Sch. 6, para. 5:

- if, under the principles of proprietary estoppel, it would be unconscionable for the registered proprietor to object to the squatter's application to be registered;
- if the squatter is otherwise entitled to the land;
- if the squatter is the owner of adjacent property and has been in adverse possession of the land in question under the mistaken, but reasonable, belief that he or she is its owner.

'Estoppel'

 STATUTE

Land Registration Act 2002, Sch. 6, para. 5(2)

The first condition is that—

(a) it would be unconscionable because of an equity by estoppel for the registered proprietor to seek to dispossess the applicant, and

(b) the circumstances are such that the applicant ought to be registered as the proprietor.

CROSS REFERENCE

For more detail on proprietary estoppel, see Chapter 10.

This exception is clearly intended to deal with cases of **proprietary estoppel**. A proprietary estoppel arises where the owner has made assurances about the land, upon the strength of which assurances the claimant has relied and acted to his or her detriment.

> **proprietary estoppel** a doctrine under which the courts can grant a remedy if a landowner has implicitly or explicitly led a claimant to act detrimentally under the belief that he or she would be granted rights in the land

There have been some objections to this provision, on the grounds that a person who moves into land under circumstances giving rise to a proprietary estoppel is unlikely to be in adverse possession. An estoppel is generally raised by the proprietor encouraging that person to move into the land, so he or she would be there by consent. This provision is more likely to be used as a defence to possession proceedings than as the basis for a claim.

The Law Commission and Land Registry (2001, para. 14.42) suggest that the sorts of case which may fall under this exception are those in which the paper owner stands by while the squatter mistakenly builds on the land, or in which there is an informal purchase and sale, and the purchaser goes into possession. LRA 2002, Sch. 6, para. 5(2)(b)—'the circumstances are such that the applicant ought to be registered as the proprietor'—means that the Registry retains a discretion whether or not to register the squatter as proprietor, even if proprietary estoppel is made out.

'Otherwise entitled to the land'

 STATUTE

Land Registration Act 2002, Sch. 6, para. 5(3)

The second condition is that the applicant is for some other reason entitled to be registered as the proprietor of the estate.

In the Law Commission/Land Registry report (2001), it was suggested at para. 14.43 that this exception is intended to deal with situations in which, for example, the squatter is entitled to the land as a beneficiary under the will or intestacy (death without leaving a will) of the previous registered proprietor, or in situations such as that in *Bridges v. Mees* [1957] Ch 475, in which the purchaser had gone into possession after paying the whole purchase price, but the land had not been transferred to him.

Boundary disputes

 STATUTE

Land Registration Act 2002, Sch. 6, para. 5(4)

The third condition is that—

(a) the land to which the application relates is adjacent to land belonging to the applicant,

(b) the exact line of the boundary between the two has not been determined under rules under section 60,

(c) for at least ten years of the period of adverse possession ending on the date of the application, the applicant (or any predecessor in title) reasonably believed that the land to which the application relates belonged to him, and

(d) the estate to which the application relates was registered more than one year prior to the date of the application.

This exception is best explained by looking at an example:

 EXAMPLE

Dave and Becci have been registered proprietors of their house since 2005. The fence between their and their neighbours' garden has always been in the same position. Recently, Andrew and Stacey moved next door. They have produced a Land Registry plan which shows the boundary as being further over into Dave and Becci's garden. Andrew and Stacey want the fence moved to recover the strip of land.

Dave and Becci should be able to rely on the exception in Sch. 6, para. 5(4), because:

(a) the land in dispute is adjacent to their land;

(b) the boundary is not fixed under Land Registration Rules 2003 (most boundaries are not);

(c) without realizing it, for the past ten years they have been in adverse possession of the land, reasonably believing it to be theirs;

(d) their estate was registered more than a year ago.

Therefore, Andrew and Stacey should not be able to move the fence.

The wording of the section means that it will not apply if the applicant moves the boundary deliberately, hoping to get more land, because in that case there would be no reasonable belief in the ownership of the disputed land.

In *IAM Group v. Chowdrey* [2012] EWCA Civ 505, it was held that the reasonable belief required is not that of a reasonably competent solicitor, but of the claimant himself. Knowledge that the paper owner disputed his title did not make that belief unreasonable in circumstances where he had occupied the disputed land since first moving into the property.

CASE CLOSE-UP

Zarb v. Parry [2012] 1 WLR 1240

The claimants (C) and defendants (D) owned adjoining land. C believed that the true boundary lay about 20m north of the established hedge, and in 2007 went on to that strip of land and began to remove fencing and plants in an attempt to take back the land by force. They were interrupted by D, who threatened to call the police.

In 2009, C made a legal claim for the boundary to be moved in their favour. D pleaded LRA 2002, Sch. 6(4). The trial judge held that C had the paper title to the strip of land, but that D had been in adverse possession of it for over ten years. The Court of Appeal upheld the decision.

It was held that the incident in 2007 had not been enough to interrupt D's possession of the land, as C did not themselves take exclusive possession of it—they were interrupted before they could do so.

It was also held that D's belief in the existing boundary was reasonable, as there was no dispute when they bought the land, and after the 2007 incident, a surveyor was employed by both parties who confirmed that the hedge was in the correct position. The CA indicated, however, that claims under this section need to be made 'promptly' or the belief of the adverse possessor may not remain reasonable.

Rejected applications

If an objection is received to the application and the case does not fall within any of the exceptions outlined earlier, the squatter will not be registered as proprietor. The landowner, however, cannot sit back at that point and do nothing more. If an application for registration is refused, but the squatter remains in adverse possession for a further two years, a second application to be registered as proprietor can be made and the squatter will, this time, be registered as proprietor whether or not the registered proprietor objects—LRA 2002, Sch. 6, paras 6 and 7. The paper owner cannot ignore the squatter: action must be taken to either evict the squatter, or otherwise deal with the situation—perhaps by offering the squatter a lease or licence.

A comparison between the Limitation Act 1980 and the Land Registration Act 2002

The effect of adverse possession under the LRA 2002 is very different to that under the old law. Instead of operating negatively, by obliging the registered proprietor to hold the land in trust for the squatter, the LRA 2002 effectively transfers the paper owner's title to the squatter by registering the squatter in the paper owner's place. The squatter takes the paper owner's estate subject to any entries in the register that bound the paper owner, with the possible exception of registered charges. If the squatter is registered because there is no objection received, he or she will not be bound by any registered charge affecting the estate immediately before registration, because the chargee was notified of the application and did not object—LRA 2002, Sch. 6, para. 9(2). If, however, the squatter was registered because the case fell within one of the three exceptions, any registered charge will be binding—LRA 2002, Sch. 6, para. 9(4).

THINKING POINT

Think about the facts of *Pye v. Graham* under the new law. Would Pye Ltd have objected to an application by the Grahams to be registered as proprietors?

Pye Ltd would have objected. It still wanted the land and had not abandoned it, as its persistent attempts to get it back through the courts prove.

As the Grahams could not have made out any of the exceptions in LRA 2002, Sch. 6, para. 5, they would not have been registered as proprietors and Pye Ltd would not have lost land worth £10m.

6.10 How do I know which law applies?

Figure 6.1 is a flow chart which may be helpful in thinking about applying the law on adverse possession.

Figure 6.1 Adverse possession flowchart

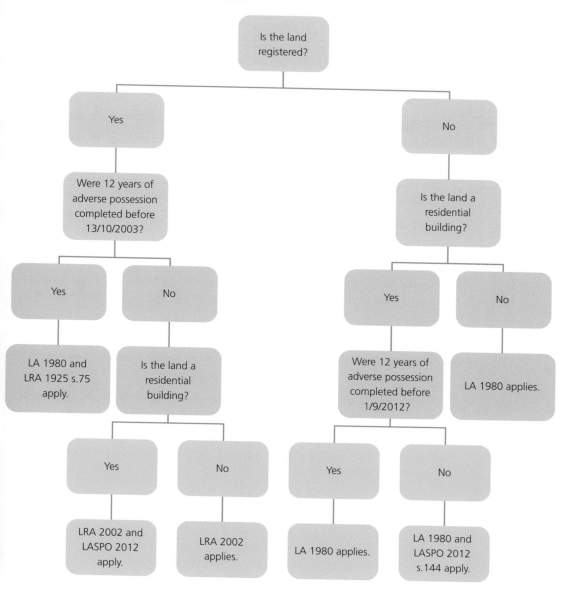

EXAMPLE

When you are looking at these examples, consider these three questions:
- Is the land registered or unregistered?
- If registered, on what date was the land adversely possessed?

1. Frances went into adverse possession of Geraldine's unregistered land on 3 October 2005. She could apply for the land to be registered in her name from 4 October 2017. Because the land is unregistered, the LA 1980 applies, so Geraldine's title is extinguished.

2. Harriet went into adverse possession of Iris's registered land on 1 October 1988. She could apply for registration as proprietor from 2 October 2000. Because this is before 1 October 2003, she is subject to the LA 1980 and the LRA 1925. The land will now be held on trust for her by Iris until she is registered as proprietor.

3. Jack went into adverse possession of Karen's registered land in November 1991. Twelve years' adverse possession was complete in November 2003. Because this is after 13 October 2003, the rules in the LRA 2002 apply. If Jack applies to be registered, Karen will be notified, and what happens next depends upon her response.

 Summary

1. Adverse possession was originally justified as providing an end to disputes over the ownership of land, ensuring that abandoned land was utilized, and ensuring that the fact of possession and the legal title never got too far apart.

2. Some of these justifications are less convincing in relation to registered land.

3. The LA 1980 works by extinguishing the title of the paper owner after the limitation period (usually twelve years) has passed.

4. For the limitation period to begin, the paper owner must have discontinued possession, or been dispossessed, and the squatter must have gone into possession.

5. Possession means a sufficient degree of physical control and an intention to possess: see *Pye v. Graham*.

6. Possession is adverse if it is without the consent of the paper owner. Possession as a tenant or licensee will not be adverse to the paper owner.

7. There was considerable controversy over how adverse possession was affected by human rights law, but the current (and presumably final) position is that the law is not in breach of the ECHR.

8. The law on adverse possession for registered land was changed by the LRA 2002 for cases from 13 October 2003.

9. The new law makes it much harder to adversely possess registered land, because the paper owner is notified of any application by the squatter to be registered, and has a chance to object and then evict the squatter.

10. LASPOA 2012 applies from 1 September 2012 to criminalize squatting in residential buildings even if the entry as a trespasser was before that date.

The bigger picture

- This is an area of law which should be of diminishing importance as time goes by, since most land is registered and the new laws in the LRA 2002 and LASPOA 2012 make it much harder to claim adverse possession. However, there have been a number of recent cases, so the law on adverse possession is not yet in decline.

- If you want advice on answering examination questions on adverse possession, see Chapter 16, 16.8.

- For more detailed information on the human rights law decisions, see the online resources.

- There are numerous additional cases on adverse possession, many of them quite old.

Consent

Hicks Development Ltd v. Chaplin [2007] EWHC 141 (Ch)

Sandhu v. Farooqui [2003] EWCA Civ 531

Smith v. Lawson (1997) 64 P & CR 239

General requirements

Markfield Investments v. Evans [2001] 1 WLR 1321

Mount Carmel Investments v. Peter Thurlow Ltd [1988] 1 WLR 1078

Ocean Estates v. Pinder [1969] 2 AC 19

Pavledes v. Ryesbridge Properties Ltd (1989) 58 P&CR 459

Seddon v. Smith (1877) 36 LT 168

Sze To Chun Keung v. Kung Kwok Wai David [1997] 1 WLR 1232

Treloar v. Nute [1976] 1 WLR 1295

? **Questions**

Self-test questions

1. Abu is aware of a strip of land adjoining the end of his garden. It appears to be unused. What should Abu do if he wishes to take adverse possession of the land? What must he show to prove adverse possession?

2. Abu receives a letter from the local council regarding the strip of land. The council claims to be the owner of the land, which it is planning to incorporate into a park in the future. What will be the effect of the letter if the council:

    (a) threatens to bring possession proceedings against Abu?

    (b) states that Abu may use the land by licence?

3. If Abu were a tenant of his land, to whom would the strip of land belong if he were to be successful in proving adverse possession?

4. If Abu were to be able to show a sufficient degree of adverse possession, how likely would he be to become the owner of the strip of land if his twelve years' adverse possession ended in November 2003 and the land was:

(a) unregistered?

(b) registered?

5. Suppose the council took no action while Abu lived in the house, but the strip of land was incorporated into the garden. Abu sold the house to Ben in 2015, not mentioning anything about the strip. In 2017, the council tried to evict Ben from the land. Ben sincerely believed that the land was part of the garden until the council wrote to him. Will Ben have any defence to possession proceedings?

Exam questions

1. Melody and Jasper met as students at the University of Woolwich in 2002. They were both short of funds, so they moved into an abandoned chalet sited behind a council block of flats. It had been left there after some building work, and was intended as a shelter for workmen, though it had a small kitchen and bathroom. The chalet was fairly basic and run down, but Melody and Jasper repaired it, insulated it, and had mains services connected. They have continued to live in it as they are struggling musicians who cannot afford a better home.

   Last week, a representative of the Woolwich Council appeared and told them that the land the chalet was standing on was registered in their name, and that the chalet belonged to them. They told Melody and Jasper that they were committing a criminal offence, and that they must leave immediately. Advise Melody and Jasper.

2. Is it still necessary for the law on adverse possession to apply to registered land?

 You will find answers to these questions online at www.oup.com/uk/clarke_directions6e/.

Further reading

Ex, L., 'What do we protect in land registration?' (2013) 129 (Oct) LQR 477

This is a case comment on *Parshall v. Hackney* [2013] EWCA Civ 240, [2013] 3 All ER 224.

Land Registry (2015) *Land Registry Practice Guide 4—Adverse possession of registered land*, available online at https://www.gov.uk/government/publications/adverse-possession-of-registered-land/practice-guide-4-adverse-possession-of-registered-land

This sets out the Land Registry procedure on adverse possession under the LRA 2002.

Land Registry (2015) *Land Registry Practice Guide 5—Adverse possession of (1) unregistered land (2) registered land where a right to be registered was acquired before 13 October 2003*, available online at https://www.gov.uk/government/publications/adverse-possession-of-1-unregistered-land-and-2-registered-land/practice-guide-5-adverse-possession-of-1-unregistered-and-2-registered-land-where-a-right-to-be-registered-was-acquired-before-13-october-2003

This sets out the law on applying under the old rules for registration of unregistered land that has been adversely possessed and registered land adversely possessed before the LRA 2002 came into force.

Law Commission/HM Land Registry (1998) *Land Registration for the Twenty-First Century: A Consultative Document*, Law Com No. 254, available online at http://www.lawcom.gov.uk/project/land-registration-for-the-21st-century/#land-registration-for-the-21st-century-consultation

See especially paras 10.1–10.19, which discuss the justification for adverse possession and go on to look at whether it should continue to exist in registered land.

Law Commission/HM Land Registry (2001) *Land Registration for the Twenty-First Century: A Conveyancing Revolution*, Law Com No. 271, available online at http://www.lawcom.gov.uk/app/uploads/2015/04/Lc271.pdf

Part XIV contains a commentary on the provisions in the LRA 2002, and explains why they were introduced.

Law Commission, Law Com, No. 227, *Updating The Land Registration Act 2002*, available at https://www.lawcom.gov.uk/project/updating-the-land-registration-act-2002/

Chapter 17 contains proposals for the reform of adverse possession law.

Milne, P., 'Mistaken belief in adverse possession—mistaken interpretation?' [2010] 4 Conv 342

This is a comment on *IAM Group Plc v. Chowdrey* [2012] EWCA Civ 505 and the 'boundary dispute' exception.

Murdoch, S., 'No trumping of reality' (2011) 1120 EG 111

Griffiths, G., 'An important question of principle—reality and rectification in registered land' [2011] Conv 331

These articles are about *Baxter v. Mannion* [2011] EWCA Civ 120.

'Residential squatting—the sting in the tail' (2015) 25(10) PLB 73–4

This discusses *Best v. Chief Land Registrar* [2015] EWCA Civ 17.

Radley-Gardner, O., 'Foisted permission and adverse possession' (2017) 133(Apr) LQR 214–16

Hickey R., 'The effect of supervening permission on adverse possession' [2017] 3 Conv 223–30

Articles on *Smith v. Molyneaux* [2016] UKPC 35.

Woods, U., 'The English law on adverse possession: A tale of two systems' (2009) 38(1) CLWR 27

This is an interesting article considering whether the role played by adverse possession in un-registered land could be replaced by marketable title legislation as commonly used in the USA.

Online Resources

For more advice relating to this chapter, including self-test questions and an interactive glossary, visit www.oup.com/uk/clarke_directions6e/.